RELIGION AND POLITICS IN SPAIN

Religion and Politics in Spain

The Spanish Church in Transition, 1962–96

Audrey Brassloff
University of Salford

Foreword by Paul Preston

First published in Great Britain 1998 by
MACMILLAN PRESS LTD
Houndmills, Basingstoke, Hampshire RG21 6XS and London
Companies and representatives throughout the world

A catalogue record for this book is available from the British Library.

ISBN 0-333-69322-1

First published in the United States of America 1998 by
ST. MARTIN'S PRESS, INC.,
Scholarly and Reference Division,
175 Fifth Avenue, New York, N.Y. 10010

ISBN 0-312-21073-6

Library of Congress Cataloging-in-Publication Data
Brassloff, Audrey, 1934–
Religion and politics in Spain : the Spanish Church in transition, 1962–96 / Audrey Brassloff.
p. cm.
Includes bibliographical references and index.
ISBN 0-312-21073-6
1. Catholic Church—Spain—History—20th century. 2. Spain–
-Church history—20th century. I. Title.
BX1585.2.B73 1998
282'.46'09045—dc21   97-18336
                                                                  CIP

© Audrey Brassloff 1998
Foreword © Paul Preston 1998

All rights reserved. No reproduction, copy or transmission of this publication may be made without written permission.

No paragraph of this publication may be reproduced, copied or transmitted save with written permission or in accordance with the provisions of the Copyright, Designs and Patents Act 1988, or under the terms of any licence permitting limited copying issued by the Copyright Licensing Agency, 90 Tottenham Court Road, London W1P 9HE.

Any person who does any unauthorised act in relation to this publication may be liable to criminal prosecution and civil claims for damages.

The author has asserted her right to be identified as the author of this work in accordance with the Copyright, Designs and Patents Act 1988.

This book is printed on paper suitable for recycling and made from fully managed and sustained forest sources.

10 9 8 7 6 5 4 3 2 1
07 06 05 04 03 02 01 00 99 98

Printed and bound in Great Britain by
Antony Rowe Ltd, Chippenham, Wiltshire

For Wolfi, who will know why

Contents

Foreword by Paul Preston	ix
Acknowledgements	xiv
List of Acronyms	xv
Glossary	xvii
Introduction	1
1 The Spanish Church and the Second Vatican Council	6
2 Aggiornamento ma non troppo (1969 to mid-1971)	25
3 The Victory of the 'Extreme Centre' (mid-1971 to mid-1973)	42
4 Preparing for a Future without Franco (mid-1973 to 1975)	61
5 The Church and the Coming of Democracy (1975 to 1978)	79
6 Learning to Live with Reality (1979 to 1982)	99
7 The Church and the PSOE Government (1982 to 1996)	119
Notes	141
Bibliography	167
Index	176

Foreword

The history of the Catholic Church in Spain in the twentieth century parallels that of the country itself. Almost every major political upheaval of an especially turbulent period had its religious backcloth and a crucial, and usually reactionary, role for the Church hierarchy. The civil wars of both the nineteenth and twentieth centuries were the struggle of a traditional, deeply Catholic, rural society against the threat of liberalism and modernisation. The gestation of the war of 1936–39 cannot be understood without some sense of how Catholics felt themselves threatened by the secularising legislation of the Second Republic and some awareness of the way in which the right legitimised its own resistance to social reform by surrounding it with a rhetoric about the defence of religion. The Catholic Church supported the Nationalist cause during the civil war. Priests said field masses, bishops blessed weapons and Cardinals mounted celebratory *Te Deum*s for Franco's victories.

The Church also provided legitimacy for the dictatorship by which the right-wing victory was institutionalised, most notably in the form of the Spanish hierarchy's Collective Letter in favour of the nationalists, 'To the Bishops of the Whole World', published on 1 July 1937. Yet the alignment of Catholicism with the right in Spain was not an absolute constant. The most prominent progressive in the Spanish Church, the Archbishop of Tarragona, Cardinal Francesc Vidal i Barraquer, and the conservative, but Basque nationalist, bishop of Vitoria, Monseñor Mateo Múgica y Urrestarazu, both refused to sign. At the beginning of the Spanish Civil War, despite enormous popularity, Vidal i Barraquer had been arrested in Tarragona by anti-clerical anarchist militiamen. The Catalan government, the Generalitat, managed to secure his release and, for his safety, secure his passage to Italy where he spent the rest of the war in various efforts to bring about a mediated peace. Franco never permitted him to return to Spain. Fourteen Basque priests were executed by the Francoists in the autumn of 1936 because of their Basque nationalist views. After the fall of the Basque Country in the summer of 1937, several hundred secular and regular clergy were imprisoned, exiled or transferred out of the region. Bishop Múgica, who claimed to support the military rebels, was the victim of frequent humiliations and death-threats at the hands of Francoist officers and Falangists. He was expelled from Francoist Spain and forced into exile in Italy where he denounced the bombing of Guernica to the Vatican, as a result of which Franco determined that he should never be permitted to return to his diocese.

Múgica and Vidal i Barraquer were, of course, exceptions. The hierarchy in general was delighted with Franco's victory. The liberalising laic legislation of the Republic was overthrown. Control of education returned to the Church. Divorce was once more illegal. The Roman Catholic Church had the monopoly of religious practice. Nevertheless, in some parts of Spain, the Church was not the embodiment of the militant values of the Inquisition which many on the extreme right longed for. In Catalonia, there was a sophisticated and cultured liberal Church. In the Basque Country particularly, and even parts of Old Castile, the relationship between clergy and ordinary peasants was one which belied the easy slur that the Church merely provided the theological justification for social injustice. It is one of the delights of Dr Brassloff's richly textured and elegantly written work that her research has been illuminated so much by an awareness of the way in which regionalist sentiments interacted with the issue of the relations between the Church and the centralist State.

In the immediate aftermath of the Civil War, levels of religiosity differed dramatically, from a high of 90 per cent attendance at mass in the north in Pamplona, to nearer 45 per cent in the centre of Spain and dropping to only 13 per cent in the south. Andalusia had probably never been fully conquered for the Church. When the Cardinal Archbishop of Seville wrote to parish priests before the Civil War exhorting them to set up committees of adult, male, practising Catholic laymen of good moral character and local standing to raise money for the maintenance of the clergy, nearly 100 per cent replied that no such persons existed. After, as before the Civil War, the urban proletariat in Madrid, Bilbao, Barcelona and the Asturian mining towns lived in virtual ignorance of Catholic doctrine and ritual. All the more so after the partisan role of the bulk of the clergy during the war, religion was seen by many as the class enemy, legitimising an unjust property structure.

That very tendency was a symptom of the Spanish Church's dominantly integrist tendency. Yet, as Dr Brassloff is fully aware, an ideological and theological pluralism within Spanish Catholicism lay behind its trajectory. As she makes clear from the very beginning, the Church is not just its hierarchy but also its community of believers. The ecclesiastical hierarchy consisted of some bishops who believed, along with Franco, that a militant, war-like Catholicism was responsible for all the glories of Spain's imperial past and liberal, foreign values as responsible for the decline of Spain. Yet at the same time, there were always subversive bishops more concerned with the Church's mission to the poor and with the political, especially regional-nationalist, aspirations of their flocks. A similar division could be traced within what Dr Brassloff calls 'the people of God', the broad mass of the faithful. The unprecedented change in stance by the Church in the 1960s was most obviously initiated by the encyclicals of Pope John XXIII and the declarations of the Second Vatican Council and their call for dialogue with the modern world. However, its sustained acceleration is accounted for by divisions between the rightist and the more liberal Church, consisting of clergy associated with local nationalist movements and the workers' movement. The attention paid by Dr Brassloff to this thread of internal tension between the pro-Franco conservatives and those progressives committed to social justice underlies each chapter of this book and makes for compelling reading.

It is hardly surprising, as Dr Brassloff shows, that General Franco himself did everything that he could to influence the Vatican Council lest its conclusions tend in any way to delegitimise his regime. Faced with clerical opposition, he and many of his followers simply concluded that the Church had been infiltrated by Communists and freemasons. Others, and many opponents of the regime, assumed that the rats were leaving the sinking ship. The role played by lay Catholic youth and workers' associations in the resistance against Franco was an immensely important one. They drew attention to abuse of human and political rights by the regime about which the hierarchy remained happily short-sighted. When the Church denounced police brutality, its standing rose among wide swathes of public opinion. The regime retaliated by threatening to reduce its financial support for the Church. This led to a complicated debate over whether the Church's educational and welfare activities were something that formed part of the regime's duty to society. Dr Brassloff is an exemplary guide through a labyrinthine issue which she demonstrates to have been a crucial step on the long road to the dissociation of Church and State in the latter days of the regime.

The contribution of the Church to the construction of democracy was every bit as important after Franco's death. Catholics were left free to vote on reform according to their consciences and politicians were enjoined to behave morally as Christians. With considerable subtlety, Dr Brassloff traces the hierarchy's comportment in this period in terms of a strategic adjustment to a situation in which the Church would no longer have State support for its pretension to a monopoly in moral and spiritual issues. She shows how, in the new situation of a free market in ethical choices, key leaders of the ecclesiastical hierarchy, most notably Cardinal Tarancón, overcame the rearguard action of the older conservatives and the pressures of younger radicals to find a role in the new democratic polity. In the most dramatically original part of her book, she then goes on to examine the consequences of the death in 1978 of the liberal Pope Paul VI and his eventual replacement by the energetic conservative Pole, Karol Wojtyla, as Pope John Paul II. Ironically, the Spanish Church passed from living in a context of a liberal Papacy and a reactionary regime to one of a conservative Papacy and a democratic regime. The second half of the book contains a lucid, and unique, account of the consequences of this reversal.

Not the least of Dr Brassloff's merits resides in her acute sensitivity to the complex changes undergone by a Church blown by the winds of change blowing from Rome and a sociological evolution which matched the far-reaching social changes of a rapidly modernising Spain. The Church made a crucial contribution to the bloodless nature of the transition to democracy after Franco by publicly dissociating itself from the dictatorship. As the regime imprisoned priests involved in Basque nationalist groups, the divisions became starker. Having reacted violently to the loss of its expected privileges of state funding and ideological hegemony under the Second Republic, the Church acquiesced in giving up those same privileges after Franco. The 53 new bishops consecrated between 1964 and 1974 acted, as the *Opus Dei* did not, to facilitate the reconciliation of the Church and the people in a democratic Spain. The significance of episcopal appointments is also a theme traced with considerable skill in this book.

Without in any way diminishing the acute critical faculty which informs this book, Dr Brassloff's own liberal Catholicism lies behind her ability to write with such insight on so many aspects of Catholic politics, culture and religiosity. However, it must be stressed that, despite this, at no point does she stray from an even-handed objectivity. Her central story of the Church's internal and external politics is placed firmly and sensitively in a context of the reality of religious practice, socio-economic change and particularly of regional differentiation. Given the conflictive broader context of the Vatican Council, the spread of liberation theology and the death agony of the Franco

Foreword

regime, and the internal reality of the complex internecine struggles within the Spanish Church, this is a difficult story to tell. The sheer complexity of the process could have resulted in an intractable text. In fact, while skilfully disentangling the threads of Spanish politics and global theological developments, Dr Brassloff tells her tale with enormous clarity. The result is an important book which has much to say, not only about the Spanish Church, but about the universal Catholic Church and about Spanish politics during the decline of the dictatorship and the transition to, and consolidation of, democracy. Moreover, it is unique in its treatment of the role of the Church in the transition to democracy, the subsequent years of consolidation, and the decade and a half of Socialist power. It constitutes a very considerable achievement.

Acknowledgements

In wrestling with the various elements of this book, I have incurred a great many debts. The first is to Professor Paul Preston who gave me unstintingly of his time and much opportune advice, not least to 'Listen to more Wagner'. I am grateful also to the late Fr Fernando Urbina and the *Pastoral Misionera* team, Professor Rafael Díaz-Salazar, Professor Joan Bada, Jordi López Camps, Fr José María Díaz Mozaz, and many other unsung colleagues in Spain and Britain who gave so much help in discussing specific issues and supplying me with appropriate material. Not least do I bless my husband to whose loving support, political acumen and agnostic discernment I owe more than I can say.

List of Acronyms

AP	Alianza Popular – (Right-wing) Popular Alliance, later PP
CCOO	Comisiones Obreras – communist-led trade union federation
CCP	Comunidades Cristianes Populares – Popular Christian Communities
CEE	Conferencia Episcopal Española – Spanish Bishops' Conference
CEPS	Comisión Episcopal de Pastoral Social – Social Pastoral Commission of the CEE
CiU	Convergència i Unió – (Christian Democrat) Catalan nationalist coalition
CNT	Confederación Nacional del Trabajo – anarchist organisation
CONCAPA	Confederación Católica de Padres de Familia y Padres de Alumnos – Catholic Parents' Association
COPE	Cadena de Ondas Populares Españolas – radio station with majority shareholding by the Catholic Church
CpS	Cristianos por el Socialismo – Christians for Socialism
EC	European Community, later European Union (EU)
EEC	European Economic Community
ETA	Euskadi Ta Askatasuna – (separatist) Basque Homeland and Freedom organisation
FERE	Federación Española de Religiosos de Enseñanza – Federation of Religious in Education
FRAP	Frente Revolucionario Anti-fascista Patriótico – ultra-left revolutionary group
FOESSA	(Fundación Fomento de Estudios Sociales y de Sociología Aplicada) – foundation for promoting sociological research
GDP	gross domestic product
HOAC	Hermandad Obrera de Acción Católica – Catholic Action Workers' Guild
IU	Izquierda Unida (communist-led) United Left coalition
JOC	Juventud Obrera Católica – Catholic Workers' Youth Movement

LOAPA	Organic Law for the Harmonisation of the Autonomy Process
LODE	Organic Law for the Right to Education
LOGSE	Organic Law for the General Organisation of the Education System
PCE	Partido Comunista Español – Spanish Communist Party
PNV	Partido Nacionalista Vasco – (moderate) Basque Nationalist Party
PP	Partido Popular – Popular Party, formerly AP
PSOE	Partido Socialista Obrero Español – Spanish Socialist Party
UCD	Unión de Centro Democrático – Democratic Centre Union
UGT	Union General de Trabajadores – General Workers' Union, traditionally linked to the PSOE
VOJ	Vanguardia Obrera Juvenil – Young Workers' Vanguard
VOS	Vanguardia Obrera Social – Social Workers' Vanguard

Glossary

base communities	informal grass-roots Christian groups
bunker	extreme pro-Franco elements opposed to any political reform
Falange	Francoism's only permitted political organisation
Cortes	Spanish Parliament
derecho de presentación	right of patronage in the appointment of bishops
Guerrilleros de Cristo Rey	(Warriors of Christ the King) right-wing extremists
integrist	ultra-conservative Catholic with pre-Vatican II mentality
liberation theology	theology of empowering the poor, marginalised and oppressed to achieve pro-actively their God-given dignity
National Movement	The Franco regime's 'umbrella' political support organisation
National Catholicism	symbiosis of Church and State under Franco
ordinary	diocesan bishop
procurador	deputy in Franco's Cortes

xvii

Introduction

It is interesting that Spain has given the universal Church... the Dominicans, the Jesuits and the Opus Dei, characterised by their zealous defence of the faith, missionary dynamism and, above all, their capacity for resolving the perennial problem facing all Churches: their need to adapt to developments in the secular world. At three different historical and crucial moments, Spanish civilisation has brought forth brilliant rescue operations, each one in line with the imperatives of accommodation. The first eradicated medieval heresy inquisitorially; the second assimilated the consequences of the Renaissance and the Reformation; the third, less far-reaching to be sure, managed to do the same with the spirit of capitalism. What we do not know, with an eye to the future, is whether there will be resources enough... for the Catholic Church to cope with the new religious pluralism [and] with the new secularisation.[1]

This book grapples with challenging socio-political and theological issues affecting the trajectory of the Catholic Church in Spain over recent decades, as it responded to far-reaching changes in society. Since there are many definitions and models of 'Church', perhaps here, the threshold of the analysis, is the appropriate place to establish that the term will be used throughout as referring both to an institution broadly identified with the hierarchy, and to 'the people of God', a community of believers.

The Second Vatican Council and its aftermath, pacts and accommodation, withdrawal from dictatorship and adjustment to democracy, Church–State relations, vested interests, internal ecclesial divisions, the challenge of secularisation: such is the backcloth to the events and the personalities which shaped this period. Some of the issues were ongoing. The (anti)capitalism controversy was a seminal feature of intra-ecclesial relations at a time when the Church was attempting to come to terms with the end of Francoism and then settling into relations with a new, democratic, regime. The opposing and shifting attitudes on the matter within the body of the Church are mapped out chapter by chapter. Another seminal issue is secularisation, 'the process by which sectors of society and culture are removed from the domination of religious institutions and symbols'.[2] Its apparently irreversible advance, which threatened the Church's whole *raison d'être* and to which there was no easy answer, even with the aid of traditional allies, is similarly charted throughout the book.

At the time Pope John XXIII summoned the Second Vatican Council in 1962, a triumphalist Spanish Catholicism appeared immutable. It was cosseted and at the same time corseted in political and social terms, by virtue of the hierarchy's close alliance with Francoism since the Civil War (1936–9), the wounds of which had not yet been allowed to heal. Catholicism was the established religion of the Spanish State. The Catholic Church enjoyed considerable privileges in its role as legitimiser of the dictatorship, willing instrument of social control and moral guardian of society. Capitalism was the overarching socio-economic system to which both the Church and the ruling power elites supporting Franco's regime adhered, and atheistic communism was their common enemy. The Council proved a difficult and often painful experience for the Spanish hierarchy, since, in the attempt both to bring the Catholic Church into the twentieth century and to stem the tide of secularisation, it called for a dialogue with the modern world, for freedom from ties with secular powers, for religious liberty, for human and civil rights.

But even before the Council, there was a leaven of renewal at work in the Spanish Church. Various Catholic workers' organisations, believing that Christianity involved a double commitment, social as well as spiritual, had become *engagés* against injustice, poverty, exploitation and repression, and were increasingly critical of the prevailing capitalist system, the 'established disorder' of the Franco regime, and the Church's alliance with them. Such commitment, shared by many of the younger priests, and by some students and intellectuals, brought conflict with both the Franco regime and the Church hierarchy. Growing at the same time was the influence of the Opus Dei, a movement with a completely different spiritual emphasis, from whose cadres sprang the Franco regime's neo-capitalist economic miracle-makers.

Vatican II, in its declarations on 'The Church in the Modern World' (more generally known as *Gaudium et Spes*) underlined the importance of human and civil rights. Gradually there came a shift in the attitudes of the Spanish hierarchy, leading – from the end of the 1960s onwards – to disengagement from their alliance with the Franco regime, and to confrontation on issues raised by the Council (and by the Church's own members) that were relevant to the socio-political situation in Spain. This change of direction became particularly evident after Cardinal Tarancón had been elected President of the Bishops' Conference. He towed the Spanish Church to what came to be called the 'extreme centre' of politics, and skilfully navigated the waters between Franco's dictatorial regime and the first stage of the transition to democracy.

However, the hierarchy found some aspects of the new alliance with democracy difficult to digest. Pluralism meant that its traditional spheres of influence – State-protected under Franco – were now subject to the vagaries of 'market choice'. The Church's stance on marital and sexual matters was challenged by society's more permissive attitudes and democracy's more liberal legislation, while the status of the Catholic religion in schools was called into question. Catholics fell away from the Church in large numbers or stayed inside, cherry-picking their beliefs. Moreover, the hierarchy's traditional antimarxism kept it in conflict with Catholic activists who saw capitalism as the real enemy of the gospel and persisted in the charge that the bishops were propping up an unjust socio-economic system. From 1981, a series of position papers showed the influence of Pope John Paul II's *Laborem Exercens* and indicated that the hierarchy was becoming more critical of the excesses of capitalism than before but was still fundamentally beholden to it.

The theology of ecclesial plurality versus hierarchical authority, the theology of the autonomy of the secular world, and the theology of socio-economics were conflated in the Church's great evangelisation dilemma of how to stem the tide of secularisation in Spain. All through history, the Church had used its system–regime alliance strategy to enable it to fight its enemies and to impose its beliefs on society. Even so, Spain had never been as completely Catholic as proclaimed by the vast majority of its prelates. There were Spaniards who, while nominally Catholic, were less than whole-heartedly committed to the Church's prescriptions. There were also those who rejected the Church's tenets because they had different world-views, different religions, or ideologies deemed by the Church to be a threat, and who, conversely, saw the Church as their enemy. Until the Council, it had been possible for the Church to counter other cosmovisions both by using State power to suppress opposition, and by pointing to its own 'superior' truth and certainties, most recently against modernity's ideological 'heresies' and scientific advances of the last two centuries. Modernity was an adversary which the universal Church fought vigorously until John XXIII called a halt in the 1960s, and attempted instead to enter into dialogue with it.

But by then, modernity itself was becoming radicalised and transmuted. The confident scientific mirror held up to the world which characterised the nineteenth century and much of the twentieth, providing coherent alternative world-pictures to that of the Church, started to crack and became fragmented. Some point to the '1968 syndrome', which had found expression in the *événements* of France and general West European movements, the civil rights demonstrations and the anti-Vietnam contestation in the United States, as marking a sea-change in society's attitudes, typified by even greater plurality, rejection of authority, and absence of specific points of reference. In turn, the certainties of science and hence the promises of its brave new world came under scrutiny and repudiation as people became more aware of its limitations, epitomised by environmental degradation and the science-based means of mass destruction. As in all aspects of life, from history and politics to art and literature, the old positivist dream that everything could be explained was in crisis; at times explanation, which is only conceivable on the assumption that there is a truth to be found, made no sense. The absolute relationship between cause and effect and the total rationality of human thought and action were called into question. Everything was now relative, and no values went undisputed.

Such an environment accelerated the process of secularisation facing the Spanish Church. In the past, alliance with the ruling elites and the monopoly of moral control had kept much of the membership inside the institution, but so much freedom, so much pluralism, so much questioning of authority could not be held in check.

The great compromise with science and politics which the Church had prepared to enter into during Vatican II and which was intended to reconcile it to the secular world, ceased to have the same relevance, or even, it may be argued, any relevance at all. In this sense Vatican II had come too late. It was no longer a question of entering into a dialogue with modernity – which had a rational world-picture – but with shattered fragments of that modernity. Such a dialogue was impossible because it would have meant introducing some aspects of the fragmentation into the Church itself; it was precisely what the Catholic Church, built on its concept of hierarchy and need to preserve unity, would not and could not contemplate. Instead of making Vatican II a point of departure for venturing a leap forward in faith, Pope Paul VI in his later years and Pope John Paul II after him even more vigorously attempted to reimpose uniformity of thought within the Church. This was to no avail, since so many of its members had

Introduction 5

drawn conclusions from the already-existing plurality of society outside, but also from the pluralism conceded by the Church as rightfully part of the secular world, and from the freedom of individual conscience inspired by Vatican II. And they acted accordingly. The Church had, in fact, been overtaken by the plurality of modernity run riot, that is, a postmodern society of increasing individualism and relativism, where there were no absolutes, no automatic respect for authority, no specific civil values, merely personal interpretations. This phenomenon was not confined to Spain but was particularly striking there because the 'counterculture' environment of the late 1960s and the repercussions of Vatican II coincided with the debilitated final years of the Franco regime. If it is true that 'the received doctrines of the Church were formed and developed in response to heresies',[3] it follows that the Church could not develop a doctrine in response to the post-Enlightenment heresy of modernity, particularly in its new, splintered form. Bishop Osés put his finger on the dilemma when he wrote in 1987, 'There is a need to evangelise man in his cultural, scientific and technical context with all its complexity... The Church has no meaning outside this reality, this world, this society, but we do not know how to deal with it'.[4] His words remain pertinent. Furthermore, the worldwide collapse of atheistic communism left the Church without a palpable enemy. The system-regime alliance strategy, at one time so important in enabling it to deliver its message, control its members and smite its enemies, became increasingly pointless. Against latter-day secularisation – diffuse, indifferent and fragmented, an intangible enemy without an ideology to confront head-on – alliances were ineffectual. A different kind of Church would have to seek a different kind of presence in society.

The distinction between *socio-economic system* – the specific way of running the economy and society, of allocating resources and of distributing incomes, by the social forces that are the main beneficiaries – and *political regime* – the specific form of organisation and authority run by political forces in the interest of the system and assuring its continuing existence – is based on David Easton[5] and, in the Spanish context, on Juan José Ruiz Rico.[6] The theory of pacts and alliances, for which the Austrian theologian August Knoll[7] was a valuable source, is here brought up to date.

1 The Spanish Church and the Second Vatican Council

The bishops – and a vast majority of priests, religious and practising Catholics – were profoundly convinced that Franco's regime, which resulted from the Crusade in defence of faith and fatherland – that was how the Civil War was considered – was like the Church's secular arm... which was always ready to defend Christianity and considered Catholic unity as a cornerstone.[1]

The 'religious issue' was one of the main factors which led to the breakdown of the Second Republic (1931–6) and spilled over into the Spanish Civil War. Although there is no evidence that the Church was directly involved in the plots leading to the 1936 military rebellion, it can be argued that its alliance over long years with the ruling political and socio-economic elites had contributed significantly to the ideological climate of the uprising. The Church legitimised the generals' revolt, giving it the status of a 'Crusade' in the defence of the Catholic faith.

Franco's victory in 1939 signified that the oligarchy which he had fought to save had triumphed, and that for almost four decades Spain would be governed by dictatorship. Tens of thousands of Spaniards were executed, tens of thousands more imprisoned. The suppression of human and civil rights, and of regional identity, especially in Catalonia and the Basque Country, ensured that there was no reconciliation between victors and vanquished. Political parties were banned, apart from the fascist Falange. Similarly, with a ban on genuine trade unions, workers' representation was reduced to the sham of 'vertical syndicates' which, by grouping together employers and employed, were presumed to avoid class conflict and resistance to what was a particularly exploitative form of capitalism. In a country devastated by war and economic ruin, the vast majority of people suffered years of poverty and hunger.

Franco's victory also signified that the Throne and Altar alliance that had been the leitmotiv of Spanish history since the Reconquest was a reality once more, and until after the Second Vatican Council there was to be no radical change in the partnership between the official Church and the State. Both the ruling elites and the Church were opposed to modernity, and to the social forces that pursued democratic political objectives, rejected privilege and sought equality and social justice. The Church legitimised the ethos, the political structures, the legislation and the activities of the State, and was a willing instrument of social control. In return, Franco abrogated the anticlerical legislation of the Second Republic and restored to the Church its privileges and its monopoly over the nation's education, faith and morals. Spain, or at least 'that section of the population which has been perverted, poisoned by corrupting doctrines' had to be 'rechristianised', said Franco in 1940 to members of Catholic Action, the 'long arm' of the Church hierarchy.

The bishops supported Franco and his regime almost to a man but that is not to say that everything always flowed smoothly in Church–State relations. Furthermore, despite the confessionality of the Spanish State, Pope Pius XII was for a long time reluctant to sign with Franco the Concordat which the General coveted as proof that his regime enjoyed Rome's moral endorsement. It was eventually signed in 1953; in the same year, the United States gave a certain respectability to the dictatorship by entering into a defence agreement with Franco as part of its Cold War policy, thus effectively ending the post-World War II international boycott of the regime. The two accords were not unrelated: Franco, Pius XII and President Eisenhower shared a visceral anti-communism and hostility to the Soviet bloc. In return for privileges to the Spanish Church, the Concordat granted Franco the right of patronage (*derecho de presentación*) in the appointment of ordinaries (diocesan bishops).[2] Auxiliary bishops and apostolic administrators, however, were appointed directly by the Vatican without reference to Franco: this would become a serious issue when the Church no longer saw eye-to-eye with the regime.

But Church–State conflict was not even a fleck on the horizon in 1953, when the Concordat was signed. The symbiosis seemed perfect. However, during the 1950s and especially from the beginning of the 1960s, there were growing signs, starting at the ecclesial grassroots, that the Spanish Church was undergoing change. The first major impetus from below came from groups such as the Christian Workers' movements, both the Catholic Action Workers' Guilds – HOAC (*Hermandades Obreras de Acción Católica*) and its youth branch – JOC (*Juventud Obrera Católica*) founded in 1946 and 1947 respectively to spread Christian ideals at work and in their daily environment, on the lines of 'See, Judge and Act' as developed by Cardinal Cardijn in Belgium. There was also the Young Workers' Vanguard – VOJ (*Vanguardia Obrera Juvenil*) and the Social Workers' Vanguard – VOS (*Vanguardia Obrera Social*), organisations usually known as the Workers' Vanguards (*Vanguardias Obreras*). The chaplains to the *Vanguardias Obreras* were Jesuits, as were those of the Catholic Employees' Movement (*Movimiento Católico de Empleados*). Catalonia was the home, alongside these groups, of Catholic Workers' Action (*Acción Católica Obrera*) and the Basque Country that of Rural Youth (*Herri Gaztedi*). Another radical minority Catholic group was the university-based FLP ('*Felipe*'–Popular Liberation Front) founded in the mid-1950s. These Catholic activists, together with worker-priests, started to participate in the great ideological currents of the clandestine secular workers' movements, examining the social realities around them in the light of the gospel, and finding them wanting. Earlier attempts by the Church to approach the workers' world had been no more than paternalistic at best and had soon become instruments of the men of property. Even HOAC and JOC had probably been set up by the hierarchy in the first place more as a means of reconquering a hostile working class that tended to identify the Church with exploitative capitalism and political reaction, and to compete with the socialist UGT and anarchist CNT trade unions, than to act as 'missionaries'.[3]

HOAC published a paper, *!Tú!*, with a circulation of 40 000 in 1949. *!Tú!* saw National Catholicism – that equating of the essential Spanish identity with the Catholic religion – as the ideology of the power elites who attempted to use religion to justify the unjustifiable. HOAC and JOC fiercely attacked the harsh social consequences for workers of the new industrialisation strategy devised for Spain in the late 1950s. Cracking down on the constant denunciation of social injustice in the incisive articles published in *!Tú!*, and its criticism of the Church's alliance with the regime and of the absence of real representation in the pseudo-trade-union syndicates, the government forced the Church authorities to cease publication of the paper in 1951. JOC's activities and its bulletin, *Juventud Obrera*, raised hackles in the episcopate itself because they aimed to demonstrate that only a Church devoted to justice and the salvation of the *whole* man could hope to awaken in young people some spark of interest in the Catholic religion.

Other journals too were an expression of new attitudes: *Incunable* (1948) was published by the clergy; *El Ciervo* (1951), the organ of a lay group,[4] became the forum for a young generation of Catalan activists, like Alfonso Comín, the first Catholic to become a member of the Central Committee of the underground Spanish Communist Party and later a key figure in founding 'Christians for Socialism'. In 1958 the first issue appeared of the more 'popular' weekly *Vida Nueva*, which, while remaining basically loyal to the hierarchy, became moderately progressive in its evaluations of Church involvement in Spanish politics and society.

Many younger – and some older – priests were greatly influenced by the radical activism of the HOAC and JOC. Under the terms of the 1953 Concordat, the State could not – in theory at least – interfere in Catholic Action, so HOAC and JOC acted with some degree of autonomy vis-à-vis both the hierarchy and the Franco regime, but their openly reformist attitude called down government wrath on many occasions. They played a prominent role in the widespread illegal strikes of 1962, working alongside marxists – socialists and communists – in a newly emerging clandestine trade union organisation, the Workers' Commissions (*CCOO–Comisiones Obreras*). Cardinal Pla y Deniel, the President of Catholic Action, was fervently pro-Franco but showed himself to be valiant in his defence of HOAC leaders and in his public declarations about labour problems. However, the failure of the hierarchy as a body to understand and empathise with the aims of these Catholic workers' movements would lead to the 'Catholic Action crisis' of the mid-1960s.

This younger generation of clerics complained of the formula-ridden backwardness of official Catholicism in Spain, and of the great divide between priest and people – criticisms not lost on Bishop (later Cardinal) Vicente Enrique y Tarancón of the Solsona diocese because of his own personal experiences. Young priests started to work in teams in poor rural and urban parishes; after the Second Vatican Council, the renewal movement of which they were a vanguard would crystallise in base (grass-roots) Christian communities and the search for new pastoral structures. Spanish seminarians studying abroad breathed in new theological airs and began to question the 'Crusade' values of the Spanish Church. An important contribution was made also by intellectuals like Xavier Zubiri, José Luis López Aranguren and Pedro Laín Entralgo. The 'nouvelle théologie' from France played an important role in the 'International Catholic Conversations' of San Sebastián, beginning in September 1947, and subsequently, from 1951–65, the Catholic 'Conversations of Gredos'. Laín later commented on the failure of the Gredos

Conversations to grapple with atheism and agnosticism and with social issues such as acute poverty and injustice,[5] but the fact that criticism and self-criticism were emerging – in the face of a generally antagonistic hierarchy[6] – showed that the Church was not monolithic, and laid important foundations for the future.

The 1950s saw also the ascent of a very different religious force in Spanish Catholicism, the Opus Dei. Founded in 1928 by an Aragonese priest, Fr (later Mgr) Escrivá de Balaguer, it was a Catholic organisation, highly conservative in tendency, created to promote the sanctification of daily life and work, but it functioned also as an elite pressure group, seeking to control the nerve-centres of national power. In the 1950s, members of the Opus began to secure important public positions and then to break the domination of the Falange over the regime's bureaucracy. The Opus technocrats aimed to modernise the economy, to end the vain attempt to achieve autarchy in Spain, and to incorporate the country fully into the neocapitalism of the West. The economic liberalism which it preached was not designed to be accompanied by political liberalisation. Members of the Opus Dei entered the government in February 1957 and would dominate politically and economically until the end of the 1960s. The harsh socio-economic consequences of their 1959 Stabilisation Plan, which laid the foundations for Spain's entry into the capitalist world of the West, drew bitter condemnation from HOAC and JOC.

Changes taking place within the Church coincided with radical alterations to the structure and values of Spanish society as a whole. A rural exodus gathered momentum, leading to rapid urbanisation and industrialisation, all on a much vaster scale than in the preceding century, and in tandem with the first sparks of faster economic growth beginning in the mid-1950s. These were among the factors that precipitated a change in people's perceptions, aspirations and life-styles. Economic development was fostered by increasing functional integration into the dynamic European economy, which led to rising industrial exports and foreign direct investment. Outmigration by Spaniards to those countries of Europe like France and Germany that were enjoying their economic miracles further accelerated the rural exodus without causing unemployment. The contacts made by Spanish migrants with other people's politics and mores, and the beginning of mass tourism to Spain, introduced different ways of thinking and behaving. Accelerated economic growth achieved by the change from agrarian to industry-based structures, and the associated move to urban life, peaked in the second half of the

1970s; then the repercussions of Europe-wide recession and deceleration of growth began to be felt.

In such shifting societal sands, the task of recapturing the soul of the nation seemed doomed to failure. During the early postwar period, up to the end of the 1950s, the Church made an attempt to bring back popular religious practices and to restore the importance of the clergy as the main agent of pastoral action. For the minority there were specialist spiritual exercises. For the majority – whether or not practising Catholics – missions were preached all over Spain, pilgrimages organised, cities, towns and monuments consecrated to the hearts of Jesus and Mary; there were popular devotions to local saints, the cult of relics, processions.

Much of what seemed a fervent response to such expressions of mass religious activity may well have been genuine, but it must also have been conditioned by the fact that people were under Church as well as State surveillance, and that a priest's recommendation was needed for a good deal of the ordinary business of daily life and work. At the same time, it was clear that in many cases indoctrination in the Catholic religion, imposed by Francoism at all levels of education, was counter-productive, as various beneficiaries of a Catholic education later revealed in their memoirs. Cardinal Vidal had warned as early as 1940 that the political attempts to reverse the aggressively secular attitudes of the Second Republic would fail. Intellectuals would not take seriously a religion which taught that the Virgin Mary had appeared in person to the apostle St James, and would be therefore equally dismissive of basic Catholic beliefs. Nor would spectacular religious displays convert 'the thousands and thousands' of people who kept their heads down because they had been on the losing side in the Civil War but had not abandoned their convictions.[7]

Increasingly, the closeness of the Church–Franco alliance, intended to be an asset to the Church in its evangelising mission, turned out to be an obstacle. Not that this was anything new: as early as 1933, Canon Arboleya had pinpointed the alliance of the Church with the ruling elites as the cause of the disaffection of broad sectors of the working class.[8] Even in 1949, at the height of National Catholicism, Fr Azpiazu SJ wrote that 'out of the seven million wage-earners, a realistic figure of the number of those going to Mass in Spain would be horrifying'.[9] In 1957 a HOAC survey showed that, of a sample of 15 491 workers, 86.1 per cent professed themselves to be Catholics in 'rites of passage', but 89.6 per cent to be anticlerical, 41.3 per cent anti-religious, 54.7 per cent completely uninterested in religion; 28.5

per cent were 'Easter duty' Catholics, 23.2 per cent 'occasional Mass-goers', only 7.6 per cent Sunday Mass-goers and 2.9 per cent members of Church organisations.[10]

Thus by the inauguration of the Second Vatican Council in 1962, Spain had not been rechristianised. Imposition of belief by coercive mass immersion had failed. The Council would propose another solution, but at the same time it would confront the Spanish Church with the need to reassess its political and intra-ecclesial relationships in line with the process of reformation which was occurring at the universal Church level.

Pope John XXIII, elected in 1958, intended to overhaul the thinking of the universal Catholic Church and, in contrast to his predecessors, to put an end to 'the Cold War between the Church and the social, political and industrial structures and realities of the modern world'.[11] In this respect, the Second Vatican Council which he summoned can be seen as the Church's attempt to respond to the growth of secularisation by coming to terms with 'modernity', an *aggiornamento* to make the Church and its message more relevant to the day and age.[12]

Pope John's encyclicals, *Mater et Magistra* in 1962 and *Pacem in Terris* in 1963, and the declarations of the Council fathers, showed an attitude of receptiveness and dialogue towards the modern world and many of its values, including freedom[13] – political as well as religious – equality, democracy, and the rights of ethnic minorities. The new thinking also embraced socio-economic matters. Whereas since Leo XIII's 1891 encyclical *Rerum Novarum* the over-riding concern of the Church had been to defend certain personal rights, especially that to private property, against the growing socialist threat, with John XXIII came a shift in emphasis to a concern for the poor and the powerless, and a critique of the structures that kept them so. In the more directly political sphere, the Church favoured some disengagement from secular powers in a marked, but not complete, reversal of centuries-old tradition. As to the specific form of secular power, the Church denounced totalitarianism and supported democracy. Furthermore, in contrast to the two previous Councils of Trent and Vatican I, Vatican II was not called to reject a heresy, not even that of communism or marxism. Instead there was to be dialogue between Catholics and atheists whenever they shared the same wider humanist goals. The spirit of détente and optimism hovered also over international diplomacy; despite ongoing Cold War confrontation, the United States under Kennedy and the Soviet Union under

Khrushchev appeared to be groping their way towards some kind of coexistence.

When Pope John declared in his opening speech to the Council that the Church in the past had been harmed by too close a relationship with 'the princes of this world', his words were taken by many as the funeral oration for the Constantinian period of the Church. But this was to a certain extent wishful thinking: the universal Church was not able or willing to release itself entirely from the embrace of such princes, the ruling political regimes and the dominant economic elites. The Vatican continued also to be a political entity, a State like other States, so as to be able to maintain its worldwide network of nuncios and apostolic delegates which it believed would facilitate evangelisation, but which at the same time strengthened Rome's centralised control of national Churches. Where it deemed appropriate and possible, the Vatican intervened as well in national and local politics. As to the socio-economic sphere, it was evident from John's encyclicals and the Council documents that there was to be no downright condemnation of the capitalist system, but of its 'excesses'. Even so, Vatican II took a great step forward, both by distancing itself to a certain extent, when it declared that 'economic development must be kept under the control of mankind. It must not be left to the sole judgement of a few men or groups possessing excessive economic power...',[14] and by reconciling itself with what it called 'socialisation', some form of 'Christian socialism', as opposed to 'really existing', that is, Soviet-type socialism.

There were demands for a new and dynamic relationship between the Church and the world, faith and politics, and the Church and the poor. However, the Christian-marxist sociologist, Alfonso Comín, pointed out that the specific field of the relations of the Church with the poor was not fully addressed at the Council nor were its implications completely taken on board. All the problematics of social restructuring – national and international – immediately conjured up the possibility of changes that were too profound to contemplate, particularly for a Church so long allied to secular powers and power structures.[15] A letter addressed by 15 French worker-priests to the Council in the course of its third session underlined the fact that the Church seemed to some workers to be 'an economic, political and cultural power which lives comfortably in capitalism'.[16]

The Spanish bishops were quite unprepared for radical change. In February 1961, they had issued a document 'Concerning the Forthcoming II Vatican Council'[17] in which there was the customary stab at the enemy, atheistic communism. They pointed to the need to reinforce the unity of the Church and to maintain the purity of the faith as interpreted by the hierarchy. Shortly after the Council actually began, and on the first anniversary of the publication of *Mater et Magistra,* they published a collective pastoral letter on 'Social Conscience'[18] in which they reiterated 'that communism is intrinsically perverse and that a Christian is not allowed to collaborate with it in any field'. They were in favour of actions furthering 'the sacred and legitimate rights of the workers', provided that such actions 'respected legal channels'. The catch was that, in Franco's Spain, there were few if any such channels. The bishops' document attempted to counter Franco's accusations that the progressive wings of Catholic Action were opening the door to communism; but at the same time it stopped short of criticising the Franco regime for its failure to recognise workers' rights. It was an appeal to finer feelings. The document urged 'beloved workers and entrepreneurs' to get to know the social doctrine of the Church and thus co-operate 'in charity and justice' in the country's economic development which was being promoted by the State 'in a noble Christian social direction'.[19]

With a few exceptions, notably that of Mgr Castán Lacoma, auxiliary bishop of Tarragona, most of the Spanish bishops had hoped for a doctrinal Council that would be a continuation of Vatican I.[20] Vatican II's call for freedom of religion, ideological pluralism in civil life, and not least the emphasis on a less close relationship with the State, especially one that was not democratic, fell on reluctant ears. That was perhaps not surprising. After all, the average age of the Spanish bishops at the Council was over 65; most of them had been ordained before the Civil War, had lived through it in the nationalist zone and had been identified with the National Catholicism of the postwar years. They were, moreover, insufficiently conscious of the pastoral and theological currents swirling in other countries which were so influential in preparing for and then shaping attitudes during the Council.[21]

Franco's speeches of the time often included a eulogy of conciliar resolutions, using carefully edited quotations to serve his own purposes. He was advised by his Justice Minister, Antonio Oriol y Urquijo, that the Spanish State 'must appear to be active and enthusiastic in carrying out the Council's norms in Spain, and not unwilling, wary or fearful'.[22] The reason Oriol gave was that it would be misguided to allow the regime's opponents to use the Council's decisions for *their* purposes. Such advice was to the point, given the way Catholic – and other – opposition groups found ammunition for their cause in conciliar pronouncements. Franco himself said to his cousin that the Second Vatican Council was pointing in a particular direction and a Catholic government had no alternative but to follow it, without protest,[23] this despite the fact that he was convinced that the Curia was infiltrated by Freemasons and communists.[24]

Franco did everything in his power to persuade the Council fathers not to support ideas, texts or decrees that might directly or indirectly delegitimise his regime. Of particular concern was the conciliar declaration on religious freedom.[25] In a clear rejection of both religious and political pluralism, Franco's adviser and confidant, Admiral Carrero Blanco, considered that allowing freedom to other religions would be suicidal 'because it would lead us into religious and consequently political disintegration'.[26] At that time Franco knew that the vast majority of the Spanish hierarchy were on the side of the regime, and thus it seems unlikely that he feared trouble from any quarter except from regional nationalist clerics like the Catalan Abbot of Montserrat, or from the 'young clergy... who have been unable to digest the real meaning of the social conflicts... and who support the agitators'.[27]

Most of the Spanish bishops were themselves hostile towards religious freedom and cautious in the extreme over ecumenism. At stake for them was the survival of the Catholic Church's spiritual and moral monopoly and its control of 'what is truth'. At the same time, they were well aware of the widespread criticism in the Catholic press of France, the Netherlands, Germany and the United States of the way religious minorities were treated in Spain.[28] Later, when the Spanish government had passed a Religious Freedom Law (1967), the bishops continued to emphasise the 'Catholic reality' of Spain, which had achieved religious unity by virtue 'of the moral principle which obliges men and societies to seek, embrace and sustain the true religion'.[29]

For all but a small minority of the bishops, Spain's 'Catholic reality' encompassed also the desirability of maintaining the confessionality of the Spanish State. Expatiating on this theme in *Ecclesia*, the organ of Catholic Action, Mgr Pedro Cantero of Zaragoza, a *procurador* in Franco's pseudo-parliament, declared that the State had not only the right but the duty to defend in law the religious unity of its nation and of its people. Mgr Cantero's 'eternal Spain' argument, in which the Catholic factor is claimed to be a national reality, was adduced not only to denounce the heretical

Protestant, but also to claim State support for the Church. This 'rightful' demand for ongoing State support, including financial subventions, continued to be made in post-conciliar times and even in the post-Franco period.

With differing degrees of emphasis, Spanish bishops spoke at the Council of the Church's concern for socio-economic justice: concern for the poor should be not only spiritual but also include improvements in their living conditions;[30] owners as well as workers had rights;[31] 'the burden of the application of the Church's social teaching lay with property-owners';[32] the remedy for inequality 'was not communism but Christian communitarianism'.[33] Vigorous Spanish voices on the (un)just distribution of wealth were those of Cardinal Bueno y Monreal of Seville and Mgr Antonio Añoveros of Cádiz-Ceuta. According to the Cardinal, businesses should be seen as an effort of a community of persons, and approaching them with too 'capitalistic' a mentality was the cause of social conflict between labour and management and also of strikes. 'The doctrine on access to ownership, control of wealth, and large estates [*latifundia*]', he said, 'should be revised so as to include the possible common ownership of land'.[34] Bishop Añoveros went so far as to say that the Council's declaration on social justice was too superficial, abstract and weak to goad people's consciences into action.[35]

As the Council proceeded, changes were beginning to take place everywhere in the Catholic Church. Those that were merely organisational were the least difficult to implement. In Spain, the Spanish Bishops' Conference (CEE) was set up in March 1966, replacing the *Junta de Metropolitanos* which had been operating since 1923 and held meetings twice a year, attended only by archbishops. In the spirit of *aggiornamento*, the bishops informed the Pope in November 1966 of their willingness to give up any rights or privileges which he deemed to be inappropriate, and they renounced a special Bull which waived for Spain the obligation of Friday fasting and abstinence at the time incumbent on Catholics everywhere.

In most matters, however, the Spanish hierarchy was slow to trim its sails to the new winds blowing in the universal Church. The Council had called into question certain aspects of National Catholicism like the confessionality of the State (which in turn affected the status of the 1953 Concordat), and the absence of political and religious freedom. Nor could a different type of regime be discounted at some not too distant date. The Spanish Church needed to fashion for itself a new model of 'the Church in the world', replying to and itself challenging the demands of Spanish society and of its own membership. Within its community a plurality of voices could already be heard, and new publications sprang up during or in the aftermath of the Council, including *Pastoral Misionera* (1965) and *Iglesia Viva* (1966). Especially influential in secular as well as Catholic circles was *Cuadernos para el Diálogo* (1963) founded by Joaquín Ruiz Giménez, who had been an observer at Vatican II. He had been profoundly influenced by John XXIII's encyclical *Pacem in Terris* and by what he had witnessed at Vatican II, and conceived *Cuadernos* as a space for dialogue and reconciliation among Spaniards,[36] of whatever persuasion, including marxists.

Pope John XXIII did not live to see the end of the Council; after his death in 1963, the task of bringing it to conclusion was left to his successor, Paul VI. The latter's 15-year pontificate strongly influenced changes in the Spanish Church and accompanied the profound political and societal transformation attending the last 12 years of Francoism and the first years of Spanish democracy. Relations between Franco and Paul VI were never easy. As Archbishop Montini of Milan, the future Pope had shown little sympathy for the Franco regime and was concerned that a particular sector of the Spanish Church (the Opus Dei) was playing a strongly legitimising role within it as members of the government.[37] Montini had incurred Franco's displeasure in 1962 by asking for clemency on behalf of two anarchists who had been sentenced to death. His election to the papacy was received frostily by the General, who was nevertheless always respectful after Montini became Pope, commenting that 'he is no longer Cardinal Montini; he is now Pope Paul VI'.[38]

For a time, changes in the official Spanish Church in adapting to conciliar declarations were almost imperceptible. Shortly after the end of Vatican II, the bishops issued a long document, 'Action in the Post-Council Period'.[39] As so often the case with bishops' documents, it was heavily larded with quotations from Vatican II. This may have been to make the conciliar principles more accessible and familiar, or simply following a tendency generalised in Catholic ecclesiastical circles for dignitaries to cite declarations of earlier dignitaries (or themselves). In view of Franco's avowed filial acceptance of papal and conciliar teaching, it may also have been a method of turning away wrath. There were admonitions for Catholic conservatives and Catholic progressives alike, couched in general catch-all terms embracing religious freedom, the liturgy, politics and economics. And in everything, said the bishops, the Church hierarchy was the custodian of the purity of the message which the membership must accept 'with perfect docility and obedience'.

Since finding an answer to secularisation had been a primary reason for summoning the Council, this emerged as a theme in several paragraphs. The Church wished to enter into dialogue with 'today's world', including the many who had lost God but could not be satisfied by materialism and atheism. The Council fathers, the bishops said – and therefore the Spanish hierarchy as well – had a message concerning marriage and the family, culture and religion, economic and social life, and civil and political harmony. They claimed that 'almost all Spaniards belong to the Church', but recognised that 'we' (the text is ambiguous as to whether the bishops are referring to themselves or to 'the faithful' as well) 'have sometimes been overconfident about Catholic unity, buttressed by law and ancient traditions'. The last six words are particularly redolent of the Throne–Altar alliance.

In view of the blatant abuse of human and democratic rights in Spain, the hierarchy's generally complacent views were contested by some of the – mostly – young clergy and lay activists to be found in the universities and in the workers' branches of Catholic Action. They translated conciliar recommendations into deeds, which resulted in clashes with the Franco regime and with their ecclesiastical superiors. One such incident in Barcelona in 1966 came to be known as the *Caputxinada*,[40] during which 130 priests staged a dignified protest against police brutality in breaking up a meeting intended to set up a democratic students' union. The priests were also subjected to police ill-treatment and insults, and vilified in the (State-controlled) press.[41] General Franco's comment was that if the priests thought that the armed police had been too harsh, they should have reported the matter to their superiors, who would have informed the government who in turn would see that justice would be done:

> The conduct of the regime and its *union with high-ranking members of the Church hierarchy* [my italics] are more than sufficient guarantee that violence will not have to be used... They accuse us of cruelties of which we are innocent... It is regrettable that these priests fail in discipline, to the scandal of the majority of Spanish Catholics.[42]

Six months after 'Action in the Post-Council Period', the CEE published 'The Church and the Temporal Order in the Light of the Council' which reflected its position vis-à-vis the political order more explicitly.[43] Towards the end came a statement that the Church should give its critical moral opinion about socio-political institutions only in the case where this was clearly demanded by the fundamental rights of the person and the family, or the salvation of souls. The statement went on to assert that the bishops did not believe 'that this is the situation in Spain'.[44] It was the last time that the majority of the hierarchy officially legitimised the Franco regime.

The document was contested by more liberal elements. *Cuadernos* maintained that it failed to tackle the problem of political parties, strikes, or ethnic minorities, that it barely touched on free trade unions or the protection of basic rights, and that it was 'restrictive' and overly-traditional in style 'especially in the most controversial doctrinal points'.[45] Shortly before this, *Cuadernos* had called for a radical reform of capitalist socio-economic structures so that all members of the national, and even the international, community, should have effective participation in the enjoyment of the spiritual and material goods of the earth'.[46]

'The Church and the Temporal Order' included a warning against communism (though not specified as such) and an admonition to Catholic Action not to operate outside the limits imposed by the hierarchy.[47] It was issued against a background of rising tension between Catholic workers' movements and young priests – very often the workers' chaplains – on the one side, and the regime on the other, and of accusations from the Catholic base that the hierarchy was abetting the civil authorities.

Catholic workers had been active participants in the widespread strikes of the spring of 1962, alongside other anti-Franco movements, especially the nascent communist-led Workers' Commissions. Franco denounced 'communist infiltration' into Church organisations. It was clear that Christian workers' movements, Catholic intellectuals and the younger clergy were responding swiftly and vigorously to John XXIII's encyclicals and, later, to the Council declarations. In many cases, of course, their commitment had preceded John and his Council, and they were carried along by the very momentum of their activities during the 1950s, in co-operation with other opposition groups, aimed at changing the unjust structures of society. For its part, the hierarchy was unable to connect with the Church's radical base, as it was in the main still locked into National Catholicism.[48] Ironically, it was the statutes drawn up by the hierarchy in 1959 allowing Catholic Action greater autonomy that gave it the runaway dynamism in the 1960s which bishops brought to a halt in the second half of the decade.[49] Nor should it be forgotten that during the Franco years, Church organisations provided the only legal vehicle of opposition to the regime.

At the same time the anti-dictatorship stance of such organisations implied the possibility of a religious 'delegitimation' of the political regime and of the overall socio-economic system, though from outside the official hierarchical Church structure. The institutional Church was not yet ready to change direction and distance itself from Francoism and all it stood for; whatever positive standing Catholicism had among the working class came from the dedication of JOC and HOAC activists. It has even been claimed, perhaps cynically,[50] that some of the bishops seemed to be hedging their bets so as to cover two eventualities: remaining faithful to Francoism themselves in case the regime survived, but allowing some leeway to their more progressive priests, in case political circumstances changed and there was a need to show that the Church too had changed.

HOAC and JOC lost their main protector when in 1966 the ageing Cardinal Pla y Deniel was replaced as President of Catholic Action by the highly reactionary Archbishop Casimiro Morcillo, now of Madrid. Secretary to the Bishops' Conference and since 1964 the hierarchy's representative on Catholic Action was Morcillo's auxiliary, the equally reactionary Mgr José Guerra Campos. Both held political appointments as *procuradores* in the Cortes, as did two other highly conservative prelates, Archbishop Pedro Cantero of Zaragoza and Mgr Almarcha of León.

With a new Press and Publications Law of 1966, Franco's government went some way towards the Vatican Council's demands for freedom of information. One of the beneficial results was that vanguard theological works from other European countries, especially Germany and France, became widely available in Spain, books by progressive theologians like Karl Rahner being runaway bestsellers.[51] However, the fact that newspapers continued to be State-controlled, that copies of publications had to be left with the authorities prior to distribution, and that the catch-all Article 2 allowed little room for manoeuvre meant that freedom of expression remained restricted. Within the first two months of its promulgation, the law had hit *Juventud Obrera, Semana*, and *Montejurra*.[52] In May 1966, the whole print-run of *Juventud Obrera* was destroyed because of an article criticising the Spanish army, and in June of the same year an issue of *Signo,* the youth organ of Catholic Action, suffered a similar fate. *Signo* was later shut down by the Church hierarchy. The government ordered the closure of *Aún*, the organ of the Catholic Employees' Movement and *La Voz del Trabajo*, that of the Workers' Vanguards.[53]

In December of the same year, the bishops issued a bland communiqué counselling Spaniards to vote according to an 'informed' conscience in the national referendum to approve 'The Organic Law of the State', one of the regime's Fundamental Laws, intended to assure the continuation of Francoism after Franco.[54] The document referred to 'citizens', not 'Catholics' and was but one of many examples of the bishops' tendency to equate the two. National HOAC and JOC leaders attacked the undemocratic political regime and the hierarchy's official part in the new law – through bishops appointed by Franco to the Council of the Regency and Council of the Kingdom – but they stopped short of advising their activists to vote against it.

Shortly afterwards, another episcopal document, 'Bringing the Secular Apostolate up to date',[55] blew the lid off the Catholic Action crisis. Members of the Catholic workers' organisations were accused of being too closely involved with 'social and political movements whose origin and strength derive from marxism and which promote atheism and the class struggle as a system'.[56] New statutes were drawn up which deprived activists of their previous independence, with the bishops claiming exclusive authority in interpreting the moral principles governing secular matters. That Mgr Morcillo and Mgr Guerra Campos were not alone among the Spanish bishops in wanting a more narrowly 'spiritual' agenda for a Catholic Action under stringent episcopal control was shown by the fact that the CEE approved these highly restrictive statutes with only 13 dissenting votes.

The climate among the bishops would not change until Cardinal Tarancón was elected President of the CEE in 1971, which unblocked many possibilities for the renewal and social commitment of Catholic Action. But new statutes drawn up in 1973 came too late, for considerable numbers of Catholic Action workers had already left, in many cases moving to secular movements of social involvement. Some went to the Communist Party (PCE) and other underground left-wing organisations. Others, 'disillusioned with the prospects for reforming capitalism' turned to co-operatives based on the experience of the communitary enterprise set up in 1956 in Mondragón in the Basque Country.[57] In 1966 membership of Catholic Action stood at 1 million; by 1972 it had dropped to 100 000.

Although HOAC and JOC had found occasional support from individual bishops, it is evident that as a body the hierarchy failed to 'defend its own' against the regime. During the crisis years of Catholic Action, it was probably beyond the capability of most bishops to understand their clergy and laity, let alone support them against Franco's repression. The appointment of 72 of them had been made between 1942 and 1962, when relations between Church and State were closest and running at their smoothest; vacant dioceses had been filled rapidly and the two nuncios of this period, Mgr Cicognani and Mgr Antoniutti, shared the Spanish bishops' support for the Spanish regime and the part they played in it.

With their seminary training in the preconciliar mould, memories of persecution during the Second Republic and the Civil War, and close links with Spain's power groups,[58] the majority of bishops did not have the breadth of vision to adapt in time to the changes required by Vatican II and by the continuing transformation of Spanish society. By the second half of the 1960s, the bishops were said to be split into three groups: the majority of elderly conservatives, ordained before the Civil War; a group of neo-conservatives appointed between 1953 and 1962 during the nunciature of Mgr Antoniutti; and some 20 'liberals', nominated between 1962 and 1967 during that of Mgr Riberi.[59] Another factor to take into account is the weight of conservative votes in the Bishops' Conference during its first six years: retired bishops – whose mentality was largely frozen in its 'Crusade' past – could not only attend Plenary Assemblies but also had the right to vote, whereas the auxiliaries (whose appointment circumvented Franco's *derecho de presentación* and who were likely to be more representative of the moderately progressive climate in Rome) could attend but had no vote. Within five years of the close of the Council, under Nuncios Riberi and especially Dadaglio, who was appointed in 1967,[60] there had been a 50 per cent changeover in the membership of the CEE,[61] and this despite the regime's laggardly pace in agreeing the names of candidates to vacant dioceses.

Franco's right of patronage was on the Church's agenda. The majority of Spanish bishops sincerely acknowledged allegiance to Franco but, as part of the universal Church, they were answerable to the Pope and to the resolutions of the Council. On 29 April 1968, Paul VI wrote to Franco, asking him to renounce his right to intervene in the appointment of bishops. It later transpired that Montini's anxiety over the *derecho de presentación* was largely linked to the fact that there was a crisis in the priesthood and activists had left the

Church in droves ('*Ha sido una separación masiva*') because they saw the bishops as too representative of the civil powers.[62] It was also clear that his prime concern over the appointment of bishops was to ensure that after Franco there would be in place in Spain an episcopate capable of taking a leading part in the new dispensation; he needed bishops who were accepted and held in high regard by the people.[63] In his reply to the Pope on 12 June, Franco stated that any amendment would require the agreement of the Spanish Parliament but that he was, in the spirit of the conciliar document *Gaudium et Spes,* 'willing to review all the privileges of both powers',[64] words which perhaps could be interpreted as a veiled threat to the Church's status, financial position and State-protected influence in Spanish society.

During this period, the semi-official Church weekly *Ecclesia,* diocesan bulletins and other documents constantly revealed evidence of the hierarchy's bad conscience about a society which the Church itself had helped to mould and which, supposedly Christian, was manifestly unjust. Furthermore, the situation was not clear-cut, since some bishops who were conservative in the domain of Church–State relations or personal morality might lean towards the progressive or even radical in the socio-economic sphere. Questions about the absence of human, political and civil rights ran alongside others about the causes of the often desperate economic plight of workers and led inevitably to questioning the prevailing capitalist order. Some of the bishops started to speak out more openly and more regularly against exploitation and came close to disowning the system.[65] Mgr Añoveros of Cádiz-Ceuta was particularly trenchant. He asked why Catholic ruling classes did not undertake essential social reforms. He spoke of the 20 000 unemployed in the Cádiz diocese, where in addition many people who actually had a job received less than half the minimum wage. 'Economic pressure groups', he said, 'are more sensitive to what is economic than to what is social, and modern capitalism suffers from many damning defects'.[66]

For their part, the working class in town and country remained alienated from the Church: many priests and bishops, it was claimed, preached the beatitudes and humility and charity from the pulpit, but what they preached was charity without justice. The workers, still finding the hierarchy as a whole on the side of the powerful, could neither understand nor accept this.[67] It was precisely what Canon Arboleya had pointed out more than thirty years earlier. People lived without reference to the Church because they saw it in a double bondage – to the privileged classes and to the public authorities; whether or not this was true was irrelevant: that is how they perceived it, and so as far as they were concerned it was true.[68]

It was not only the workers who continued to be lost to the Church. An editorial in *Cuadernos* pointed to the general crisis of confidence among young people: in the home, at work and at university, but also in the seminaries and among priests.[69] This was ascribed to the generation gap but more importantly to young people's greater awareness of their own responsibilities and of the need for their elders and superiors to be open to new ideas. The situation was paralleled by a slump in vocations to the priesthood and an increase in the number of priests becoming laicised.[70]

Underlining the decline in religious affiliation, a 1970 sociological report by FOESSA[71] carried a significant heading: 'Spanish religiosity at a time of change and secularisation'. It discussed symptoms of disaffection among workers, the poor and, above all, university students, indicating the last group as 'the bridgehead of a hypothetical process of secularisation of our Catholicism'. This is an interesting comment, italicised in the report, as the students of this period would form the dominant political class in the second half of the 1970s and in the 1980s.

2 Aggiornamento ma non troppo (1969 to mid-1971)

The impact of the Second Vatican Council on our public life, in its double – social and political – aspect, is full of apparent paradoxes. As is well known, Spanish Catholicism played a relatively small role in the Council proceedings; future generations, however, may come to the conclusion that in no other country has the apparent impact of Vatican II on Catholicism been greater.[1]

Although more independent and progressive bishops were beginning to alter the balance of the CEE, staunchly pro-Franco voices remained strong during this period. Mgr Morcillo, who only recently had brought about the emasculation of HOAC and JOC, was elected President of the CEE, narrowly defeating Mgr Enrique y Tarancón, 'the Pope's preferred candidate';[2] Tarancón had recently been translated from Oviedo to Toledo to become the Primate of Spain and would soon play a leading role in Church–State affairs. Like other conservative forces in the Catholic world, Spanish prelates were appalled by the example of a 'runaway' Church in Holland, by the Medellín (Colombia) meeting in 1968 of Latin American bishops which heralded the widespread diffusion of liberation theology, by the ongoing Christian-marxist dialogue, and by the Vatican's *Ostpolitik*. The civil rights movements in the United States, the May 1968 *événements* in France and upheavals in Western Europe generally threw up the concept of 'contestation' to authority and served as a background to what was thought at the time might lead to the break-up of the established political, economic and social order.

The Spanish bishops increasingly had to contend not merely with a contestatory clergy and Catholic activists on the left but also with mounting aggression from the anti-Council Catholic right, who did not want to see an end to the prevailing social and political system. They belonged to what was already known as the 'bunker', which included, apart from integrist clerics, the majority of high-ranking army officers, hard-line Falangists, the 'ex-combatants' who had fought on the winning side in the Civil War, and the economic elites, including bankers, industrialists and landowners. Clergy clinging to

National Catholicism set up their integrist Priestly Brotherhood (*Hermandad Sacerdotal*) in 1969, while lay groups organised themselves into gangs such as the Warriors of Christ the King (*Guerrilleros de Cristo Rey*) to terrorise the left, break up meetings on Church premises and threaten or even beat up progressive priests. The weekly *¿Qué Pasa?* reflected the reactionary mood of the right, as did *El Cruzado Español*, *Iglesia-Mundo* and *Fuerza Nueva*, the vehicle for the views of the right-wing extremist lawyer, Blas Piñar.

It was Blas Piñar who in January 1969 left for the Caudillo a highly critical report[3] on the diocese of Santander, purporting to show that its seminary had become too 'progressive', that the previous Rector had been against the National Movement and that the philospher Julián Marías gave lectures whose contents were at odds with the teaching of the magisterium. These 'evils', he claimed, had been discovered and reported to the Holy See, but the damage had been done: the bishop appointed in August 1968 was Mgr José María Cirarda who had proceeded to surround himself with people known to be hostile to the regime, and to absent himself from events that he knew to be pleasing to the General.[4] Franco commented to his cousin that Cirarda had been considered subversive in his previous diocese of Jaén, and said he was going to keep Blas Piñar's report on file.[5] Mgr Cirarda would indeed continue to prove a thorn in the regime's flesh when he became in addition Apostolic Administrator of the Basque diocese of Bilbao later in 1968.

The Basque Country was a political flashpoint because the frustrated demands of its more extreme nationalists had already exploded into violence with the founding in 1959 of ETA, a terrorist organisation whose acronym signified Basque Homeland and Freedom. The attitude of the official Church to the 'regional question' in the Basque Country, as in Catalonia, the other high-profile community, depended on the proclivities of individual bishops in each diocese and was always interlocked with other political, social and human rights issues. The situation in Barcelona was complicated by the fact that the Archbishop, Mgr Marcelo González Martín, appointed in 1966, was not a Catalan and had been selected against the wishes of the diocesan clergy. In fact, ever since his appointment to Barcelona in 1966, he had had a history of co-operation with the police when they carried out raids on church premises, and he held scant sympathy for his more radical priests. An increasing number of clergy, and not only in Catalonia and the Basque Country, found themselves fined, arrested, tried and imprisoned for the allegedly subversive content of their sermons; their premises were searched and their publications banned.

With the deterioration of the political situation in the Basque Country, splits began to appear in the ranks of the hierarchy, despite attempts to give an appearance of unity.[6] Following attacks by ETA, including the murder of the San Sebastián Chief of Police, a state of emergency had been declared in Guipúzcoa in August 1968 and in the following January extended to the rest of Spain. On 8 February 1969, bishops' representatives went to the Ministry of Justice asking for a swift return to normality. The government issued a communiqué accusing some of the clergy of using the state of emergency as a pretext to attack the regime. It also reminded the bishops that they had sworn an oath of fidelity, and undertaken not to take part – nor allow their clergy to take part – in any activity that might be harmful to public order and to the State.

The hierarchy as a body condoned the state of emergency, via a communiqué from its Standing Commission, with a reference to the 'need to preserve peace and public order' and to place 'temporary restriction on certain rights'. However, some bishops were more valiant. Bishop Cirarda, now Apostolic Administrator of Bilbao, stated in a pastoral letter that one had to analyse the underlying causes that had brought the state of emergency about; he was clearly referring to the hardships caused by redundancies and by economic exploitation. Cirarda, possibly pushed by his more militant clergy, had already gained a reputation for robust defence of the priests and Catholic activists of his diocese. A similar line was taken by Mgr Arturo Tabera, Archbishop of Pamplona, who, along with all the bishops of Andalusia, sent a telegram expressing disagreement with the Standing Commission's communiqué. There were other protests, including those of 40 lecturers and 294 students of the Barcelona Theology Faculty and 250 priests from Navarre. Bishop Jacinto Argaya of San Sebastián attacked the situation in his 1969 Lenten pastoral letter, saying that

> The prolonged state of emergency, which has meant a temporary suspension of some of the basic rights of the human person, has resulted in arrests, deportations, grave suffering and economic and professional breakdown. We are living through labour conflicts which, besides anxiety and severe economic hardship, especially for the weakest, have brought about the dismissal of workers.[7]

On 27 April 1969, Mgr Cirarda let it be known that he had, for reasons sanctioned by the Concordat, refused the Spanish authorities permission to put his Vicar-General, José Angel Ubieta López, on trial on a charge of taking part in terrorist activities. The background to Mgr Cirarda's statement was the fact that the Franco regime was starting to find it troublesome to honour the so-called 'clergy charter' (laid down in the 1953 Concordat) which prevented priests being charged for criminal offences without the consent of their bishop. The government had therefore issued a decree in July 1968 altering the interpretation of the relevant article 16 of the Concordat, and a special prison for priests was opened in Zamora. Some of the inmates were Basques who were supporters, or alleged supporters, of ETA.[8]

In June 1969, a pastoral letter by Mgr Infantes Florido entitled *Christians and Public Life*[9] called for a society which was pluralist in ideology, and for 'indispensable civil liberties' so that people in free association might fully participate in public life. The next month, in an article in *Ecclesia*,[10] he made an energetic defence of all the human rights that the Council had called for and especially the right to freedom, to truth, to work and to access to culture.

In October 1969, Mgr Cirarda sharply criticised aspects of a trial in which four priests were convicted of violating the government's Banditry and Terrorism decree. He accused the Commander of the Sixth Military Region of falsely stating that the trial was closed to the public at his – Mgr Cirarda's – request, and he challenged the court's findings which questioned the priests' humanitarian motives in aiding a wounded fugitive.[11]

In 1970, the bishops of Andalusia and Murcia issued a joint statement about the problems facing the workers of the South. They spoke of most of the ills – from unemployment to the need for emigration – that the bishops as individuals had condemned on previous occasions.[12] A year earlier, the bishops of the Tarragona diocese, in a joint statement to commemorate 1 May,[13] had expressed similar concerns. In Huelva, Mgr González Moralejo organised a collection for 71 miners' families when the El Olvido mine was shut down.[14]

Following a strike of building workers in Granada, the police opened fire and three strikers were killed on 21 July 1970. In response, the Archbishop, Mgr Emilio Benavent, condemned police brutality and defended the worker-priests of his diocese against the accusation of being 'instigators of violence', quoting all the rights that had been enumerated at the recent CEE meeting.[15] Mgr Díaz Merchán supported his priests against the accusation that they had used their sermons at Mass 'for political, even marxist ends'.[16] (Tape-recordings by the police of homilies were routine and fines and imprisonment often followed.) In this case, Mgr Díaz Merchán was referring to the gaoling of a priest-miner, Carlos García Huelga, parish priest of Barredos, the denunciation of several Asturian priests for the 'political' content of their sermons, and a letter to the press by the provincial Council of the National Movement, alleging profanation of churches by traitorous clerics with their anti-Spanish and marxist activities. *Vida Nueva*[17] made an analysis of two so-called subversive sermons – one of which was composed almost entirely of quotations from papal encyclicals and Council documents – printing both what the priests had actually said and the scandalised reaction of right-wing Catholics.

Events in Spain did not of course pass unnoticed in Rome. On 23 June 1969, having spoken of the wars in Vietnam and Biafra and the situation in the Middle East, Pope Paul turned 'not without some disquiet' to the situation in Spain. He urged the Spanish bishops to demonstrate greater boldness in promoting social justice and went on, in a veiled reference to the Church–State tensions that hindered the appointment of diocesan ordinaries (as opposed to that of auxiliary bishops or apostolic administrators), to express his desire that vacant dioceses would soon be filled. He also made a special reference to the healthy, if sometimes intemperately expressed, aspirations of young priests (who thereby felt that their socio-political commitment had been vindicated). Significantly, he failed to send any word of greeting to Franco as Head of State or to any of the other Spanish authorities.[18]

As if in defensive response to the Pope's reference to the Spanish hierarchy's lack of valour in facing up to Franco, Mgr Morcillo, Archbishop of Madrid and now President of the CEE, wrote an article in *Ecclesia*[19] which clearly reflected his desire to keep on good terms with the regime:

> In the history of Spain of the last thirty years the Bishops have issued prudent communications, which have always been well received by the Head of State and his governments, and they have always been beneficial for Spain and for Spaniards of the lowest condition. Nor has there been a lack of episcopal teaching, whether individually or collectively, concerning the main problems of social concern. But it is also true that the bishops have avoided political

intrusion, about which it has so often and so unjustly been attacked.

This kind of 'national or cultural Catholicism' was criticised in the 1970 FOESSA sociological report on Spain which, at the end of the chapter on 'Religious Life',[20] drew attention to the need of the Church to renounce its role as legitimiser of the norms and values of a specific society, and to be bolder in its prophetic denunciation of oppression and exploitation.

The regime was stung by the Pope's address which it considered an unwarranted interference in Spanish national affairs; especially offensive was the apparent inclusion of Spain in a list of Third World countries suffering from conflicts and underdevelopment. All this on top of the implicit defence of the priests involved in the workers' movements of Catholic Action, and veiled criticism of the absence of social justice in Spain.[21]

Franco was the more irritated at what was perceived as interference by the Church in political matters because he could not afford to ignore its influence. Three days after the Pope's address of 23 June 1969, mentioned above, Laureano López Rodó, Opus Dei Minister in charge of Economic and Social Development Plans, warned the General that he thought that the Pope's speech was even more important than the condemnation of the regime by the United Nations in 1946, because of the greater prestige and moral authority that the Pope enjoyed in Spain. López Rodó seized the opportunity to propel Franco into making up his mind at last about the appointment of a successor: to show the Vatican that the regime was not on the verge of collapse, Prince Juan Carlos ought to be designated as future King and Franco's successor as Head of State, so as to guarantee continuity and give Spain 'another thirty years of peace'.[22] Prince Juan Carlos was the grandson of Alfonso XIII, the last king of Spain and son of the Pretender, Don Juan, whom Franco considered too liberal and unreliable to be his political heir.

It was then in fact that Franco settled the matter and on 22 July 1969 Juan Carlos swore fidelity to the principles of the General's National Movement. The question of the succession had at long last been resolved, but amid differing, sometimes overlapping, sometimes colliding, visions of the future perceived by the regime's variegated political 'families' of monarchists, army officers, Falangists and Catholic groups. Hardline Falangists attempted to seize what might be a last opportunity to break the political hegemony of the Opus Dei technocrats and thus be in a position to dominate the post-Franco political scenario. This opportunity seemed to have arrived with the revelation of what came to be known as the 'Matesa scandal', allegedly involving prominent Opus members, but in fact the Falangist attempt to cover their main political rivals in opprobrium backfired.[23] For the time being, *opusdeístas* retained Franco's confidence and held dominating positions in the subsequent Cabinet reshuffle.

The Franco regime was evidently no longer finding National Catholicism an unmixed blessing. In place of enunciating ritual eulogies of the oneness of Church and State, both parties now preferred to emphasise the 'healthy co-operation' and 'mutual independence' enjoined by Vatican II; this shadow-boxing over non-interference in each other's sphere of competence would characterise exchanges between them till the death of Franco, and even beyond.

'Healthy co-operation' was subject to constant stress. When the regime ordered what came to be known as the 'Burgos' show trial of 16 Basques, two of them priests, who had been arrested for terrorist attacks including the murder of the San Sebastián Police Chief, Mgr Cirarda and Mgr Argaya published a joint pastoral letter on 22 November 1969, measured in tone but explosive in content.[24] It made three requests: that the trial should be held in public, in a civil, not military, court, and that, were any of the accused sentenced to death, the penalty would be commuted. Quoting Paul VI, the bishops condemned all kind of violence, 'structural, subversive and repressive', so their letter was tantamount to an attack on the regime as well as on Basque terrorists. It provoked a series of furiously hostile reactions: the Justice Ministry fumed that it was wrong to consider the violence of a delinquent and that of established legal procedure on an equal basis.[25] It was also attacked by the ultra-right-wing *Hermandad Sacerdotal*.

At its XIII Plenary Assembly of 1–5 December 1970, the Bishops' Conference supported Cirarda and Argaya and, echoing an appeal by the Pope, asked for clemency for the ETA militants, two of whom had by then been sentenced to death (later commuted to life imprisonment). A significant minority of right-wing bishops dissociated themselves from the majority declaration and tabled a complaint about what they saw as the disproportionate amount of time devoted to socio-political matters in CEE Assemblies to the detriment of the Church's 'real', spiritual, mission. To avoid the embarrassment of showing up the CEE as divided – since the dissenting bishops threatened to publish 'parallel' episcopal documents – the President, Mgr Morcillo, did not read out their 'diatribe against the Conference',[26] but shortly afterwards it was published without authorisation by the right-wing *Iglesia-Mundo*.

The regime continued to emphasise the exclusively spiritual dimension of the message and mission of the Church, in a bid to counter the forays by bishops and priests into such sensitive temporal matters as human and civil rights. A lecture entitled 'Church and State' given in 1970 by the Undersecretary of Justice, Alfredo López Martínez, alluded to 'the treasure of the Catholic Church' as being 'the word of God', before going on to deplore the 'temporal commitment' of priests who had 'a late political vocation' and Catholics who were 'pawns in the chess-game of politics' manipulated by 'some members of the hierarchy'.[27] This last reference was linked to criticism of Vatican diplomats making unjustifiable 'incursions into the field of politics', and was an interesting reflection on what was indeed occurring: Pope Paul VI had started, through the papal nuncio, Mgr Dadaglio, to reshape the corporate mentality of the Bishops' Conference. The Undersecretary's strictures on politicised priests accorded well with the thinking of right-wing members of the Spanish hierarchy: Cardinal Marcelo González commented that 'much of the crisis in the priesthood has been brought about by priests themselves' because they were tempted by revisionism (as opposed to revision, which had been necessary), which made priests forget evangelisation and thus they ended up 'as politicians and trade union leaders'.[28]

Franco's end-of-year message referred once more to Church and State having parallel aims, but shortly afterwards the Minister of the Interior averred to the National Council of the Movement that 'the Catholic faith is no longer the principal neutraliser of our familiar demons',[29] implying that the Church could no longer be relied upon to act as the regime's instrument of social control. Franco saw that the CEE was changing direction, pushed by the prevailing attitude in the Vatican, by the more progressive, even radical, priests and laity, and by some of its own members.

Church initiatives on social justice came within the province of the Spanish national branch of the Justitia et Pax Commission, set up by Paul VI in 1967. 'Justice and Peace' became, in effect, the Church euphemism for politics in the way it sought to make Catholics aware of socio-political problems. As Bishop González Moralejo, the first President, stated in his message for the 1970 World Peace Day, the

Commission had been launched to 'mobilise men of good will, especially Christians, to work in solidarity for peace in the world'. He spoke of some of the conflicts that had to be resolved in the Spanish context, including those of social and political life, between victors and vanquished in the Civil War (by now three decades in the past), between workers and employers, government and governed, between centralist and regionalist tendencies. The Commission entitled its 1971 statement 'Every Man is My Brother' (*Todo hombre es mi hermano*). It defended the rights of ethnic and linguistic minorities, attacked discrimination, oppression, and class warfare, and, while condemning 'outdated marxism', it also denounced right-wing extremists (*ultrarreaccionarios*) who 'claim to safeguard our peace by identifying it with law and order, rigidity and intransigence in the exercise of power'.

In 1971, while a bill was before the Cortes concerning conscientious objection to compulsory military service, the Commission was prevented from publicising the fact that at the time there were 189 conscientious objectors in prison, and from sending relevant information to the hierarchy. Representatives of the conscientious objectors then contacted each one of the bishops, reproaching them for their lack of commitment. The hierarchy issued a statement but not until two years later, in December 1973,[30] and even then it was confined to solutions that had been suggested by Vatican II without putting them into the specific Spanish context.

Though well aware that the Vatican Council had endorsed the principle of democracy, the hierarchy remained cautious and imprecise in its pronouncements. Mgr Díaz Merchán, then of Guádix-Baza, claimed that harmony between Church and State must not be confused with 'compromising support' for the government, but by the same token the bishops' declarations on socio-political problems must not be confused with support for political groups of the opposition. The great unknown was what would happen to Spain after the death of Franco because, he said, it was unlikely that people would accept another regime like that of the General which had emerged in special historical circumstances.[31]

But while the Spanish Church was being prodded into loosening its political ties with the regime, it had no intention of relinquishing claims on its traditional spheres of influence, especially in education, marriage and sexual mores, which Francoism had protected. Significant markers were laid down for a future in which Church doctrine might no longer be enshrined in Spain's legislation. Education was already on the agenda and at their Assembly held on 11 July 1970, the bishops issued a communiqué concerning a new Act.[32] Though welcoming its emphasis on the 'Christian concept of education', they regretted the priority to be given to funding places in State schools, claiming that this ran counter to the Francoist Spaniards' Charter of 1945, under which the government was to 'foster and protect' private schools.[33]

Clearly the hierarchy not only wanted to maintain its hold on education, but to continue to be paid from the State coffers, thus maintaining influence in society while not severing financial dependence on the regime. The education issue, particularly the Church-influenced 'parents' rights to choose' the kind of school they considered most appropriate for their children in the context of 'the socio-religious reality' of Spain, would feature again and again in their documents. All of them echoed Mgr Cantero's demand in 1963 for State protection for the historical, sociological and political 'reality' of a Catholic Spain in which 'national community' was equated with 'Catholic community'. Moreover, to show that they intended to remain the moral watchdogs of the nation, despite their public acknowledgment of the 'autonomy of civil society', the bishops indicated in a document on 'The Moral Life of our People'[34] that they would co-operate in showing the authorities what laws ought to govern public morality.

Divisions among the bishops, which had become apparent at the XIII Plenary Assembly over the Basque issue, surfaced again over a 'Trade Union' bill. Though originally (in 1966) they had been in favour, most of them had by now come to reject it – along with the Catholic Action and secular workers' organisations – as being incompatible with basic freedoms. Even Mgr Cantero criticised it in an interview with Associated Press,[35] declaring that as a deputy in Parliament he would propose amendments. He agreed, he said, with the verdict of the International Labour Organisation, which considered that there was consensus about the way trade unionism ought to develop in Spain and, astutely quoting Franco himself, he recalled that 'the survival of any regime depends on its being embodied in public consciousness'. Mgr Guerra Campos, however, stoutly maintained that the draft law was in line with Catholic doctrine[36] and a minority of bishops (those who in December 1970 had threatened to publish 'parallel' episcopal documents) stated that they were not defending the trade union law specifically but the autonomy of the law-givers.

About this time, reports that a new Concordat was imminent came to trouble not only Church–State but also CEE–Vatican relations. Without prior consultation with the CEE, Franco and his ministers appeared to have come to an agreement with Paul VI, over a draft (known as the Garrigues–Casaroli draft, named after the Spanish Ambassador to the Holy See and Mgr Casaroli, then Secretary of the Sacred Congregation for Extraordinary Affairs) which barely modified the 1953 Concordat.[37] Cardinal Tarancón, as Vice-President of the CEE, wrote to the Vatican Secretary of State, Cardinal Villot, protesting that the CEE's voice should be heard, and that any new Concordat would serve only to prolong the life of a dying regime. He suggested that a partial agreement putting an end to the priests' charter would suffice. In response, Villot sent a copy of the Garrigues–Casaroli proposals, to be discussed by all the Spanish bishops at diocesan and then at Plenary Assembly level.

The CEE debated the proposals on 20 February 1971. Although their discussions were held in secret, rumour had it that the old guard of bishops who wanted no change to the Concordat status quo had been heavily defeated, by a vote of 60 to 10.[38] The figure was influenced by absence through illness of Mgr Morcillo (who as President should have presided) and some 30 other bishops, most of them, like him, conservative in tendency.[39]

The meeting was chaired by Cardinal Tarancón, as CEE Vice-President. At the end he caused a frisson of expectancy among the bishops by announcing that he was about to read out two letters concerning the Concordat. He had not done so earlier in the meeting, he said, so as not to inflame the discussion. One was the copy of a letter to the Holy See from the Justice Minister, laying down new conditions, including one whereby auxiliary bishops and apostolic administrators would be included in Franco's *derecho de presentación*. The other – received two days after the Assembly had begun – was from Cardinal Villot, being a copy of his reply to Oriol, stating that the Vatican could not yield on the issue of the appointment of auxiliary bishops, let alone on that of apostolic administrators. For the assembled bishops this was sensational: Tarancón recalls in his memoirs that their reaction was that there might easily be a complete breakdown in relations between the Spanish government and the Vatican.[40] A special four-man commission was set up, including Tarancón himself, to hold conversations with the government and the Holy See in the name of the Bishops' Conference, so as to take the heat out of the situation. Tarancón sought a pretext to go to

Rome where he consulted Villot, Casaroli, Mgr Benelli (the Deputy Secretary of State) and finally Pope Paul VI, who thought that the Spanish government would not accept the CEE's proposal for the Concordat to be replaced by partial agreements, and that negotiations ought not to be delayed for too long.[41]

There were further rumours before the year's end about the existence of another draft which, while mentioned by Mgr Guerra Campos in meetings of the CEE Standing Commission, came to nothing. Progressive Catholics criticised the absence of consultation and many thought that any Concordat at all was anachronistic: when *El Ciervo* took soundings among its 5 600 readers, 61 per cent were found to be in favour of abrogation.[42]

The Spanish bishops were also wrestling with the problem of finding an appropriate answer to the inequalities in Spanish society. At times condemnation of the unacceptable features of the socio-economic basis of the regime bordered on, or even shaded into, condemnation of the system itself. That is not surprising: Franco's repressive political regime allowed a particularly virulent form of capitalism to operate.

The ambivalence of the bishops' attitude can be seen in the major document, 'The Church and the Poor'[43] (drawn up at the XII Plenary Assembly), which spoke of the Church's need not only to be poor but to be seen to be poor, and to show solidarity with those suffering poverty. They admitted, however, that they had difficulty in prescribing how the Church's evangelical poverty was to be achieved. One of the problems, which they set out in churchspeak even more convoluted than usual, was how the Church would finance itself and its activities; they could not bring themselves to ask for absolute personal poverty 'for not everyone is called to the same degree of witness in virtues'.

With regard to the material privations of the people, the bishops' concern remained at the level of lamentation and petition: lamentation about the 'often inhumane conditions in which our brothers frequently live', petition that 'those who have political or economic power should, while they attempt to increase collective wealth, also give an example of austerity'. They entreated the authorities to do more to eliminate unjust disparities of income and wealth (though they used the milder term 'differences') between people and between regions, to promote agrarian reform, to build decent housing 'for the human and Christian development of so many modest families', to eliminate speculation, to make emigration unnecessary, and to adjust minimum salaries to real needs. The Church itself would do as much as it could for the poor via its charitable organisation *Cáritas*.

In another section of the same document, this time more boldly and without hiding, as was their wont, behind papal or conciliar words, the bishops affirmed every person's right to free association and assembly, to representative trade unions, to freedom of expression and information, and to a just legal system. With regard to moral poverty, they said, this was reflected in the decline in behavioural standards (*devaluación de las costumbres*) and a loss of the meaning of the Christian faith; this was especially dangerous for young people who were surrounded on all sides by eroticism and consumer fever.

The majority wanted to 'renew' or 'transform' society, with a degree of political and social change. They were looking for capitalism with a human face: they did not want a thorough change of structures, of the balance of forces within society. More specifically, they seemed to be advocating as well as accepting a model of neo-capitalist society which recognised *formal* liberties and social rights, but without demanding a transformation of socio-economic structures as the *sine qua non* of real (social) democracy. The bishops appeared not to see a contradiction inherent in accepting an ideology much of which was in flagrant opposition to human dignity and then attempting no more than to palliate its worst features. They appealed only to the better nature of exploiters, but did not encourage the exploited to examine the source of their exploitation, as did marxists and liberation theologians. However, given the desire of the bishops for reconciliation at long last in Spanish society, such encouragement might have smacked to them of opening old wounds. The fact remains that it was not suggested that the exploitative system, into which even the exploiters were locked, should be abandoned.

Arguably the oppression was so severe because the politico-economic system was presided over by an unaccountable small and powerful establishment: with their intertwining relationships, the banking and industrial elite, the landed aristocracy, high-ranking civil servants and politicians, and the upper echelons of the military,[44] backed by the Francoist State machinery, wielded a power that seemed impregnable. Their writ ran in both public and private enterprises, either through multiple directorships, or marriage, or social and political influence. In such a situation of inter-relationships, where political power largely coincided with economic power, there was no room for real social concern, genuine agrarian reform, nor for real worker-participation in industry.

Together the oligarchic groups ran a tightly-controlled, low-wage, high-profit economy, well suited to produce fast rates of capital accumulation and economic growth. But the set-up was at the same time rigid, corrupt and inefficient. Modest attempts to reform, liberalise and streamline it, to prepare for and then launch the 'economic miracle' had fallen to the expertise of technocrats, many of whom 'happened to be' members of the Opus Dei, themselves by now firmly enmeshed in the close-knit old-established economic and political elites.[45]

Under the premiership of Admiral Carrero Blanco (not an Opus member himself but a sympathiser), whom the dictator had cast in the role of co-ordinator of Francoism after Franco, López Rodó continued as Minister for Economic and Social Development Plans, with wide powers. The Opus Dei technocrats held key ministries; they first had chastened the old financial elites (over the nationalisation of the Bank of Spain and the Institutes of Official Credit) and then developed close relationships with them. In Europe the economic boom of the fifties and sixties and the consequent success of economic integration signalled the triumph of neo-capitalism on the continent and underlined the need for Spain to abandon autarchy and adjust to liberal economic orthodoxy. Development demanded foreign capital and technology and increasing participation in world trade.

López Rodó's economic reforms were accompanied by administrative restructuring, backed up by *opusdeístas* in other ministries. Their influence extended beyond the political sphere to industry, construction, banking, commerce, insurance, the media, advertising, tourism, cinema groups, and publishing. The Opus had its own University in Pamplona and in 1957 had opened the Institute for Higher Business Studies (IESE – *Instituto de Estudios Superiores de la Empresa*), which was part of the University and a prestigious hothouse for the nurturing of technocrats and managers.

Authoritarian in its politics, conservative in its Catholicism, liberal-market in its economics, the Opus can be seen as 'a symbolic synthesis in theory and practice of the traditional values which triumphed in 1939 and the demands of neocapitalist modernisation'.[46] It seems ironical that the Opus, with its emphasis on 'spirituality', should have held the reins of economic decision-making and cultivated the materialistic values of capitalism. Its members sought out-and-out economic development, which led to greater prosperity for some strata of society but exacerbated the harsh inequalities condemned by the bishops either as individuals or as a body.

Critics within the Church claimed that, despite their rhetoric, none of the bishops had seriously tackled the grave problem of the poor, that the denunciation of injustice by the hierarchy was not translated into action. Specifically, 'there is no recorded case of a single bishop who has taken part in a demonstration or in a just strike in solidarity with his people; nor a single one who lives the real poverty of the poorest, like Hélder Câmara. Not one in gaol'.[47] Alfonso Comín maintained that as long as the members of the institutional Church failed to sever their links with the capitalist system, they were supporting oppression.[48] At the same time, priests were criticised, execrated, fined and imprisoned by the regime for what was called 'politicisation of the gospel', for their interpretation of what it meant in terms of defending social justice.

Beset as they were with such issues, the Spanish bishops had to contend also with the decline in their moral authority, reflected in the drop in religious observance. Their concerns echoed those of Paul VI who was only too aware that the Second Vatican Council had not succeeded in making the Church relevant. During one of his weekly audiences, the Pope pointed to the very paradox deriving from the Council's attempt to come to terms with modernity. He asked 'How is religion to be presented to our generation?... How to make it understandable, acceptable, welcome, effective, modern?' when the 'effort, very laudable in itself, to make religious doctrine acceptable to men of our times, hides a danger... which we can call doctrinal relativism'; doctrine must not be adulterated.[49]

Following the Pope's exhortation to the bishops of the world on 5 January 1971 to keep guard over the integrity and purity of the faith, the CEE issued their own declaration on 25 March. It recognised that new times demanded new ways of expressing the message of the gospel, but voiced the same concern as the Pope over the 'accumulation of ambiguities, uncertainties and doubts' among Catholics about basic tenets and other demands of the faith. In referring to 'the indissolubility of marriage and due respect for life', the bishops were speaking of issues that Spanish Catholics generally, along with others, had begun to approach with a greater breadth of individual conscience than before Vatican II: divorce, contraception and abortion in particular. After the publication in July 1968 of Pope Paul's encyclical *Humanae Vitae* condemning 'artificial' birth control, which provoked 'rebellion, reservations and upset in many Catholic quarters',[50] the Spanish bishops had issued a document showing their full support of the Pope's teaching. They now reminded theologians that the authentic teaching authority was not invested in them but in the hierarchy.

Both the Pope and the Spanish hierarchy had put their finger on new aspects of secularisation. Vatican II, by admitting freedom of conscience, had opened up the possibilities of à la carte Catholicism, apparently allowing a choice of tenets to be held or rejected, according to individual taste. On the other hand, insistence on the full menu of tenets came up against a resistance to authority which had increasingly characterised life especially since the 1960s, both inside and outside the Church. Although the bishops continued to speak of 'Catholic Spain' in their documents, they had begun to recognise that Catholicism was no longer the spiritual mantle covering the whole nation. Pointing to what he saw as the need for new missionary methods, the auxiliary bishop of Huesca stated, 'We constantly hear that people no longer go to confession; that in a large number of cases fulfilment of Easter duties is purely routine and not rooted in faith; that many Christians treat the sacrament of marriage as a merely social occasion'.[51]

What the 1970 FOESSA report said about the growing awareness in Spain of a 'crisis of Catholicism' continued to apply and in spades. Apart from the vast number of those who were no more than on the fringe of belief, or of unreasoning religiosity, there were those whose 'atheism, agnosticism, practical irreligiosity, secularisation, anticlericalism' were now bolder and more clearly identifiable; the number involved might not have risen dramatically since the previous decade of the 1950s–1960s but their 'social visibility' had. The report ascribed this phenomenon to the personal anonymity deriving from the process of urbanisation, greater openness to the rest of the Western world, increasing social scepticism towards the myth of Catholicism as the 'national religion', and greater ecclesiastical understanding towards the 'deviant' forms of religiosity. It also identified a weakening of the function of religious validation of social norms and values, and an increasing awareness of the dysfunctions of Catholicism in Spanish society in such matters as birth control, ethical pluralism and freedom of expression.

In short, by the end of this period, mid-1971, almost all the Spanish Church, along with Spanish society, had undergone immeasurable changes. In the sphere of political alliances, it was already looking to the post-Franco period. Democracy and human rights were firmly on the CEE's agenda and, under Cardinal Tarancón as its President, would soon provoke open hostilities with the Franco regime. Future alliances or pacts would have to be negotiated with whatever democratic forces emerged in the post-Franco era. Foreseeing a loss of political support for its 'rights', the Church would emphasise its claims to social influence founded on its perception of the Catholic identity of Spain. As to the prevailing socio-economic order, the CEE remained a Church Reluctant: reluctant to bestow its *nihil obstat*, but reluctant also to commit itself to real transformation. All the while, the great heresy, marxist atheism, continued to be perceived to be the main threat to the Church's influence and relevance in Spain. But in reality the main threat was the onward march of secularisation.

3 The Victory of the 'Extreme Centre' (mid-1971 to mid-1973)

The crisis generated in the Church at the time of (not because of) the Second Vatican Council was so grave that the consequences were being felt a quarter of a century later. A Christian who was firm in his faith – and who knew of similar periods in the history of the Church – would bear this time of Babel with fortitude, but perhaps the same could not be said of the 'average' Christian. The latter, browsing through the daily press, might see that there was more or less accurate talk of some cardinal who defended the abolition of celibacy, of bishops who favoured a 'socialist option', of hundreds of priests who were requesting laicisation.[1]

As the resolutions of Vatican II worked their way through the Spanish Church and as the likelihood of fundamental political change drew closer, the first half of the 1970s found the Church manoeuvring within the constraints of an increasingly tense relationship with Francoism while preparing for a different regime. At the same time it had to decide to what extent to turn away from the prevailing socio-economic system, the defects of which were increasingly offensive to many Christian consciences. Recognising structural injustice in capitalism or even admitting its flaws did not, of course, necessarily mean opting for all models – or indeed any model – of socialism. Divisions ran deep despite attempts to show a united front. On basic tenets of dogma it was not difficult to be united but socio-political issues threw up strong divergences which were clearly reflected in personal statements or diocesan bulletins.

Any understanding of these developments within the Spanish Church and of its relations with the Spanish *res publica* during the last years of Franco and the fledgling years of democracy must take into account the figure of Cardinal Enrique y Tarancón. With his finely-tuned political sense and undoubted fidelity to a democratic ideal on the lines of Italian Christian Democracy, which had been encouraged by Rome since Vatican II, Tarancón attempted to build a bridge between the left and moderate right of the Spanish Church, and between the 'two Spains' of victors and vanquished still divided so many decades after the Civil War. He was a man of the 'extreme centre'.[2]

The tributes paid to the Cardinal in both the Catholic and secular press after his retirement in 1983 and again after his death in November 1994 emphasised the unique part he played in this key period. Under his leadership, the institutional Church ceased to be considered the enemy of democracy, and, without budging far from the centre ground, even ventured in the end to envisage the possibility of accepting certain elements of a moderate socialism. But 'socialism' was never defined.

Tarancón could be said to be 'Paul VI's man' since the Pope, anxious to support a change within moderation in the Spanish Church and its disengagement from Francoism, and to prepare the ground for the post-Franco situation, had appointed him Archbishop of Toledo, Primate of Spain, a mere month before the CEE elections of 1 February 1969,[3] to enhance his candidature to the presidency. When he lost narrowly to Mgr Casimiro Morcillo, Archbishop of Madrid-Alcalá and leader of the conservative wing of the Church, Tarancón was offered and accepted the vice-presidency. This was to be a crucial factor two years later. Morcillo died at 12.30 a.m. on 29 May 1971. On that same morning the Papal Nuncio, Mgr Dadaglio, indicated to Tarancón the Pope's personal decision[4] that he should become Apostolic Administrator of the Madrid diocese. This 'ecclesiastical coup', accepted immediately by Tarancón, scuppered the plans of the Madrid (Alcalá) diocesan chapter to appoint a prelate – all speculation points to Mgr Guerra Campos – more faithfully allied to the regime. Within six months (on 4 December 1971) Tarancón would be appointed Cardinal Archbishop of Madrid, and elected President of the Bishops' Conference.

He faced a mammoth task.[5] There was the fact that Franco was growing old, and the Church would have to prepare for the as yet unknown political set-up which came after him. On the one hand, the Church was still in hock to a regime which had saved it from the 'red hordes' of the Second Republic, and which had granted it all manner of privileges, including generous State financing. On the other hand, the general mood of the universal Catholic Church, reflected in a growing groundswell of opinion in Spain, was for disengagement from regimes which respected neither political plurality nor human rights. Furthermore, there was the paradox of a government, which was by its constitution Catholic, fining clerics for preaching 'subversive' sermons, imprisoning priests and monks for their dissidence, and supporting a press which was not averse to attacking Tarancón himself, the Nuncio and even Paul VI. The Church itself was not united in the face of these challenges. There were divisions within the hierarchy, and in the wider ecclesial community the tendencies ran from the radical left – close to liberation theology – to the right-wing preconciliar movements grouped around the 5000-strong integrist *Hermandad Sacerdotal*.[6]

The major ecclesial event of 1971, in fact one that was pivotal in the Church's evolving understanding of itself, the regime and society, took place in the autumn. Between 13 and 18 September, following a sociological survey of all the Spanish clergy, and soundings taken at diocesan and interdiocesan level, Tarancón presided over a Joint Assembly of bishops and priests from all over the country.[7] Debates centred on seven areas: six on the role and pastoral activity of priests, following on from the first which covered 'The Church and the World in the Spain of Today'. This first schema, questioning as it did all the issues affecting Church–State relations, was bound to provoke a hostile reaction from the regime, since its conclusions concerning all manner of human and civil rights and freedoms struck right at the heart of Francoism.

The Assembly advocated the mutual independence of Church and State, an end to Church involvement in government bodies, the elimination of 'all real or apparent situations of mutual concession of privileges', a revision of the Concordat and a stop to government intervention in the appointment of bishops. It expressed regret that Church schools had been elitist in the past and declared that 'we do not wish them to be so in the future'. Resolution 49 called on the Church to be evangelically poor and to reject links with 'economic powers'.

A HOAC report published about the same time fleshed out this last resolution: it highlighted the plight of many Spaniards after the implementation of two – in many other ways successful – Economic and Social Development Plans ushered in by the Opus Dei technocrats. Unskilled workers, for instance, worked desperately long hours in increasingly dangerous and unhygienic working conditions and often had to juggle their time and energy over two – or more – jobs a day in order to make ends meet, for which they received little over half the minimum subsistence wage. It spoke of 'a fabulous redistribution of wealth but in the wrong direction: financial resources were taken from the workers and placed at the disposal of capital'.[8]

Especially arresting was an Assembly resolution which, with reference to the Civil War, affirmed that 'We humbly recognise and ask pardon because we did not know at the time how to be true "ministers of reconciliation" towards our people, divided by a war between brothers'. It attracted more than 50 per cent of the votes but failed to achieve the two-thirds majority needed for ratification;[9] even so, as the *New York Times* commented, it represented 'a historic examination of conscience by the Spanish Church' as to its uncompromisingly pro-Franco role in the Civil War.[10] The split on this resolution was fairly predictable: Mgr Antonio Montero, then auxiliary bishop of Seville,[11] later stated[12] that it had been most ardently advocated by young priests in their twenties who had not lived through the religious persecution of the Civil War. While he himself had abstained, he could understand the attitude of those older bishops who *had* been persecuted and refused to ask for pardon. Mgr González Moralejo of Huelva said that he had abstained because he considered that the resolution was badly worded and, rather than a humble admission of guilt, it seemed like an accusation. He too thought that the majority of those pressing for this motion to be passed were the young priests who had not lived through the Civil War.[13] Mgr Elías Yanes of Oviedo[14] similarly considered that some priests who had lived through the Republic and the Civil War felt closely attached to the person of Franco; this emotional link prevented them from expressing open criticism.

The Assembly had been called largely to respond to issues faced by priests: their theological training, their way of life, their need to adapt evangelisation to the immense changes in Spanish society. In soundings on their political options taken among the clergy before the Assembly began, the first choice was some kind of socialism (24.8 per cent among diocesan priests and 23 per cent among male religious orders); traditional or constitutional monarchy came second among priests (21.7 per cent) and 'the prevailing situation' was second among monks (20.2 per cent).[15] The 'democratic' style of the Assembly and the radical motions discussed would never have been possible without pressure from the more progressive priests, religious and laity over the previous 10 or 15 years, but they provoked a fierce backlash from the clerical right. All the pent-up tensions within the clergy were released in a public display of internal dissension. With the death of Mgr Morcillo, what had originally been conceived by the hierarchy as a mere survey of the views of priests in Spain became an instrument of struggle to wrench the dominance of the CEE from the conservatives.

Ecclesia and progressive journals such as *Pastoral Misionera, Iglesia Viva,* and *Cuadernos para el Diálogo* ran enthusiastic commentaries.[16] The English Catholic weekly *The Tablet* commented that

> the September assembly of bishops and priests marked a climax of the new spirit that has been making its way in the Church in Spain since Vatican II. That assembly made a break from the Catholic-Nationalist conception that had previously been characteristic of the Church's self-understanding in Spain, calling for disengagement from ties with the State.[17]

Indeed, among progressive elements in the Church there was initial euphoria about the conclusions reached by the Joint Assembly. A good number of chaplains who had worked alongside Catholic Action workers and students believed that with the Assembly would come a revival of genuine attempts to transform society.[18] After all, every one of the conclusions of the first discussion area were pointing in this direction. A group of 36 priests, many from university faculties, petitioned the hierarchy to implement the findings of the Assembly. They were particularly concerned that the bishops' position should, in true fidelity to the gospel, be clearly in defence of every human being, 'which demands a struggle against all forms of political, social, economic and cultural injustice'.[19] Full discussion was postponed, a sure sign that consensus was not to be achieved easily, until the XVI Plenary of the hierarchy to be held between 6–11 March of the following year. In the event there was a majority of 51–10 in favour of assuming the Assembly's conclusions.[20]

Right-wing hostility had flared even before the start of the Assembly. In February 1971 the *Hermandad Sacerdotal* had spoken of the fearful consequences if 'this Assembly with its democratic air and Babel-like confusion is not stopped in time',[21] and it later held its own counter-Assembly. Attacks came also from the government-controlled press and the right-wing Catholic paper *Iglesia-Mundo*.[22] The *opusdeístas* were offended by Assembly conclusion 49, which was widely taken to be critical of them in that it called upon the Church to renounce all real or apparent wealth and to reject alignment with any powerful or privileged group.[23]

Nor was General Franco slow to react to the conclusions arising out of the Assembly's first schema, especially to a motion which questioned the 'Crusade' interpretation of the Civil War. Just over a month after the close of the Assembly, the Caudillo made an attack on what appeared to be the Church's rejection of its past. Affirming that the Civil War had been fought 'in defence of the spiritual patrimony of Christian civilisation', he reminded his audience that most of the Spanish bishops of the time called the war 'a Crusade', whereas 'today there are some who try to give another interpretation to the nature of our war of liberation, in the vain hope that new generations... can be led along the paths of confusion, weakness and disorientation'.[24]

Despite soured relations, towards the end of the year the Spanish government and the Vatican patched together a compromise on appointments to several major dioceses. Tarancón, previously Apostolic Administrator, was confirmed as Archbishop of the Madrid diocese; Archbishop Narcís Jubany, who followed a similarly moderately progressive line, was appointed to Barcelona, while the highly conservative Mgr González Martín became Primate of Toledo.[25]

Violence and political agitation continued to rage throughout the country. A Public Order Law issued in 1971 raised to three months the one-month limit for arrest without trial. In effect it extended indefinitely the state of emergency declared during the tense days of the Basque nationalists' trial in Burgos in December 1970, and aimed at mollifying powerful right-wing elements, particularly the Army, with their phobia about any political liberalisation.

Incidents involving clashes between the police and protesting or striking workers multiplied, with priests and some of the bishops continuing to provide support and shelter in defence of human and civil rights. Since strikes and unauthorised meetings were illegal, churches and church premises had become sanctuaries for sit-down demonstrations, and clandestine meetings of various kinds. On one occasion members of the Workers' Commissions, including 'Fr Paco' (as Francisco García Salve, formerly a Jesuit priest, now a leader of the Madrid construction workers, was widely referred to), met secretly in a spiritual retreat house in Pozuelo, on the outskirts of Madrid. Police went to arrest the group, since 'nobody believed they were there just to say the rosary',[26] even though, under the terms of the Concordat, the police were supposed to ask for permission before entering church premises. Some of the bishops protected their 'turbulent priests' (albeit at times with some chagrin) by denying permission for court proceedings to be taken against them, and they continued to denounce instances of injustice.

In fact they were becoming increasingly outspoken. In April 1973, Mgr Jubany of Barcelona blamed social injustice for the death of a striker, a construction-worker killed by the police in a nearby town. Mgr Jubany's statement, while condemning all violence as being unevangelical and unchristian, included a strong, if implicit, criticism of the regime: 'One cannot condemn violence lightly without serious analysis of what brings it about. There are unjust situations which oppress and impede the free exercise of the most basic rights'.[27]

Right-wing thugs frequently aided the police in repression. After a prayer meeting on the eve of May Day 1973, Catholic workers and five priests, including the national JOC chaplain, were beaten up by *Guerrilleros de Cristo Rey* who threatened to attack Mgr Oliver, auxiliary Bishop of Madrid and Vicar of the Workers' Apostolate. Using iron bars, they clubbed people leaving the church while Mgr Oliver was taunted with shouts of 'Down with red priests'.[28] The *Guerrilleros*' leader, Mariano Sánchez-Covisa, denounced by Cardinal Tarancón in connection with the attack, was questioned by the authorities but released without charge.[29]

On May Day itself, following the murder of a secret police inspector by a member of the ultra-left terrorist group, Revolutionary Antifascist and Patriotic Front (FRAP), thousands of Spanish nationalists and hard-line Falangists marched through Madrid shouting anti-government slogans (*'Franco sí, Opus no'*) and, naming Cardinal Tarancón specifically (*Tarancón al paredón*) called for 'red bishops' to be sent to the firing squad.[30] The fact that the authorities allowed this demonstration to go ahead can be interpreted as an indication that Franco was being pressurised by hard-line Falangists and other groups of the political 'bunker' to impose more repressive measures than those of his Opus ministers. The attempt to discredit the Opus was part of a campaign against Franco's plans for installing a monarchy under Juan Carlos after the Caudillo's death.[31]

The *Financial Times* correspondent reported that, while there was general revulsion at the murder of the policeman, it was increasingly common to hear people ask why there had not been similar expressions of official regret and memorial services for the worker killed by police in Barcelona that spring, or for the two shipyard workers shot dead in El Ferrol in March 1972, or for the protesting SEAT worker who had died in similar circumstances in 1971, or for the three people who had died when the police opened fire on demonstrators in Granada in the summer of 1970.[32] It was at times like these, when churchmen denounced police brutality – as they did on all the above occasions – that the Church's social and political standing rose in public opinion.[33]

It was also at times like these, or when some Church document touched a political nerve, that State–Church relations were most under strain. A case in point was a two-thousand-word document drawn up by the national Justice and Peace Commission for World Peace Day (1 January 1972), entitled 'If You Want Peace, Work for Justice'.[34] This was a full-blooded attack on the Franco regime and the myth of the Crusade which had subjected Spain to a 'false peace' characterised by official repression and social injustice, and created a society in which depoliticisation was the price to pay for an increasing number of material goods. It went on to demand that

> At the same time that the Church proclaims the principles which concern justice and peace, and strives to apply them to the real events of the world in which it lives and which take place within the Church itself, it must also assume the risk of prophetically denouncing injustice, wherever this be found or attempts to install itself, even when doing so draws upon the Church, upon the members of its hierarchy or of its laity, criticism, lack of understanding and even contempt and persecution by the powerful in the land.

It called upon the Church to assert its freedom, abandon all privilege and to be poor with the poor. It ended by asking whether as individuals or collectively the Church was willing to follow Christ in paying the price of defending peace with justice: Christ had paid a high price indeed, since for those who were against him, those in power, 'his attitudes were uncomfortable for the established "order" '.[35]

The document was banned by the Ministry of Justice,[36] but the government could not prevent it being read out in churches throughout Spain at Mass on Sunday 19 December.[37] It was the object of legal proceedings by the Public Order Court, and provoked a protest to the Papal Nuncio from the Ministry of Foreign Affairs; the Ministry said that it ran counter to the recent more favourable climate of understanding between Church and State which had followed agreement on recent episcopal appointments.[38]

The President of the Justice and Peace Commission, Mgr González Moralejo, resigned. He said later[39] that he had done so in protest against the banned document because he did not agree with some of the wording of the text, but *before* conflict with the government had arisen. He considered that the Justice and Peace members wanted to 'make politics', to attack the government, whereas he believed that this was not the Church's mission: the Church must do what the gospel demanded and this sometimes meant denunciation, not for its own sake, but for the sake of the gospel. Likewise there had to be disengagement from the regime, not for disengagement's sake, but because the Church was aware of its mission and this is what its mission demanded. An article in the French Catholic journal *Informations Catholiques Internationales*, quoting a layman from Barcelona, put a different gloss on this incident, claiming that Mgr Moralejo's refusal to sign the document, after being involved in drawing it up, was symptomatic of the fact that at bottom the bishops remained too authoritarian and too clerical to envisage a break with the regime. In fact none of the bishops protested against the government ban.[40] Interestingly enough, only a few weeks before the publication of 'If You Want Peace Work for Justice', the 1971 international Synod of Bishops in Rome had stated that 'the struggle for justice is a *constitutive* [my italics] dimension of the preaching of the gospel'[41] a declaration which, of course, could be perceived by Spanish Catholic activists as vindicating their battles against the Franco regime and organised capital.

The right-wing press described the Justice and Peace document as 'a plot against the State' and called for the severest penalties to be meted out to those responsible; it also accused the Nuncio of inciting the Spanish Church to adopt 'non-pastoral' attitudes.[42] In a speech delivered in León on 18 December, the Undersecretary for Justice attacked what he saw in the document as an 'alliance of a marxist view of life with old heresies reborn', which rejected any spiritual dimension and reduced human progress exclusively to social progress, seeing Jesus Christ 'as a precursor of modern social struggles, like a hero who has come to effect a violent change in politico-social structures'.[43]

Right-wing anticlerical feeling erupted again at a gathering held in December 1971 in honour of the fascist lawyer, Blas Piñar. Amid shouts of 'Down with Councils', telegrams and letters of support were read out from political, military and ecclesiastical dignitaries including the President of the Cortes, the Information and Tourism Minister, various civil governors, and the retired Bishop of Valencia. Blas Piñar himself attacked ecumenism for breaking up religious unity and for contributing to the loss of the (Catholic) faith. He spoke of 'national indignation and patriotism' against separatist propaganda 'which has its lairs in many religious houses'.[44]

Franco's 1971 end-of-year message showed that he was still smarting from the 'political' resolutions of the Joint Assembly, and was stung both by the Justice and Peace document and an increasing number of incidents involving Church pressure for political and social reforms. He warned that a fearful social crisis would be brought about if the aims of the Church and the State were at odds: 'what the State cannot do is stand idly by in the face of certain attitudes of a temporal nature assumed by certain ecclesiastics'.[45] Government and Church attitudes were clearly on a diverging course. Following a labour dispute in Franco's birthplace of El Ferrol (Galicia), in which two workers were killed by the police and others were injured, the Civil Governor of the region, representing the government position, attributed responsibility to the illegal Communist Party, but the local bishop, Mgr Araujo, authorised a homily under the title 'Thou Shalt not Kill', which unambiguously condemned police repression.[46]

Early in 1972, a clumsy attempt was made to discredit the 1971 Joint Assembly and its conclusions, which the bishops had undertaken to 'assume'. On 21 February, the news agency *Europa-Press* (linked to Opus Dei and representing conservative attitudes in the Church) printed an item referring to the existence of a 'Roman document' which was alleged to torpedo the Assembly's conclusions. It later transpired that the document had been concocted without the knowledge not only of the CEE but also of the Pope and his Secretary of State, Cardinal Villot: Mgr Guerra Campos, conspiring with members of the Opus Dei[47] and with the help, inside the Vatican, of the Prefect of the Sacred Congregation for the Clergy, had intended to use the document as part of an anti-Assembly campaign designed to show that the CEE was out of favour with the Vatican, to ensure that close Church–State ties were maintained and to undermine any Church moves in favour of democracy.[48] By coincidence, Tarancón was already due to go to Rome on 28 February, and took the opportunity to give his version of events. He received the personal support of Paul VI and returned to Madrid with a letter of clarification from Cardinal Villot.

The anti-Assembly campaign was also – and most notably – aimed at preventing Cardinal Tarancón's election to the Presidency of the CEE, so as to halt the progress towards more moderate attitudes being assumed by the hierarchy.[49] But in the event the whole affair boomeranged on its instigators and Tarancón emerged strengthened. In the elections held during that XVI Plenary Meeting (March 1972), not only was he elected President of the CEE by a handsome majority[50] but the ultra-conservative Mgr Guerra Campos was ousted as Secretary to the Conference, albeit by a narrow margin.

The political conservatives within the hierarchy were now fighting a rearguard action to maintain the Church's alliance with the Franco regime. As Primate of Toledo, Mgr González Martín took his seat *ex officio* in Franco's Council of State on 23 March 1972. He claimed after his investiture that it did not signify a lack of commitment to the principle of disengagement but rather that 'noble, respectful and cordial co-operation with the State can be useful'.[51] Mgr Cantero Cuadrado, Archbishop of Zaragoza, and Mgr Guerra Campos continued to attend the Spanish Parliament as *procuradores* nominated by Franco.[52] Guerra Campos came to be magnified by his right-wing supporters as 'the Bishop of Spain' – as representative of the 'true values' of the Church – and for some years he appeared on Spanish television in a religious programme called *The Eighth Day* in which he presented ultra-traditional dogma.[53]

The regime was understandably irritated by the Church's strategy of circumventing the dispositions of the Concordat concerning the *derecho de presentación* by the appointment of auxiliary bishops.[54] According to the 1953 Concordat, the Holy See had undertaken to initiate contacts over appointments as soon as a diocese became vacant or if it was considered necessary to appoint a coadjutor with right of succession. Ever since Church–State relations had become strained, the Vatican had ceased to appoint coadjutors, and tended – as in the case of Mgr Tarancón in Madrid – to appoint apostolic administrators, who could remain indefinitely in the post and whose appointment, like that of auxiliary bishops, was not subject to State approval. The number of auxiliary bishops increased considerably: six were appointed in 1972 alone.[55]

There was more to it than this, for during the XV Plenary Meeting (December 1971) the hierarchy introduced a change in its internal regulations, which radically altered the relative weight of conservatives and centrists in the CEE votes. Hitherto retired bishops – in an age-group most apt to be in favour of the Church–State alliance – had been entitled to vote in Conference matters,[56] and auxiliary bishops were not. The situation was now reversed,[57] and the recently-appointed auxiliaries were more likely to be in tune with the democratic leanings of the Pope, the Nuncio and Tarancón than with the dictatorship. As this represented of course a considerable shift in the composition of the episcopate, it was not surprising that government-inspired attacks appeared in the press about the Vatican's 'back-door' appointment of bishops and apostolic administrators who were not subject to the regime's right of patronage and should not, it was claimed, have voting rights.[58] These attacks gathered momentum as time went on.

As to actual relations between the regime and the Vatican, what little contact there was proved stormy. In the spring of 1973, the Foreign Minister, Gregorio López Bravo, had a meeting with Pope Paul, whom he accused of fomenting subversion among certain priests and bishops and supporting separatism in the Basque Country. The Pope told Cardinal Tarancón soon afterwards that he had found the Foreign Minister's conduct intolerably impertinent.[59]

Also at issue between Church and State was the 'priests' charter', originally conceived as a means of avoiding publicity over offences committed by the clergy, both secular and regular, mainly connected with sexual and financial offences. Under the terms of the Concordat, the State was obliged to seek permission from the ordinary of a diocese to prosecute a member of the clergy in State courts; in addition there was to be no publicity about the case, and any prison sentence was to be served in a special detention centre.[60] From the late 1960s onwards, however, the type of offence committed by the clergy was more likely to be one of political opposition. In such cases, the last thing the priests wanted was lack of publicity, nor did they want a special prison like the one designated for them in Zamora, but rather to share the lot of other political offenders in State prisons. The Church no longer desired this particular 'privilege', while the State, anxious to avoid publicity about anti-regime activities by the clergy, now demanded strict observance of the relevant section of the Concordat.[61]

Admiral Carrero Blanco furiously berated the Spanish bishops for their ingratitude. He recalled that the Caudillo – without any thought save of God and Fatherland – had rescued them from an anticlerical Second Republic and spent some 300 billion pesetas on building and maintaining churches, seminaries, and charitable and educational centres.[62] In reply, Tarancón claimed that Carrero seemed to suggest that the Church was an enemy of the regime, but he, Tarancón, was a man of dialogue and the bishops did not want to break with Franco.[63] Carrero did not understand the way the Church was evolving, but he respected the hierarchy 'before all and above all',[64] and Tarancón even commented later that he thought that the two of them might have reached a better understanding had Carrero's life not been cut short.[65]

Franco's end-of-year message, three weeks after this 'Carrero drubbing' (*mazazo Carrero*),[66] piously underlined his government's disinterested service to the Church over more than three decades, 'willingly granting it all manner of facilities and assistance in the fulfilment of its sacred mission'. But there was a sting in the tail as he gave yet another clear warning to the bishops not to overstep the limits of the God–Caesar relationship, saying that 'if it is the mission of the hierarchy to illuminate the conscience of the faithful in the fulfilment of their socio-civic duties, it is not their mission to invade the domain of the civil authority'.[67]

As if to underline the financial dependence of the Church on the State, the government had a short time earlier stopped subsidising some twenty seminaries[68] – admittedly surplus in the light of the drop in the number of seminarians – and officials spoke of a reappraisal of the problem of financing private (Church) secondary schools and the clergy's stipends.[69] The Spanish Church, although wealthy in terms of real estate, gold and art treasures, would find it challenging, if not impossible in the short term, to maintain itself without State subsidies, for congregations were dwindling and anyway unaccustomed to making an open-handed contribution to supporting their pastors. Although the Joint Assembly had urged financial independence from the State, the bishops, while recognising that the normal upkeep of the Church – personal, material and apostolic activities – ought to depend on the voluntary contributions of its membership,[70] continued to find themselves unable to give up State subsidies.

In January 1973, an episcopal document, 'The Church and the Political Community',[71] late offspring of the Joint Assembly of September 1971, emerged after a difficult and protracted labour,[72] swaddled in rumours, similar to those that a year earlier had accompanied the 'Roman document'.[73] It was passed by the narrowest of majorities,[74] which highlighted the divisions within the CEE, even though in order to achieve consensus[75] some of the document's teeth had already been drawn during the various drafting processes, to the extent that the quite explicit conclusions of the 1971 Joint Assembly, which had been included in earlier drafts, were omitted from the final version.[76]

The document was divided into two sections. The first, 'The Church and the Temporal Order', discussed in the abstract the variety of political options open to Christians and the necessity for them to work for justice in the world; it spoke of the prophetic mission of the Church vis-à-vis 'social sins' and the role of the priest who, while maintaining a 'certain distance from any political post or endeavour', could 'contribute much to the introduction of a more just social order'.

The second section, 'Church–State Relations', reaffirmed the need for the Concordat to be revised, for the Church to renounce its privileges and the presence of bishops in official political organisations, and it again asked the State to end the *derecho de presentación*; the confessionality of the State was left open but religious freedom for everyone was to be guaranteed. Clearly, for sound theological and practical reasons (insights brought by Vatican II, internal pressures, and the Church's anticipation of a democratic Spain in the post-Franco period) the hierarchy was bringing the alliance to Franco's regime to an end, and since various aspects of 'The Church and the Political Community' could be interpreted as confrontational – a break with the regime *avant la lettre*[77] – it received a hostile reception from the government-controlled media.

The bishops' statement trod a very delicate path through the issue of what it called 'economic help'.[78] Declaring that State subsidies given to the Church were now considered to be a service to the people, enabling them to develop their religious dimension, the document emphasised the historical role of the Church in providing all manner of schools, hospitals, old people's homes, housing and social services. In such circumstances, it claimed, State subsidies could not be considered a privilege. In any case, a distinction had to be made between the (modest) stipends allotted to the clergy and the larger sums allocated to the Church's educational and social services, maintenance of religious monuments and the building and repair of church buildings. The document seemed to imply – realistically, perhaps – that, even though the Church must make its members aware that they ought to give it proper financial support, that would not be enough; it did not propose to turn away help given by the Spanish people via the State. The burden of argument in this part of the document was on 'freedom for the Church for the sake of serving the community', in an attempt to show that what it received from the State was its due, not a grace and favour subsidy.

Deep down the bishops were aware that the Church occupied a privileged position – both legal and de facto – in society in general and in education in particular, within a regime where for others the margin of freedom was very narrow. The bad conscience aroused in them by this led to constant self-justification.[79] The section of 'The Church and the Political Community' concerned with education was headed '*Rights* [my italics] of the Church' and claimed that its rights in education were often wrongly confused with privilege.[80] The first right enabled the Church, strictly for the common good, to teach any subject in conditions of equal oppportunity. The corresponding duty of the State was to offer the Church the necessary means to achieve its educational aims insofar as the country's general economic situation allowed and without discrimination in favour of State schools. The second right was that of all Spanish Catholics to receive religious instruction in State schools.

There had already been a spate of episcopal documents on this issue, and the hierarchy's argument continued to be that the existence of Church schools and religious instruction were the wish and the inalienable right of Spanish society which knew itself to be Catholic: religion on the school curriculum was the only viable way of reaching all children. The bishops were here still harking back to a never-never land of unanimity in the faith, and so to a Church *rightfully* supported by the secular authorities.[81] They based their arguments on the premise that Spanish society had always been and still remained Christian and, specifically, Catholic.

Although progressive Catholics for the most part welcomed 'The Church and the Political Community', they had reservations. Leaving aside the 'rights' the Church still claimed in the financial, educational and ethical spheres, there was regret, for example, that the Concordat was to be merely revised, and not abrogated[82] as outdated. Furthermore, it was not clear to whom the document was addressed: Spanish society as a whole, the Catholic community, or the Franco regime.[83] It might also seem to be an opportunistic, poorly digested, assumption by the Church of the values and language of progressive *secular* groups working for a more just society.[84] It was even referred to as the bishops' 'collective agreement' as if a bishops' trade union were negotiating wages and working conditions with the government.[85]

In the matter of political pluralism, the bishops' attitude was observed by some[86] to be positive in that it was implicitly asking for a change of structures which would make such pluralism possible, but by others as being too theoretical, not spelling out precisely the options open to Christians,[87] whereas the Church's relations with the State were stated clearly. The bishops' rejection of marxist analysis and praxis was thought to be not only proof of the corseted nature of the pluralism they proposed but was also an indication of the Church's knee-jerk reaction to its old enemy.[88] It was suggested that the incompatibility between marxist ideology and Christian faith as presented by Paul VI's *Octogesima Adveniens*,[89] published almost two years earlier (May 1971), had shown a much greater wealth of nuances,[90] and unfavourable comparisons were also made with a recent document by the French bishops which included a section on marxism and the class struggle.[91] Clearly, however, given the particular historical and political circumstances, it was much more difficult for the bishops of the Spanish Church to be specific than for the French bishops living in a democratic country, or for the Pope as head of the universal Church.[92]

Evidence advanced against the Church's claim that it genuinely desired real freedom centred on the issue of how the institution was to be financed if the State ceased to pay priests' stipends, withdrew financial support for educational establishments and the maintenance of church property, and discontinued tax exemptions.[93] Although they had started to realise that subventions generally came with dangerous strings attached and although they had moved away from the regime *politically*, the bishops could not bring themselves to make a complete *financial* break.[94] But the alliance with the Franco regime could not finally be buried so long as the Church continued to accept financial dependence on the State, and claimed specific areas of influence in society. The same would evidently apply to any regime coming after Franco.

The Church was reluctant to go into society naked of power, influence, and economic backing, with the gospel as its only source of credibility. Its 'extreme centre' mind-set made it back off both from an overhaul of its own structures and from social revolution in the sense of the far-reaching restructuring of society as demanded by its radical base.[95] Having 'lost' the working class in the nineteenth century because of its alliance with capitalist forces, it had moved a long way since Vatican II in recognising the need for greater social justice but its more radical members thought it had not gone far enough in helping to bring that about.

'The Church and the Political Community' must also be examined in tandem with another CEE document – 'Pastoral Guidance on the Secular Apostolate'.[96] Whereas the first had been more abstract and had one eye on the political establishment, the second had practical implications, being a call to personal involvement by Catholic activists in transforming the world, exactly the kind of commitment that the Church had condemned in the 1960s. Activists were urged to voice their opinions 'on their own responsibility' about the realities of Spanish socio-political and economic life and to act in accordance with the prompting of the gospel. 'Pastoral Guidance' did not indicate, however, what backing activists would have from their bishops should they find themselves in gaol for doing precisely what the bishops had urged them to do. 'The Church and the Political Community' could be interpreted as little more than an exercise in rhetoric, unless it were taken to a logical conclusion and thereby involved the commitment of all the Catholic community, including the official Church, not just that of activists.[97]

What was happening in the Spanish Church has to be seen in the light of thinking in Rome, where the Pope favoured formal democracy but could not accept radical socialism, which he saw as overturning the structures of society. Papal political strategy appeared to favour a centrism embracing enlightened conservatism and moderate reformism, excluding both revolution and reaction. It was based on the hope that the power elites and beneficiaries of capitalism could be cajoled into themselves softening the harshness of their system, eliminating the more flagrant imbalances and disparities in the First World as well as vis-à-vis the Third World. Thus good relationships with the powerful capitalist countries of the world, especially the United States, were imperative. Parallel attempts must be continued to bring about a liberalisation of Soviet socialist countries, which would allow the Church there a certain freedom of movement, while opposition to communism must remain unyielding.[98]

Such absolute anti-communism in effect implied pro-capitalism. The class struggle was rejected as it was seen almost exclusively as a policy option, freely and perversely chosen, hardly ever considered[99] an inescapable reality expressing a genuine and in part irreconcilable conflict of interest between capital and labour. Pope Paul's *Octogesima Adveniens* had condemned marxism (the philosophy of communism) more harshly than liberalism (the philosophy of capitalism) and made it clear that a Christian would need a very long spoon to sup with socialism. What seriously limited the Church's realistically available socio-economic options was that all too often it saw the alternatives as polarised exclusively between full-blooded Soviet-type 'really existing' socialism and full-blooded 'really existing' capitalism.

By now Paul VI 'was entering a period of dark night, of depression, of deep agonising over his stewardship'.[100] He attempted to contain the Catholic faithful throughout the Catholic Church within the limits imposed by doctrinal unity[101] and the papal authority which guaranteed it, and to affirm that unity all the more energetically the more the social and political spectrum was opened up. In March 1972, 33 theologians, including three Spaniards,[102] wrote a manifesto criticising *inter alia* the feudal, authoritarian mentality of a Church hierarchy more interested in addressing matters of secondary importance than major issues; this, they declared, resulted in passivity on the part of many members of the Church and the growing apathy of public opinion vis-à-vis Church pronouncements.[103] It was also about this time that the Swiss theologian Hans Küng published his book questioning the infallibility of the Pope. 'The smoke of Satan', Paul VI declared, 'has entered God's temple', the devil had come 'in order to spoil and wither the fruits of the Vatican Council'.[104] And while to 'save' Vatican II Rome increasingly insisted on 'right teaching' which emanated from the magisterium alone,[105] there came also an increasingly revisionist attitude to some of the Council reforms. Both the primacy of the magisterium and a certain revisionism would feature prominently and consistently in the pontificate of Paul VI's successor, John Paul II.

Following Paul VI's lead the Spanish bishops individually and collectively referred constantly to the need for unity within the Church based on respect for the teachings of the Pope and the hierarchy. The latter, they said, 'in communion with the Pope and under his authority have the mission received from Christ to guarantee the integrity of the faith' and thus are empowered to see that Catholic activists act 'in accordance with the teaching of the ecclesiastical authority'.[106]

Right teaching – whether viewed from Rome or Madrid – was part of evangelisation, which was the *raison d'être* of the Church's existence. The Church had to know how to deliver its (orthodox) message to a clientèle that was increasingly disinclined to listen. The omens were not good. The social and economic changes related in the fifties and sixties to the breakdown of the agrarian and artisanal structure of Spanish society were accentuated in the 1970s. By then, the Church's traditional interpretation of the world and of life, the goals and behavioural norms it sought to impose on its membership, had been widely rejected or ignored and it seemed unable to find an answer.[107] Even the 'loyal opposition' who remained inside the Church continued their criticism of institutionalised authority of all kinds, and this was accompanied by a crisis in the religious orders, a drop in vocations to the priesthood, the haemorrhage of men leaving the priesthood, tension between the generations and devaluation of some of the Church's sacraments, especially that of penance.[108] The situation was unprecedented, a plurality of views inside the Church – some of them heterodox – being freely expressed by individiduals or groups, priests and lay people and certain organs of the Catholic press.

Social analysis pointed to a wide range of attitudes: a sizeable minority of Catholic activists who tried not only to adapt to the postconciliar Church but also to bear witness to their religion in temporal commitment; a small liberal Catholic minority associated with certain sectors of the upper classes; the vast majority of baptised but indifferent Catholics whose religious observance was nil or negligible, and whose religiosity, overlaid with superstition, would give way in the next generation to attitudes bordering on agnosticism or even atheism; then there was a rural traditional Catholic minority whose religious belief had little theological content and was fed by pious routine.[109] In the case of most practising Catholics – and this must be in large part due to the way the Christian faith had traditionally been taught – religion was concerned with private morality, and did not extend to public morality: it did not have a social dimension.[110] These attitudes were not, of course, confined to Catholics in Spain.

The Church's once sure foundations had become shifting ground. Its political alliance with Franco was in tatters, so it could not obtain loyalty by the back-up of political force, but at the same time it lost credibility because of its financial dependence on the State. It had mounting qualms about its links with organised capital, but it continued to reject any alternative that was more than filing down capitalism's sharpest edges. Its doctrines were contested even by those who remained inside, either through passive resistance or through attempts to bring change about. How could it connect, reach the unevangelised, recover those, like so many intellectuals, students and workers, who had embraced atheism or agnosticism or, even more starkly perturbing, those who simply opted out? Roads continued to lead away from Rome.

4 Preparing for a Future without Franco (mid-1973 to 1975)

> What has always filled churchmen with panic is that someone should actually dare to put the social dimension of the gospel into practice with all its implications. And panic is induced by the possible contamination of marxism which this practice might entail. Hence the never-ending calls for prudence and moderation when social problems are being judged. 'The Church has in the past yielded frequently to the temptation of the middle course. It has reined back evangelical radicalism so as to make it possible for a camel to pass through the eye of a needle. It has invented... the dwarf camel'.[1]

With the General now in his eighties and in failing health, the establishment's key 'political families' jockeyed for position to ensure for themselves a dominant role in post-Franco Spain. Embryonic political parties in and outside the families started to take shape, and 'by the mid-1970s, the shrewder elements would be negotiating with the left and the more reactionary ones would become involved in desperate attempts to put the clock back'.[2]

From Rome, Paul VI supported and guided the hierarchy in Spain in its move towards a democratically moderate stance and, even if many Spanish Catholics remained fervent Francoists, by now the Spanish Church as a whole had ceased to be a legitimiser of Franco's regime and was certainly no longer its instrument of social control. It became instead a rallying-point of opposition. An increasing number of churchmen became part of a swelling movement of intellectuals, students, workers and peasants thirsting for an end to dictatorship. But the intra-ecclesial climate remained heavy with conflict and confrontation.

In June 1973 Franco reshuffled his Cabinet and nominated his *éminence grise*, Admiral Carrero Blanco, as the first Prime Minister of his long dictatorship. The Admiral's appointment was intended to be the linchpin of Franco's last plans to leave Spain's political future all sewn up *(atado y bien atado)*, his brief to oversee the post-Franco situation according to the Caudillo's wishes: Carrero would supervise the monarchy Franco had 're-installed' in the person of Prince Juan Carlos, and the National Movement would continue as the umbrella not for real political parties but for the anodyne 'legitimate contrasting of opinions' allowed by Franco's laws.

The Cabinet reshuffle signalled the eclipse of the Opus Dei in the Spanish government, with the exception of Laureano López Rodó, who took over as Foreign Minister. The Concordat came sharply into focus with the arrival in Madrid on 1 November of the Vatican's Mgr Casaroli on what was supposed to be merely a 'protocol' stop-over between Washington and Rome. Despite the fact that areas for negotiation had already been agreed between the Holy See and the Spanish Bishops' Conference, all the indications were that Casaroli and López Rodó had stitched up a deal about a new Concordat behind the backs of the CEE, the Nuncio in Madrid, and the rest of the Spanish government. Cardinal Tarancón surmised that the Holy See had agreed to what it thought would be little more than a private visit because the Pope wanted to show goodwill towards Spain and reduce anti-Vatican hostility in the Franco regime.[3] The Cardinal told Casaroli that, far from reducing tension, his visit would allow the authorities to persuade people that they had the backing of the Vatican and provide them with an excuse to sideline the CEE. He added that he feared some radical Christian groups would use the goodwill gesture to bring about confrontation between Rome and the CEE.[4]

Casaroli's visit indeed served as a catalyst for a demonstration by radical Catholics. Just a week later, on 11 November, armed police surrounded the Nunciature in Madrid as hundreds of priests and laymen in the capital and other Spanish cities staged sit-ins in sympathy with priests who were political prisoners of the regime, kept isolated in the 'priests' prison' of Zamora. The Madrid sit-in started on a Saturday evening when five bus-loads of demonstrators arrived at the Nunciature, and asked to see Mgr Dadaglio. Most had left the building by the following afternoon but 111 stayed overnight. They had been joined there for a time by three auxiliary bishops of Madrid – Mgr Estepa, Mgr Oliver, and Mgr Iniesta – who, at the request of the demonstrators, signed a document supporting their action which included a call for amnesty for political prisoners. *Europa-Press* and the *Hermandad Sacerdotal* used the occasion to attack the CEE, the Nuncio and the Holy See.[5]

The sit-in at the Nunciature was as much in protest against the apparent hijacking by López Rodó of Casaroli's very public private visit as an expression of sympathy with the Zamora priests. The demonstrators complained that the conversation between Mgr Casaroli and López Rodó had been bilateral, marginalising the Bishops' Conference and the Catholic laity, that the conclusions of the Joint Assembly and the Bishops' document 'The Church and the Political Community' regarding a new Concordat had been ignored, and that Mgr Casaroli's statements lacked transparency. They argued that recent declarations by the Spanish hierarchy on the situation in the country were inadequate, being merely 'words', whereas what was required were clear-cut declarations, especially regarding rights of assembly, association and expression, and the right to strike. In a note addressed specifically to Cardinal Tarancón, they asked (through the three Madrid auxiliary bishops present at the sit-in) that their protests and demands should be read out at the next Plenary Assembly of the episcopate.[6]

In Bilbao about 50 priests took part in a similar sit-in at the offices of the bishop, Mgr Añoveros. The next day priests throughout the Basque Country denounced from the pulpit the regime's policy of segregating priests from other political prisoners. It was denounced also by the bishops of the Bilbao, San Sebastián and Segovia dioceses, who in a letter to their priests stated that the CEE had repeatedly asked the government to do away with the special prison at Zamora.[7] The priests' protest and the bishops' letter followed a riot at the Zamora prison earlier in November. The inmates had set fire to books and furniture to call attention to their demand to be interned in ordinary prisons and treated like other political prisoners. They were subsequently placed in solitary confinement, whereupon they went on hunger strike. Of the seven prisoners then at Zamora, six were Basques, serving long sentences for political offences, two of them having been convicted in the much-publicised court-martial of Basque nationalists in Burgos in 1970; the seventh, 'Fr Paco', along with nine other alleged leaders of the banned Workers' Commissions, was awaiting trial – which would become similarly famous under its case number, 1001 – for their illegal meeting at the Pozuelo monastery.

Short shrift by both Church and regime was given to another group of some 85 members of the grass-roots 'Popular Church' (*Iglesia Popular*)[8] of Madrid, who on 29 and 30 November attempted to set up a Christian Assembly in the diocesan seminary of Madrid. Taking advantage of the fact that the XIX Plenary Assembly of the bishops was being held in the capital, the group tried unsuccessfully to speak with them 'on some urgent and important matters which affect our Church'. Instead Mgr Estepa, as Rector of the seminary, went to meet them. It was then that the police arrived and arrested several members of the group.[9] Later, in a blow-by-blow criticism of the pastoral letter on reconciliation which Tarancón and his Episcopal Council had issued at the end of the Plenary Assembly, the grass-roots communities attacked the bishops' failure to respond to the group's invitation to parley and to prevent the police violating the Concordat by making arrests on church premises. Fr José Mariá Llanos, a respected progressive, who had not been involved in the sit-in, wrote a letter of protest to Tarancón about his (mis)handling of the episode.[10]

On 20 December, Spain was rocked by a terrorist attack of unprecedented gravity and far-reaching consequences. Franco's plans for the country's future were dealt a severe blow by the assassination by ETA of Admiral Carrero only a few months after his appointment as Prime Minister. Events following his death highlighted the divisions between progressive elements in the hierarchy and the increasingly hardline government and its extremist supporters, the *ultras*. As Archbishop of Madrid, it fell to Cardinal Tarancón to preside over both the funeral and burial services, where he was met with insults and shouts of 'Death to the red bishops' from the *Guerrilleros de Cristo Rey* who were among the crowds paying their last respects to the dead Prime Minister. The police made no attempt to intervene.[11] Tarancón himself said that the two-part exequies were 'a *via crucis*' for him because of right-wing extremists: 'The threats during those days were constant and the government came to fear for my physical safety' to the extent that they attempted to find a solution that would mean someone else saying the funeral Mass. 'But I refused and when I refused there came the lot: the demonstration, the insults and all the rest'. He added, not without black humour, that he was not afraid because he knew that 'a Catholic government could not afford the luxury of a cardinal being assassinated, especially at such a time'.[12]

In the explosive atmosphere surrounding the murder of Carrero Blanco a show trial was held, the *proceso 1001*, of ten leaders of *Comisiones Obreras* charged with illegal association. None of the bishops, not even the most progressive, took a clear stand – in public at least – against the harsh sentences handed down.[13] Yet only two months before, three of the Catalan bishops had publicly denounced a police raid on the parish of María Medianera (Barcelona) and the subsequent arrest of 113 political suspects, and called for rights of assembly and association. The detainees were members of the

Assembly of Catalonia, a group attempting to obtain recognition by the regime of the rights of man enshrined in the United Nations Charter. 'We are aware', said Mgr Camprodón of Girona, 'that the intervention of the Church in this field might be interpreted as a political act, but we cannot avoid this if we want to be consistent with the spirit of the Lord'.[14]

On 12 February 1974, Carrero Blanco's successor, Carlos Arias Navarro, made a celebrated speech which seemed to offer half-promises of broader political openness, but he took fright at the unyielding hostility to change on the part of 'the bunker' and in the event nothing of substance emerged. Reiterating the regime's insistence that the Church must not become involved in political affairs, he stated that

> The government will maintain the conditions which will allow the Church to fulfil, without hindrance, its sacred mission and the exercise of its apostolate; but it will reject with equal firmness any interference in questions that, falling within the temporal jurisdiction of the community, are reserved to the judgement and decision of the civil authority.[15]

The former Minister of Public Works, Federico Silva Muñoz, went even further in a speech made a few months later, airing views representative of a harder line: the Church itself could define and the State could agree a range of matters on which the Church could pronounce only as a collective body, for example through the Bishops' Conference; another range of matters would be left to the discretion of bishops in their respective dioceses; the remaining subjects were those on which priests could preach within the limits imposed by the Church itself.[16] It was a kind of 'social pact' between Church and State to avoid conflict by defining once and for all what matters were considered suitable as homily material.

In effect, the regime appeared here to be threatening to replace unilaterally the 'mutual independence', currently professed by both parties, with a modified version of National Catholicism:[17] the Church would be 'domesticated' so that, in return for certain economic and social sweeteners, it would fit in with the *government*'s blueprint of what a Church should be. The regime did not want *political* liberalisation and it did not want the Church to change in any way that might help to bring such liberalisation about. For its part the Church – at least the majority of Church leaders – did not want *ecclesial* liberalisation, a radical transformation of its historical institutional self, nor to bid adieu to all its past glories: thus it would be prepared for continuing dependence on and connivance with the *'protectoris fidei'*,[18] so as not to lose the financial support of the State and to preserve as far as possible its officially guaranteed control over the country's mores.

But in a way this was kite-flying, and contrasted with the more positive developments which had seemed to be taking shape in Church–State relations. The new Foreign Minister, Pedro Cortina, informed Cardinal Tarancón that nothing would be done to revise the Concordat without first hearing the views of the Spanish bishops.[19] Following a meeting with Arias on 17 January 1974, Tarancón is said to have spoken of a thaw (*distensión*) in relations between the Spanish government and the Vatican, and alluded to declarations by both Church and State concerning mutual independence and cordial collaboration.[20] He suggested that, since a complete renewal of the Concordat was a lengthy process, it would be better to tackle the thorniest problems first.[21] As part of this 'truce' with the government, Tarancón sent a letter to each one of Spain's bishops, asking them to avoid anything that might rock the boat.[22]

However, the Church–State crisis that Tarancón had wished to avoid exploded with the publication by Mgr Añoveros of Bilbao of a pastoral letter,[23] calling for a more sympathetic understanding of the Basque people, their culture and traditions. Drawn up by diocesan pastoral workers with the co-operation of the Bilbao Vicar-General, José Angel Ubieta,[24] the pastoral letter stated that the Basques, like other national minorities in Spain, were entitled to their own identity, and it attacked discrimination by the civil authorities against the Basque language.[25] All but three of the 750 priests of the Bilbao diocese read out the pastoral letter at Mass. *Sábado Gráfico* managed to publish the sermon in full but other publications were seized or suffered sanctions for daring to publish even extracts.[26] The government reacted clumsily, claiming that it contained a very serious attack on national unity, placed the bishop and Mgr Ubieta under house arrest and threatened to deport them.

Añoveros' letter came at a politically volatile moment, with the Spanish police still vainly hunting for the Basque terrorists they believed were responsible for the assassination of Admiral Carrero Blanco, and yet only two weeks after the new Prime Minister's 12 February speech apparently pledging more freedom of expression. Añoveros is said in fact to have published the homily precisely to see how genuine the opening-up promised by Arias Navarro would be.[27] He refused to leave Spain, declaring that he would do so only if he received direct orders from the Pope, and threatened with excommunication any Catholic who attempted to expel him, as a violation of the Concordat. Cardinal Tarancón, who was presiding over a meeting of the Bishops' Conference in Madrid when he received a telephone message about the expulsion threat, confirmed later that for three days he had carried in his pocket a document excommunicating the government.[28] Mgr Añoveros received the solid backing of most of his fellow bishops, even though some made him aware that they believed the pastoral letter not to be opportune and others also deplored its content.[29] Tarancón recounts in considerable detail in his 'Confessions' the delicate manoeuvring and second-guessing needed to bring the 'Añoveros affair' to a diplomatic conclusion.[30]

The stand which Mgr Añoveros had made in Bilbao was paralleled by boldness from other bishops and priests: a letter, in Catalan – a language *non grata* to the regime – from the vicars of the archdiocese of Barcelona and read in many churches on 10 March, declared that they suppported Bishop Añoveros absolutely. It called for recognition of the rights of assembly, free association and free speech, as well as the rights of the ethnic minorities in Spain.[31]

The Añoveros case detonated another bout of Francoist fury against the role and number of auxiliary bishops. The *Boletín de las Cortes* recording the parliamentary proceedings of 10 May 1974 stated that

> The Spanish government considers that there has in fact been a change in the figure of the... auxiliary bishop and that the present auxiliary bishop has *de facto* jurisdiction and presence in certain organisations of the Church which confer upon him a real influence which would justify his inclusion in the *derecho de presentación*. There are at the moment 21 auxiliary bishops... named directly by the Holy See.[32]

When the same *Boletín*, coming so soon after the Añoveros affair, went on to state that the government considered a revision of the Concordat to be opportune, this seemed no idle menace. The Justice Minister threatened to break off diplomatic relations with the Holy See if the latter did not accept that the government's right of veto be extended to include auxiliary bishops.[33] Whatever Church attitudes *within* Spain might be – from discarding the Concordat to maintaining the status quo – the Vatican must have been dismayed at a possible break in diplomatic relations. Quite apart from the problems abrogation of the Concordat would create in Spain, the political repercussions might be extremely harmful to the Holy See in its international relations, particularly those with the Italian government: there was at the time a growing movement in Italy to end the Concordat signed with Mussolini in 1929.

The damage done to Church–State relations by the Añoveros affair – seen by many as finally marking the end of the Church–State alliance in Spain – was never to be repaired in Franco's lifetime. Foreign Minister Cortina and Mgr Casaroli held several meetings but no further moves were made before the death of General Franco in November 1975. In Cortina's words, negotiations continued to prove 'inevitably laborious'.[34]

It is still not entirely clear whose feet dragged more over renewing the Concordat. It was partly that neither the Holy See nor the Spanish government wanted to yield on certain issues and partly the CEE's determination not to be left out of any negotiations affecting the Spanish Church. According to José María Areilza (who was to be Foreign Minister in the first post-Franco Cabinet), neither the Vatican nor the regime wanted a new agreement but, instead of saying so openly, lied to each other for years.[35] The State went through the motions of consultation over the years without any apparent intention of agreeing to a revision of the Concordat.[36] Similarly, broad sectors of the hierarchy and clergy in the Spanish Church were against a thoroughgoing revision of the Concordat despite their protestations to the contrary. What they did want was that the State should renounce its one real privilege – the *derecho de presentación*, that the Church should be relieved of the burden of the 'priests' charter', and that the impression should be given in Spanish society that its relations with the Spanish State were no longer governed by the alliance which had brought about the Concordat in the first place.[37] Cardinal Tarancón says that he had at first favoured merely amending the 1953 Concordat but, after the 1972 tensions, he became convinced, as did many other bishops, that partial agreements were preferable, reasoning that it was more prudent 'not to sign a Concordat with a dying regime, given that in all likelihood such a Concordat would be swept away by whatever came afterwards'.[38]

In a measured opening address to the XXI Plenary Assembly of the CEE in November, Tarancón offered the Church's services to help solve the nation's political problems, declaring that it would work with all groups supporting civil liberties in Spain, 'such as association, assembly and expression'.[39] Putting the stress on reconciliation between Spaniards, he condemned violence of *any* kind and in this context made an oblique reference to right-wing extremists who continued to evoke the horrors of the Civil War[40] in order to prevent that reconciliation coming about. Though there was a certain opaqueness in Tarancón's address, it was the strongest definition yet made of the role of the Church, as he envisaged it, in the change from authoritarian rule to democracy. But the regime had no intention of permitting any meaningful move in that direction. A mere week after Tarancón's address, the Prime Minister made a speech which closed the door on any 'political association' that did not fit within the framework of the National Movement.[41]

The number and size of fines on priests for so-called subversive sermons[42] or for 'abetting' strikers and opposition activists rose to astronomical heights.[43] In January 1974, the prosecution asked, in addition to a sentence of six years' imprisonment, for a fine of 100 000 pesetas to be imposed on Fr Lluis Xirinachs, accused of 'illegal propaganda'. In October, a priest was fined the same amount, without benefit of trial, for attending a strikers' meeting in a Madrid church; three more priests were arrested along with other detainees. The sermon 'penalty record' was held by Fr Bernardo Maisterra of the Pamplona diocese who within two weeks was fined first 500 000 and then 600 000 pesetas. He joined in Carabanchel jail (Madrid) other priests who had rejected the privilege granted by the Concordat to carry out their sentence in monasteries instead.

In 1975 there was an escalation of terrorism by ETA. The police responded with arrests, torture, beatings and mass intimidation. The Basque Country was almost permanently under a state of emergency, which in July was extended via an anti-terrorist law to the rest of Spain. Among priests arrested under suspicion of collusion with ETA was Fr Anastasio Erquicia, who was taken half-dead to hospital in Bilbao after being beaten up at a police station. His bishop, Mgr Añoveros, called for an end to violence 'on both sides'.[44] The ensuing general silence of the hierarchy over this incident can be contrasted with the great pro-Añoveros mobilization of high-ranking prelates: in the case of Fr Erquicia it was 'only' the rights of an individual priest and not those of the institutional Church that had been at stake.[45]

In March the government suspended at the last minute what was to have been the First Christian Assembly of Vallecas, in a working-class district of Madrid. This was not merely an incident of political intervention in a Church matter; it also pointed up different stances within the Church. The Assembly was to have been the culmination of months of preparation on the part of base Catholic communities in an attempt to find Christian solutions to the problems of the area, including housing and schools. Cardinal Tarancón was aware of the Assembly's programme, drawn up by progressive priests, knew that it had aroused the hostility of Opus Dei and *Hermandad Sacerdotal* priests with influence in the regime and feared that a 'religious–political struggle' would ensue.[46] He allowed it to go ahead but forbade his auxiliary bishop, Mgr Iniesta, to permit the Vallecas gathering to be called a '*Joint Assembly*', as being too reminiscent of the 1971 Joint Assembly of Bishops and Priests which had raised such a storm, and would have preferred the word 'Assembly' dropped as well. In an attempt to ensure that no inflammatory positions were assumed, Tarancón decided to attend all the sessions himself, but his forebodings about an unhappy outcome were justified. The authorities tried to force him to suspend the Assembly and, when he refused, they sent in the police on the pretext that political extremists were intending to intervene and create a climate of hostility against the government.[47] The authorities suspended another Assembly in Las Palmas in May on the grounds that it would promote separatist ideas among the people of the Canary Islands.[48] In July a HOAC regional Assembly was interrupted in a college chapel in Alicante and, despite the fact that it had been authorised, the police arrested those present and suspended the gathering.[49]

On 26 May the Justice and Peace Commission had called for an end to indiscrimate police action and demanded that the authorities take action against ultra-right terrorist groups.[50] However, the police – the *Gristapo*[51] – continued to attack left-wing lawyers, priests and workers, and to use violence in breaking up strikes and demonstrations. In the Basque Country they operated blanket repression in answer to ETA's terrorism. In September, death sentences passed on two Basques and three members of the ultra-left group FRAP were upheld despite a huge international outcry. Urged on by priests and people, the Standing Commission of the CEE had unanimously asked for clemency.[52] From the Pope, who had four times sought mercy for the men, came stern denunciation of the regime.[53] In diplomatic protest against the Pope's words, Spanish government representatives, who would normally have had the place of honour in St. Peter's Square on 28 September for the canonisation of a Spanish missionary priest, were conspicuously absent.[54] The EEC suspended negotiations to renew the Preferential Trade Agreement signed with Spain in 1970. Two documents circulating clandestinely – the text of a sermon writ-

A Future without Franco

ten by Mgr Iniesta and a letter signed by 832 priests – expressed strong condemnation of the anti-terrorism decree, of the death penalties recently imposed and carried out and of other violations of human rights.[55] Such was the bitter political climate in which Francisco Franco died on 20 November 1975.

Throughout this period, intra-ecclesial debate and struggle had run parallel to the conflict between Church and State. The hierarchy found itself buffeted ever more by virulent right-wing anticlericalism and pressure from below, from groups of clergy and people who clamoured for structural changes in society and for a more specific, more outspoken and more fundamental denunciation of abuses of human and civil rights. While distancing themselves increasingly from the more blatant abuses, the bishops could not bring themselves to cut off ties, especially financial ties, with the State. Nor, despite references to the need for 'radical changes', did they respond favourably to the various – at times unrealistic – socialist options espoused by some Church groups.

Exceptional in the way it accepted the existence of class conflict leading to class struggle was a working document published in 1974 by the Catalan bishops under the title 'Paschal Mystery and Liberating Action'.[56] It devoted several pages to the issue, and attacked the structural violence of the prevailing unjust socio-economic system seen as being responsible. This is interesting because Church documents tended to vilify Marx for 'inventing' the class struggle and attributed it to hatred (an anti-Christian attitude) on the part of the victims of exploitation, rather than blaming it on the exploiters. Quoting traditional Church doctrine on the right to active resistance, the Catalan bishops stated that 'When the oppressed party resists and fights the oppressive party, using all and only the means of just defence and just action, its struggle – by contrast with that of the other party – is praiseworthy'; the moral means used, 'including strikes, political pressure, attempts to change economic and political structures are no more than specific expressions of the rights of man'.[57] The fact that the bishops recognised the difference between the violence of the oppressor and the violence of the oppressed, that they saw that one could not be neutral in the face of injustice, and that in general terms in this document they urged Christians to participate in the struggle, was encouraging to those committed to social change. But, armed though such Christians might be with the moral weaponry provided by the hierarchy, in the final analysis it was they who were directly in the line of fire from the system and the regime.

Two further, related, documents came out almost simultaneously in September 1974, both with the title 'Christian Attitudes to the Economic Situation'. The first, shorter and somewhat anodyne, was published under the aegis of the CEE Standing Commission.[58] The second was in many respects the most trenchant indictment of the socio-economic ills afflicting Spanish society hitherto published by a group of Spanish bishops,[59] with strong demands for political and civil freedoms, and for a more just distribution of national economic wealth, at regional and personal level. Like the Catalan bishops' statement homing in on the marxist–capitalist confrontation, this document did not emanate from the Spanish hierarchy as a whole, and it is significant that the CEE as a body chose not to make it their own.

Dialogue was attempted between the 'centrist' bishops headed by Tarancón and the more radically progressive Catholics, though it might often seem one of the deaf. The centrists disavowed what they perceived as 'left-wing clericalism', conceived in reaction to the traditional right-wing clericalism that had brandished the gospel to legitimise the Franco political regime and the whole socio-economic system or seen it as a private matter between an individual and God. Now, it was said, the gospel as wielded by the radical left-wing had its meaning reduced to no more than an 'ideology of revolutionary social change for Christians' or used to justify – on poor theological grounds – the ideology behind the class struggle.[60] A forceful rebuff to these left-wing Catholics came in April 1975, in a pastoral letter from the whole Spanish hierarchy,[61] which declared that

> A hasty identification of the evangelical preferential option for the poor with the so-called 'class option' presupposes confining the poor to their specific social sector and canonising the class struggle from within the Church itself. Such a position, besides being based on an analysis of doubtful scientific value, is openly opposed to the consubstantial universality of the Church, and through its lack of critical spirit and coherence with the faith places in grave danger the very credibility of a Christian community which adopts it.

It is also possible that, perhaps unconsciously, some of the clergy, accustomed to the power to command, meant to hold on to it even when they moved left in their thinking, trying to 'maintain domination over the laity' from their new position.[62]

While many of the Spanish middle classes remained moulded in preconciliar socio-economic ideas, others went into perplexed crisis when they realised that the gospel had previously been hijacked by the political and economic establishment. Anti-capitalism and various hues of pro-socialism remained the political option of the majority of Catholic progressives. This applied to the base communities, some of whom came from HOAC, JOC, VOS and VOJ, savaged a few years previously by both State and Church. HOAC maintained that there had to be a 'revolution against theologies which, being built on ideologies of domination and made up of conservative ideologies of the established disorder, hijacked the liberating message of Jesus';[63] some of its members – as individuals, not as an organisation – aimed to join in creating base Christian communities, in an attempt to bring about a renewal of both Church and society based more directly on the gospel. This was not an easy task for it presupposed a profound change of mentality and praxis in the hierarchy, since 'priestly, episcopal and papal functions have over the centuries assumed the same cultural forms as the powerful of the land', whereas the gospel demanded a spirit of service and a sharing of responsibilities.[64]

In his opening address[65] to the XXI Plenary Assembly of the CEE on 27 November 1974, Tarancón, while speaking of a plurality of political options, laid down certain limits that excluded undemocratic regimes of both left and right, and groups who 'exercise violence, albeit verbal'. Many of the declarations he made were clouded in churchspeak, but one was unambiguous: Christians must reject left-wing systems that were 'intrinsically inseparable from their atheistic doctrine and contradict Christian principles'. In this context, his preferred option was once again an 'extreme centre'.[66] The more liberal bishops were caught in crossfire: they continued to be pressed from below by progressive priests and lay people, a fact that appears to have made them less rather than more understanding, to harden their attitude and resort to demanding obedience to their authority; at the same time they were at odds with their conservative brethren and frequently subjected to vicious attacks from right-wing extremists.

A persistent socialist thorn in the side of the episcopate as well as that of the regime[67] was the Justice and Peace Commission. It had originally been fully responsible to the hierarchy but in December 1972 was granted a statute of autonomy, although the President and the Secretary were still appointed by the bishops.[68] It was fundamentally anti-capitalist.[69] According to the then Secretary, it did not in general enjoy the support of the bishops because of its progressive and therefore contentious line, and also because of the relative autonomy of movement it had recently acquired. The bishops had a strategy of their own in their conflicts with the regime and did not want interference. They had become more open-minded but they did not want to break entirely their bonds of dependence (*desenfeudarse*) on the regime; in any case, their preferred political option was Christian Democracy, whereas that of the Justice and Peace Commission was close to a Christian marxism on the lines of liberation theology;[70] the few bishops thought to be basically sympathetic to the Commission's activities were Mgr Díaz Merchán of Oviedo, Mgr Osés, auxiliary bishop of Huesca, Mgr Iniesta and Mgr Echarren of Madrid, and Mgr Palenzuela of Segovia. Justice and Peace was involved in a great number of human rights issues, including the abolition of the death penalty and the defence of freedom of expression, association, assembly and demonstration. To mark the Holy Year of 1975 proclaimed by Paul VI, it obtained 160 000 signatures to a petition calling for amnesty for exiles, political prisoners and conscientious objectors to military service which, after various vicissitudes,[71] it persuaded Cardinal Tarancón to deliver to General Franco. The petition was repeated in July 1975.[72]

A new group had sprung up in January 1973, called Christians for Socialism (CpS). Taking their lead from events in Chile, some two hundred Christians issued what came to be known as the 'Avila document', which stated that they had met to reflect on the meaning of their faith from a marxist, class standpoint.[73] CpS did not claim that theirs was the *only* example of a faith that is lived authentically. But they had come to see in socialism the only option that would struggle against man's exploitation by man and that remained truly faithful to the gospel demands for freedom and justice in the circumstances in which they lived. They pointed to an official Church which was on the one hand still serving the system, and on the other hand advocated a selective kind of pluralism which excluded their, CpS, marxist political option.[74]

Such an attitude was not likely to endear the group to the majority of bishops[75] although a few, like Mgr Iniesta, auxiliary bishop of Madrid, were sympathetic, with some reservations.[76] Mgr Iniesta later stated that the Church as an institution had not learned to *be* – as opposed to proselytise and preach – among working-class people and learn from them, and was failing to 'live alongside, hope, suffer, communicate with and if necessary die for and with those with whom it lives'.[77] As an institution it had failed to 'connect' with the working class. Given the harsh living conditions of many Spaniards, and the previous socio-political history of Catholicism in Spain, the commitment of activists to a radical, utopian, version of Christianity was not surprising, even though its 'curious blend of primitive Christianity and communism' met with criticism even from some of those who were themselves critical of the institutional Church.[78]

The thinking and activity of well-known priests[79] – as well as of student and workers' chaplains – could be considered as aligned, though not necessarily completely identified, with the aspirations of the radical groups. Fr José María de Llanos had a previous history as a Jesuit of the elitist school, fully imbued with the spirit of National Catholicism, who had been General Franco's confessor. In later life he moved to Pozo del Tío Raimundo, a poor working-class district of Madrid where he made no secret of his marxist Christianity.[80] Closely linked to him was Fr José María Díez-Alegría SJ, formerly a lecturer at the Gregorian University in Rome but proscribed by the hierarchy for views considered theologically unsound. Díez-Alegría explained his anti-capitalism most clearly in his book *I believe in Hope*.[81] Canon José María González Ruiz, of Málaga cathedral, also condemned capitalism explicitly,[82] while having reservations about CpS.[83]

With all the apparent contradictions, ambiguities and nuances of its various – joint and individual – utterances, the *official* Church had come down on the side of 'moderation'. This stance was most clearly defined in an address[84] in Rome made before the Synod of Bishops of the whole Catholic Church by Cardinal Jubany speaking on behalf of all the Spanish hierarchy. Jubany rejected three 'biased' and 'misleading' tendencies in evangelisation before describing the orthodox view. He discounted the tendency that was concerned exclusively with personal morality and had no explicit concern with societal problems, the tendency, he said, that was the most widespread among Spanish Catholics. He then dismissed what he called the 'temporalist' tendency for which humanity was divided between oppressors and oppressed through the fault of the prevailing capitalist socio-economic structures, and then the third, the specifically marxist tendency which discovered 'in marxist socialism the only valid way out of the internal contradictions of capitalism'. By calling all these tendencies 'biased' and 'misleading', Jubany presented them as contrary to the official position of the Church hierarchy; furthermore, those very adjectives underlined the 'centrist' or 'moderately reformist' majority stance of the hierarchy under Tarancón.

The impression that remains is that the bishops wanted to improve society, but without fundamentally changing the balance of forces within it, and that the Church 'appears to give its blessing to a neocapitalist model of society which does not go beyond recognising *formal* liberties and social rights'.[85] In the opinion of some Catholic activists, explanation of the ambiguity of the Church's attitude – on the one hand urging *them* to socio-political commitment but on the other hand balking at the sacrifice of *its own* place of privilege in society – lay in opportunism, the institutional Church's concern for self-preservation. Activists could have expected from the Church's preaching about the poor that its conduct would be qualitatively different from that of the rest of society, whereas in reality the Church appeared to be no more than the 'sacred face' of an unjust society.[86] The hierarchy seemed to be playing a double game so that it always came out the winner, and if it did allow a measure of freedom to Christian activists, that was because it wanted to use their commitment to social justice as a kind of insurance policy for the Church's credibility.

In contrast to the new Christian groups on the left, such as CpS or the Popular Christian Communities, whose faith of necessity went hand-in-hand with socio-political commitment, there were others that operated on a more 'spiritual' plane. These included the 'Kikos', after Kiko (Francisco) Argüello who, together with Carmen Hernández, founded the Neocatechumen Communities in 1962, and the Charismatic Renewal Communities, largely inspired by American Pentecostalism, which made their first appearance in Madrid in 1973. Some Catholics were disconcerted by the apparent turmoil within the Church and kept or retreated to more traditional pious practices.

Fr Díez-Alegría thought that people felt few links with *institutional* Catholicism, but that did not mean that they shut the door on a world of genuine faith. Rejection was bound up with the fact that in the past the Church had been concerned with private morality, in which it shared values with the ruling elite.[87] According to a 1973 *Vida Nueva* survey, the majority of Spaniards lived their religion as something peripheral, conventional, formal and with no great depth of conviction and corresponding commitment. The findings confirmed the ongoing march of dechristianisation, what Pope John Paul II would later call Spanish neopaganism.[88]

The hierarchy, meanwhile, continued to assert the visceral identification of the Spanish people with Catholicism. Cardinal Tarancón expressed the Church's claim to influence in a Spain quasi-identified with Catholicism in the following convoluted sentence:

There is no doubt that in Spain, where Catholicism was so fundamental to social life that it shaped many of its customs, and where the ecclesial community and the political community are almost one and the same, because the immense majority of Spaniards are Catholics and where, for that very reason, the religious and the ecclesial have an almost decisive influence in social life, and the socio-political has, for that very reason, a decisive influence in religious life and in the life of the very Church, our mission to society, in its human aspect – in what we call social harmony – has a special importance.[89]

A Map of Religious Practice in Spain published in September 1975[90] recorded various sociologists' opinions as to why Spain's most recent phase of dechristianisation had come about: the abrupt jump from a pre-industrial to an industrial society without a proper period of adaptation; a reduction in the number of children deemed desirable; immediate access to the media, with many people going straight from illiteracy to a TV culture; access to the world of comfort and consumerism without matching cultural understanding; moving from an environment of routine religious observance, often conforming to social pressure, to one in which religion had to involve personal commitment. Secularisation had accelerated in the sense that people did not need God to improve their lot, so that 'today the economy offers the worldview which previously was offered only by religion'.[91]

Nor did this appear to be a passing phenomenon. The outlook was equally bleak, as a survey of the ideas of young people – who would be expected to be the future hope of the Church – showed in various surveys. Fewer young people now believed in the divinity of Christ (20 per cent) or an after-life (25–30 per cent) and fewer still in the Church (40 per cent).[92] José Luis Aranguren blamed lack of prophetic vision, dogmatism, empty ritual and the blinkered mentality of an outmoded institution for causing desertion by the young.[93] A *Vida Nueva* survey found that the young were

> neither in nor out of the Church. And what is more serious, it is a question which really does not worry them. Many no longer expect anything from it. Only a troubled minority becomes impatient and dreams of a different Church. Young people follow events in the Church as something distant. If the Church speaks, it leaves them indifferent, they accept or reject whatever they like, without thinking whether to oppose or abandon it.[94]

The room for manoeuvre for both priest and 'good' lay Catholic was, in theory at least, circumscribed by increasing centralisation, in fact re-centralisation from Rome, and a hardening of official attitudes towards whatever was considered heterodox. The 'clear and authorised voice of the bishops, at diocesan and national level',[95] was to be heeded, and not that of others in the seminaries: a reference to the more progressive stance taken by some of the seminaries' teaching staff. The hierarchy, as 'preachers of the gospel and authentic teachers of the Church in faith and customs', must help Christians to discern when 'a political or social option is compatible with the Christian concept of social harmony'.[96]

An impassioned integrist version of this view is found in a statement by Francisco López Hernández Herrera, for five years a HOAC chaplain, at the national meeting of the women's branch of HOAC in Cuenca, July 1972, and recorded in its Proceedings: 'There are those in the Church who say that "desacralisation" is good and that it is good to import, like fools, Anglo-Saxon morality, that is Anglo-Saxon paganism, theology from Holland... In the midst of internal strife, one laments the lack of solid doctrine, apostolic fervour....'[97]

The Church had moved a long way since Vatican II in its greater openness to 'the world'. However, it then took fright at the links being forged by some of its members with the secularised culture of the times, and by internal changes that it had itself initiated but that it saw as threatening to become unstoppable. To continue the process of reform begun in the Council would imply allowing the possibility of building a new theological framework based on the complex secular humanist neo-pagan culture – be it atheist or not – of the twentieth century. It has been claimed that this could have been done in the 1970s, just as in his day Augustine had assumed the Platonic system or Thomas Aquinas that of Aristotle: 'In a word, the acceptance of the person of Jesus Christ made through the complex mental system which is the framework of contemporary society would give... a new dynamism to Christian faith. But all this is too much adventure for... men whose eyes are still full of preconciliar dogmatics'.[98] All the Church's evangelisation programmes tended to be conditioned not by an open-minded and forward-looking mentality shaped by the spirit of Vatican II but by an authoritarian backward-looking Counter-Reformation mind-set.

While the tangible external marxist-atheist enemy still hovered within ecclesiastical gunsights, the intangible enemy, secularisation – combining a polytheism of values outside with supermarket Catholicism inside – was moving ever further out of range in a silent schism of indifference.

5 The Church and the Coming of Democracy (1975 to 1978)

> It is a question of achieving a change of regime (generally on the basis of the existing institutional order), but in no way altering qualitatively the configuration of the classes placed in positions of power. Change of regime, but not of system. Or, more precisely, change of regime to achieve the persistence of the system. If one thinks like this, more than one fiction based on the immediate images of the political role of a 'modernised' Spanish Church collapses.[1]

Following Franco's death in November 1975, political and social activity, both legal and clandestine, by regime insiders and by opposition movements, assumed new and dramatically different forms. Under the monarchy of King Juan Carlos, a process of change was set in motion which culminated in the creation of a democratic regime on a par with that of most West European nations of the time. The manner in which dictatorship gave way to parliamentary democracy and the country began to come to terms with pluralism in its many guises aroused the surprised admiration of both Spaniards themselves and foreign onlookers.

Among the majority of people there was now a conviction that democracy was the only viable political option and, although political reform was imposed from above by the very people who had been part of the Franco machine, it was achieved by negotiated agreement with the opposition, now emerging from clandestinity. There was an overwhelming desire to avoid a repetition of the civil strife of the 1930s and to heal a nation which Francoist policy had kept divided into victors and vanquished: right from the start of his reign, King Juan Carlos made it clear that he wished to be King of *all* Spaniards. Consensus politics, together with a tacitly-accepted collective amnesia regarding certain aspects of the Franco years, ensured that stress was laid on what united rather than what divided those laying the foundations of Spain's future. Even so, in some respects democracy and the new pluralism presented Spaniards with confusing choices, since little during the preceding four decades had prepared them for the political changes into which they were now plunged.

Franco's Prime Minister, Carlos Arias Navarro, remained in office after the dictator's death for a brief period marked by intense political and social turbulence. Fraga Iribarne, as Minister of the Interior, imposed a repressive clampdown. In Vitoria, a demonstration held on 3 February 1976 during an all-out strike which had lasted several weeks was broken up by police with truncheons and tear gas. On 3 March, the riot police behaved with particular brutality in dislodging 5000 strikers and demonstrators from the Church of San Francisco. Driven out by smoke bombs, the workers were met by indiscriminate shooting which left several dead and over 70 badly injured. The homily preached in the packed cathedral of Vitoria during the funeral of the first three victims was written jointly by the local clergy, who had been strongly supportive of the workers throughout the labour dispute. Rounds of applause interrupted the sermon as the priest reading it condemned the deaths as homicide. He went on to say that the churches would continue to be available for workers' assemblies. This was in clear defiance of a government announcement saying that the police considered themselves justified in raiding churches in order to break up unauthorised meetings.[2] Events in Vitoria had the effect of ratcheting up local backing for Basque separatism and at the same time discrediting the civil authorities.

Church members themselves were not immune from brutality or hounding by the police. Fr Jesús Cubillo was arrested for preaching a sermon during which he denounced the way that the security forces had treated a group of youths in his parish.[3] 'Fr Paco' (the former Jesuit prominent in the '1001 trial') was arrested in Chamartín railway station, Madrid, and the large crowd that had gathered to meet him was broken up by the police.[4] Police raided HOAC premises and arrested several activists, and a few weeks later the same premises were attacked by armed thugs widely understood to be operating in connivance with the authorities.[5]

There were calls for justice and reconciliation. In the last days of 1975, HOAC was demanding amnesty for all political prisoners, abrogation of anti-terrorist laws, suppression of the Public Order Tribunal so that political cases would be tried before civil and not military courts, and the abolition of the death penalty.[6] The Justice and Peace Commission launched a national campaign on human rights.[7] Mgr Iniesta, Mgr Echarren, and Mgr Oliver of the Madrid diocese were among the signatories of a request to hold a demonstration in favour of freedom for political prisoners and the return of exiles.[8] When the bishops of San Sebastián, Mgr Argaya and Mgr Setién, wrote a letter to all the priests of their diocese condemning both the violence of terrorists and the repressive response of the security forces, the Ministry of Information and Tourism attempted to block its publication.[9]

The King replaced Arias Navarro in July 1976 by Adolfo Suárez in what to many was a surprising choice, since Suárez had been a Franco *apparatchik*. However, along with other insiders, he had nurtured reformist ideas and accepted democracy as the only viable political option for Spain's future. Democracy was also the political medium that allowed the ruling socio-economic system and elites to continue in power and privilege. Suárez's strategy was to block the *'continuistas'*, those sectors of society faithful to the project that Franco had devised for Spain's future, and at the same time to neutralise the opposition by consultation. His political allies would come to form the nucleus of a centre-right coalition, the Democratic Centre Union (UCD), which, for much of the period led by Suárez, governed Spain between the first post-Franco election of June 1977 and that of November 1982.

With a new Prime Minister in position, it became apparent that democracy would be given a more vigorous impetus. In the summer of 1976 Suárez introduced, subject to the approbation of the Francoist Cortes and to public referendum, a Political Reform Law, which would force Franco's non-representative Parliament to vote itself into extinction and bring in an elected assembly based on genuine political parties. Over the next months, the bishops issued no fewer than three documents giving guidelines on political and social matters. The faithful were left free in conscience to vote either for or against the Political Reform Law, but there were provisos about 'basic moral demands' addressed to both government and governed, 'especially if they call themselves Christian'.[10] Once the law had been steered through the Cortes – the last act of Franco's sham Parliament – and ratified by referendum in December 1976, attention was turned to further dismantling the Franco legacy and preparing for a general election, to be held in June 1977.

The Church's problems in democracy were to be different from those it had encountered under Francoism. By the time the General died, it had already survived one identity crisis. It had learned from the Second Vatican Council and also from its base to take a stand on human rights and freedoms, and in the regime's latter stages had provided sanctuary for those in opposition. But now it faced another crisis. How was it to react to the new pluralism in Spanish society that was not only political but affected almost every aspect of life? What place did the institutional Church have in such a society? In some respects it had been easier to be anti-Franco (on basic human rights issues) than it would be in the future to be pro-democracy, because of what democracy implied in people's overall range of choices. The relationship with the State and society was now different and so were the accompanying extra- and intra-ecclesial difficulties. Cardinal Tarancón reminded his fellow bishops of the Church's need to adapt to change and to use its creative imagination so as not 'to miss the train of the new culture – we could even say new civilisation – in which the Church not only has to be immersed but also continue its evangelising mission with the same efficacy as before'.[11]

The Church could see that the post-Franco game of political chess was to be played according to different rules, and the strategy not so much for survival as for maintaining influence must vary accordingly. It no longer had official monopoly of the country's ethics and was at a loss as to how to proceed in a liberal atmosphere where belief in God and the practice of religion were not actively opposed, but neither were they State-promoted. The bishops wanted the Church's continuing social and cultural relevance to be made secure. At first the hierarchy seemed to have difficulty in realising that its clientèle was not now the whole Spanish nation but was, rather, restricted to that decreasing number of Spanish Catholics who were prepared to listen. It continued to appeal to the Church's rights conferred by Catholic tradition.[12]

The Spanish Church had not made a complete break with Francoism so long as the dictator ruled. Nevertheless, the increasing distance it put between itself and the regime had provoked different reactions: Franco stalwarts continued to reproach the hierarchy for its ingratitude towards a regime that had showered the Church with favours, while others construed the Church's new stance as opportunistic manoeuvring to be in the right place when Spain's new political future became reality.[13] The centrists among the hierarchy attributed any change of attitude to fidelity to the imperatives of the Council, and Cardinal Tarancón stated his conviction that it had been in the belief that such a regime was the best possible political solution for Spain that the Spanish Church had prepared itself for democracy some four years before Franco's death.[14] It was the centrist bishops who defined the public attitude of the Church, although the minority of prelates whose conservative ideas remained unchanged had the effect of making other bishops seem more liberal than they actually were.[15] The few more progressive bishops maintained a discreet profile. Helping to orchestrate right-wing clerical anti-democracy fever was the ferociously National Catholic *Hermandad Sacerdotal*, for whom freemasonry and marxism were still the greatest enemies Spain had and for whom the Church had gone to near-anarchy.[16]

Often during the course of the 'transition' the bishops were to complain of sniping from the ecclesial progressives and radicals on issues to which they were convinced that the magisterium alone held the key. Cardinal Tarancón's opening address to the XXIX Plenary Assembly provides an example. He said that Conference documents and positions had been contested by individuals or groups of Catholics whose attitudes were presented as an important part of ecclesial 'public opinion'. Putting other points of view could be healthy but he objected especially to a certain 'obsession for publicly discrediting what they call the Church-Institution'; he also resented accusations of dirigisme on the part of bishops by people who were themselves attempting 'to direct the conscience of all the people of God with more intransigence perhaps than that which authority has used'.[17]

Radical Catholics denounced both what they saw as the Church's role as legitimiser, this time of a monarchy thrust without consultation upon the nation, and the aim of the Church to ensure 'with new pacts, the survival of its power, masked by allusions to "mutual independence and healthy collaboration"' with the dominant classes.[18] Such groups welcomed democracy, but were not clear which way to turn when they found themselves up against a democracy which had not made a complete break (*ruptura*) with the old regime, whereas they had been looking for a real political and socio-economic revolution. Moreover, accustomed to struggling against the dictatorship, they did not always understand how the rules had changed and so they tended to denounce the new situation in terms similar to those in which they had condemned Francoism, even though the very fact that there were now genuine political parties and trade unions meant that *blanket* condemnation was no longer always the appropriate response.[19]

Changes in Rome would also affect the course of the Spanish Church in the post-Franco period. Paul VI's papacy had been eventful. In 1963 he had been called upon to take the Second Vatican Council to its conclusion after the death of John XXIII at a time when

Catholicism started to come to terms with other religions, Christian and non-Christian, with unbelief, with a wide variety of cultures, ideologies and sciences. After the Council, Paul had seen the Church riven with divisions and defections and the debilitation of papal authority, particularly after the publication of his 1968 encyclical *Humanae Vitae*. He died in 1978, followed to the grave a few weeks later by his successor, John Paul I. With the next Pope, John Paul II, the Church entered a period of renewed conservatism, the strategy the Vatican deemed most likely to restore the old fabric of Christendom.

Following his accession there was at first a reversal of Paul VI's *Ostpolitik*. John Paul II made ferocious attacks on Soviet communism, and intervened directly in his native Poland. The Vatican volte-face may be explained in part by the Pope's experience while a Bishop in Poland of seeing his country – and others that had formerly been Christian – under the heel of atheistic Soviet communism. There was also the fact that his pontificate coincided with a hardliner, Brezhnev, in the Kremlin and a fervently anti-communist President Reagan in the White House. The Church's need for allies during this period meant that a necessary corollary of anti-communism was a pro-Western, especially pro-United States, stance, irrespective of the way that the United States installed or propped up anti-democratic and exploitative regimes. Latin America provided vivid examples. Consequently, 'Christianity was identified with Western civilisation; the marriage of religion and politics became once again very close, and the condemnation of atheistic communism...served the interests of capitalism, imperialism and colonialism'.[20]

Against this background, the Spanish Church entered into a positive if critical engagement with democracy, more precisely, with democratic governments, professing independence in all matters but reserving the right to issue moral judgements, on all – not excluding political – matters. It claimed to accept, following Vatican II, 'the autonomy of secular matters, which have their own laws and demands which must be respected by the Church, *albeit this may involve a reduction in its importance and social influence*' [my italics],[21] though in fact it showed a remarkable reluctance to accept such curtailment of its influence. This may in part be due to its difficulty in distinguishing between rights and privileges. In practice, its 'political independence' would allow it to be on the side of whatever party came to power, irrespective of political colour, provided its stance on matters that it believed to fall within its spiritual or material sphere of interest was not opposed: especially education, marriage, divorce, abortion, financing. Thus its profession of political independence can only be accepted with important reservations, since it was always conditioned by the defence of the basic interests of the Church as understood by the CEE. Independence did not mean 'equidistance'.

In the early stages of the transition to democracy the hierarchy focused on human and civil rights and freedoms (including amnesty for political prisoners) as part of the reconciliation process. It urged Catholics to take an active part in political life and not to vote for marxism or unbridled capitalism. Regarding Church–State relations, it called for a revision of the 1953 Concordat, including complete freedom in the appointment of bishops.[22] Both in this early period but especially after the nuts and bolts of the democratisation process were more or less in place, the Church intensified its push for *social* influence, particularly on 'family matters': education and marriage, with total rejection of divorce, birth control and abortion.

The parameters of its critical alliance with democracy were set out by Cardinal Tarancón in the course of the homily[23] he preached during the Mass celebrated on 27 November 1975 at the Jerónimos Church in Madrid to mark the accession to the throne of King Juan Carlos I. It could be interpreted as highly political as well as moral in content, as Tarancón set out his view of the future of Church–State relations within a framework of co-operation and mutual autonomy. The beginning of the homily was a theocratic evocation of the ancient splendours celebrating the alliance of Throne and Altar, 'of a broad and ancient tradition: that which throughout history seeks the light and the support of the Spirit of wisdom in the coronation of popes and of kings, in the summoning of conclaves and councils...'.[24] Speaking not merely in his own name but for the whole Spanish Church,[25] the Cardinal outlined a democratic programme for King and country to follow, and thereby to receive the support of the Church, which must have its 'room for freedom'. He stated that while the Church, following the teaching of the Council, favoured no specific political ideology nor specific options in the temporal sphere, it had the duty to enlighten consciences with the gospel message, even when its preaching might be critical of society. This part of the homily has resonances of the conciliar document *Gaudium et Spes*. The scope – and limits – of the Church's 'room for freedom' would emerge, not always uncontroversially, as the transition to democracy progressed.

The ongoing quasi-identification of 'what is Spanish' with 'what is Catholic' was also suggested in Tarancón's homily. In exchange for sound and just government, the Church gave assurance of the obedience of the people, to whom it taught the moral duty to support legitimate authority in all that was conducive to the common good. The implication was that the Church might demand obedience of *all* Spaniards ('the obedience of citizens') rather than the obedience only of members of the Catholic Church. This is one of the issues that bedevilled the Church/State/society relationship particularly in the first post-Franco years, centring as it did on the profound socio-political and cultural changes in Spain and the concomitant plurality of beliefs and non-beliefs. The Church claimed to respect this plurality and yet it not infrequently spoke as if it held the monopoly of ethics for the whole, or at least the majority of the nation, and as if the nation were fundamentally Catholic[26] in its beliefs and practices. The fact that there was no specific alternative code of ethics laid down for a State that had for so long been tutored by the norms of Catholic doctrine also tended to cloud the issue. Tarancón's homily was widely acclaimed at the time as being 'positive for the democratic process'[27] that the country was initiating, although not every response was applause.[28]

At the XXIII Plenary Assembly of the CEE, postponed to mid-December 1975 because of Franco's death, part of the Cardinal's opening address[29] was a justification of both the hierarchy's pro-Franco attitude in previous years and its conversion to democracy. He maintained then – and repeated in his memoirs – that from the very first days of the Second Republic Spanish Catholics had confronted the government, uniting Faith and Fatherland in one single concept since 'Spain could not cease to be Catholic without ceasing to be Spain'.[30] In the new dispensation, he said, those who accused the bishops of opportunism because they had not remained committed to the Franco regime were wrong, as were those who now wanted to push the hierarchy in another political direction.

The agenda of the CEE XXIV Plenary Assembly of February 1976 included an item that followed on from political issues that had been discussed at the December 1975 meeting, and from a confidential questionnaire sent in advance for reflection and response.[31] The issues covered were the Church's position vis-à-vis Spanish society, independence from and collaboration with the State, financial problems, the resolution of intra-ecclesial questions and, perhaps especially interesting, the bishops' attitudes towards capitalism, socialism (marxist and non-marxist). The findings were never officially published, and in any case the usefulness of the exercise was marred by the relatively low number of answers received.[32] However, according to the journal *Posible*,[33] which claimed to have had access to the confidential replies, there was a majority opinion that the evils of capitalism could not be reformed, and some bishops considered that the 'social doctrine' of the Church had hitherto favoured capitalism because of its concept of the right to the ownership of property, because of its condemnation of socialism, and, conversely, because of the inadequacy of its critique of capitalism. 'Worst of all, not a few consider that the Church has led people to believe that only those Christians – workers or owners – who accepted the style and forms of the capitalist system were acceptable'. All respondents thought that the Church in part and indirectly favoured the capitalist system in its economic and social interests, and most that it had lacked courage in denunciation. All but one accepted a non-dogmatic, non-marxist socialism that did not defend the class struggle; most stated categorically that Christians could not keep their Christian identity if they joined a marxist party, though some responses were much more nuanced. CpS came in for especial criticism on the grounds of theological and moral reductionism, and for proposing a Popular Church as against the institutional Church.[34]

The March–April issue of *Iglesia Viva* published a statement by a group of theologians[35] which was also in part concerned with marxism and capitalism. They considered that the Church had not sufficiently emphasised the contradictions between some of the basic criteria of capitalism and the demands of the gospel. If Christians had to live in a capitalist society, they would have to seek to change it insofar as it was incompatible with recognition of the dignity of all people; at the same time there was a danger that Christians who rejected capitalism would opt for socialism without subjecting it to sufficient analysis. The Church ought to explain the main objections to the structures and the ethics of capitalism and marxism.

A document issued after the national Justice and Peace Congress[36] of May 1976 went further. It criticised capitalism's individualistic basis and lack of solidarity: fragmentary and functional modifications of capitalism were not enough, since it was rotten to the core of its internal dynamics, and the whole system must be replaced by another in which man was the authentic protagonist of his fulfilment. The Justice and Peace Commission also urged a gradual decentralisation of decisions and appropriate control of economic management, so that workers and regions could participate fully in economic planning.

It advocated limiting the power of multinational corporations, and redistributing income via measures including fiscal reform, targeting public investment and improving social security.

A similar document[37] was presented to the bishops later in the year. It was signed by 49 priests, most of them highly regarded for their theological or pastoral expertise, expressing the view that Spain would soon have the characteristics of a European-style neo-capitalist society. Within the capitalist system, 'the Church has a place assigned to it and is called upon to legitimise the system and create the kind of person the system needs'. The group warned that 'accepting the economic means offered by capitalism is tantamount to accepting the logic of the system itself' and warned also, in a telling juxtaposition of ideas, that 'the economic temptation tends to produce a model of "Church" which gives priority to the institutional over the "community of believers"'.

The Spanish Church's professed independence vis-à-vis all political forces meant not favouring any single party, and accepting the legitimacy for Christians of all political options, albeit within certain limits.[38] It did not imitate some other West European Churches in creating or sponsoring a political party under the banner of Christian Democracy. According to Tarancón, about 12 bishops favoured this, but the majority agreed with him that, in order to preserve the Church's independence, no political party should be offered the 'Catholic' or 'Christian' label.[39] Such a party might be seen by the public as being the only genuine expression of the gospel message or of the attitude of the Church.[40] It might also be divisive.[41]

However, while it was not appropriate to have parties operating in the name of Christian Democracy, it was 'licit, appropriate and even...necessary to constitute parties which are Christian in inspiration'.[42] The bishops who were 'centrist' in religious terms would as a consequence find a natural partner in the UCD, a coalition which claimed the centre ground of politics and in which Christian Democrats figured prominently.[43] The political pluralism defended by the bishops was so hedged around with caveats that it was the political centre that, either explicitly or implicitly, was favoured. After all, it was this centre, and not a nascent left-leaning version of Christian Democracy that they had chosen – politically and socio-economically – in their claim to be defending Christian values and a just society. Despite their implicit endorsement of Christian Democracy in Spain, it has been suggested that the Vatican was displeased with Tarancón's refusal to endorse explicitly a Catholic party on the lines of Italian Christian Democracy.[44]

UCD claimed to hold the values of 'Christian humanism' – the ideological concept espoused by the Spanish bishops – and became the functional equivalent of Christian Democracy in Spain. The wide ideological diversity of its composition, from Liberals and Independents through '*Tácito*'[45] Christian Democrats to Social Democrats, from the religiously conservative *opusdeístas* to agnostics, made internal controversy inevitable, especially when, later, UCD came to draw up party policy on specific issues affecting the Church's concerns.

UCD had the advantage over other parties in that it was headed by the Prime Minister, Adolfo Suárez, and could therefore capitalise on his success as principal actor – along with King Juan Carlos and Torcuato Fernández Miranda, the King's former tutor – in the early stages of the transition to formal political democracy. Its members, largely proceeding from Francoism, retained their connections with banks, business and industry. Accordingly, it

> was the ideal instrument to ensure that in the transition from a dictatorial to a democratic regime, real government power would remain in the hands, if not of the same people as before, at least of sufficiently conservative individuals to guarantee the existing structure of the economic and social power.[46]

Left-wing Christian Democracy in Spain comprised very disparate elements, which eventually fused into a Christian Democracy Federation (FDC), headed by Joaquín Ruiz Giménez, but it failed disastrously to attract votes partly because of internal disunity, partly because of infrastructural shortcomings. It was also partly 'as a result of the leftist ideological thrust of its campaign, which was inappropriate for the relatively conservative Christian democratic electorate of Spain',[47] emphasising as it did workers' ownership and control (*autogestión*) of firms, federalism as the structural model for the State, and collaboration with socialists and communists. Its programme was closer to the positions of grass-roots Christian communities than to the strategy envisaged by the centrist elements of the Spanish episcopacy.

To the right of UCD was the Popular Alliance (Alianza Popular – AP) headed by Franco's former Minister of Information and Tourism, Manuel Fraga, and embracing other leftovers from the Franco regime of the 1960s and early 1970s. Fraga himself had been Minister of the Interior in Arias Navarro's post-Franco Cabinet. The

AP's conservatism came under the category of 'liberal-authoritarian' which moved further right the more Suárez's UCD took up the centre and centre-right space.[48] None of the groups comprising the Alliance had a large membership and they overestimated the extent of residual Francoism among the people as a whole. Fraga failed in his attempt to get the Church to commit itself further in specific political questions, although on moral questions his attitude 'always tallies with the Church's stance'.[49] It seems likely that, quite apart from the Church's proclaimed political independence, AP was too tarred with Franco's dictatorial brush for a democracy-supporting hierarchy to want to sticky its fingers by too close a contact.

The Spanish Socialist Party (PSOE), from being traditionally anticlerical and aggressively secular, showed a new sensibility towards the need to harness the co-operation of Christians and an awareness of the religiosity still underlying Spanish society, a religiosity which in some instances was now combined with socialist sympathies.[50] At the X PSOE Congress held in Toulouse in 1967 it had affirmed that although socialism was secular and its ideology and action had no reference to the transcendental, it was not anti-religious. Socialism and Christianity, insofar as the latter was a religion of love for one's neighbour, were perfectly compatible. In 1979, the PSOE abandoned marxism as the basis of its ideology. Nevertheless, still mindful of the Church's traditional interference in politics and its traditional support for the political centre and right, the PSOE continued to advocate a secular, non-confessional State. Freedom of religion was to be guaranteed as a private and 'spiritual' matter.

The Communist Party (PCE) agreed to accept a monarchy and to offer support for a future social contract.[51] From the mid-1950s, it had collaborated with groups of progressive Catholics (mainly HOAC and JOC) in the workers' struggles and, in a bid to maximise the number of possible voters, it now encouraged the membership of Catholics, some of whom, including priests, became leading party officials. Tarancón remarked ironically in connection with the four clerics who were members of the PCE, 'Clericalism in Spain is so strong that even the Communists want to have priests'. The first Catholic to become a member of the executive committee of the PCE and the Catalan Communist Party (PSUC) was the longstanding activist Alfonso Comín.

In the first stages of the transition the PCE was temperate in its attitude towards the Church, in an attempt to overcome its red badge of anticlericalism, and to demonstrate its moderation. But in a second phase, dating from the constituent period, the party became more critical, accusing the Church of not knowing its place in a secular world. In the view of the PCE, the Church, with its 'wars of religion' over education and divorce, continued to press for perpetuating privileges associated with the powers and practices of a confessional State.[52]

By the time of the first post-Franco election, the bishops had issued so many pronouncements about Catholic involvement in the political arena that they were suffering from repetition-fatigue.[53] On the one hand, they claimed, people constantly requested guidance 'at important moments of national life', and yet on the other hand if the bishops spoke out or kept silent they would fail to please one or other sector of the population; the Church was in an awkward position for it had great social strength which might easily be manipulated politically; even saying or doing nothing might be considered tantamount to adopting a specific political attitude.[54]

Since divorce now featured on the agenda of all the major political parties except AP, the bishops had to come to terms with the inevitable; in fact, Tarancón conceded in private that he approved of civil divorce. The bishops defended the indissolubility of canonical marriage but accepted – within such clarity as was permitted by churchspeak – civil divorce for non-Catholics: 'There may be a conflict of values in the face of which the authorities have to use political prudence for the common good, which, even if it cannot do without ethical values, cannot ignore the force of social realities either'.[55]

Education also powerfully concentrated the Church's mind. According to an opinion poll carried out by the General Sociology Office of the Episcopate, 93 per cent of parents wanted their children to receive a religious education.[56] CONCAPA, the Catholic Parents' Federation, under its leader, Carmen Alvear, fought for 'Catholic rights' in season and out of season,[57] and in its stance sometimes proved to be 'more Papist than the Pope'. For the bishops at the XXVI Plenary Assembly of June 1977 there was no such thing as 'neutral education'; the State had no right to fix the educational model without reference to society and the rights of parents (as indicated by the Church).[58] In a pastoral letter to the diocese of Zaragoza, Mgr Elías Yanes, Chairman of the Episcopal Education Commission, insisted on the rights of parents in education and protested that an attack on the 'historical identity of our people' would be perpetrated if there were to be schools where the children of Catholic parents could not hear Christ spoken of in a religious sense.[59] On the other hand, the bishops of Pamplona-Tudela, San Sebastián and Vitoria, without denying the legitimacy of a Church presence in State schools, considered that the essential places for religious education were the Church's own institutions, like parishes and Christian communities.[60]

Despite the bishops' professed independence vis-à-vis political parties, there was a general awareness that the majority favoured the political centre,[61] an attitude encapsulated in the chant of 'UCD, your cassock's plain to see' ('*UCD, la sotana se te ve*'). Cardinal Tarancón always rejected the charge that he favoured UCD. Interviewed later by the priest–journalist José Luis Martín Descalzo, he said,

> Many politicians came to see me. But of all tendencies. I gave all of them my opinion and to none of them my support as a bishop. Least of all on the eve of elections, when I do not receive anyone. Naturally what I cannot avoid is that the moderate attitude which the Church had adopted, and that I have always fought to maintain, should coincide with the parties that wished to be moderate. And that is what happened to me as regards UCD. But also with the moderate currents in the PSOE.[62]

In the same interview, he made the point that all parties liked to have the Church at hand (or at least not as an enemy) and all – even its enemies – wanted to make use of it. By contrast, the Socialist leader Felipe González, looking back in 1980 to the mid-70s, thought that the Church distrusted the PSOE immediately before and after Franco's death and that when the electoral process began there was clear – if not explicit – support by the Church for the UCD.[63]

In the run-up to the June elections, priests and members of the religious orders were instructed not to become candidates, barring exceptional circumstances.[64] However, several did stand, mainly for regionalist and/or left-wing parties, and four were elected.[65] There appear to have been few instances in 1977 of local priests' intervening directly in the elections; those who did intervene generally confined themselves to attacking the left rather than advocating specific parties.[66] During a Communist Party meeting, the Secretary-General, Santiago Carrillo, invited Fr Llanos – who was a card-carrying member, not of the party but of the communist-inspired trade union Comisiones Obreras[67] – and Fr Díez-Alegría, to go up onto the presidential platform, which they did.[68] Fr Llanos, it will be remembered, was the Jesuit priest who had turned from supporter of the regime's elite to supporter of the poor and marginalised. The radical theologian Fr Díez-Alegría had similar views and spent time with him every summer in Madrid's deprived quarter of Pozo del Tío Raimundo.

Some of the bishops continued to play a strongly anti-marxist hand. They included four from the province of Burgos[69] who denounced marxism for its 'atheistic materialism, dialectic of violence and class struggle and a view of life incompatible with our faith', and thereby implicitly disqualified the PSOE and PCE electoral programmes.[70] By contrast, Mgr Iniesta of Madrid declared in a statement to the leading daily paper *El País* that he thought that 'Christians who believe that a certain type of marxism is compatible with Christianity cannot be denied their place in the Church'.[71]

A year before the election, CpS had demanded a pluralism in the options open to Christians that should include marxism-inspired socialism.[72] It forecast that the Church might well favour parties that were 'Christian in inspiration' as their 'secular arm' in obtaining via elections what it used to obtain by privilege or transaction.[73] CpS supported the left-wing parties,[74] though the Asturian regional branch decided not to recommend a vote for the left out of respect for the ideological pluralism that came with democracy.[75] The Popular Communities of Madrid warned that certain political and ecclesial sectors had mounted an anti-marxist campaign intended to discredit left-wing parties.[76] The Madrid HOAC Committee said the bishops' teaching had to be borne in mind but was not binding, while the Justice and Peace Commission left the matter to the individual conscience.[77]

Adolfo Suárez's centre-right UCD won the election with 34 per cent of the vote but well short of an overall majority. There was strong showing from the Socialists, with 28.5 per cent. Fraga's right-wing Alianza Popular trailed with only 8.4 per cent, below even the Communists' 9.3 per cent. AP had sedulously wooed the Catholic vote, flaunting its own 'guardianship of Christian values' and its anti-communism; in what was probably a counterproductive move, it went so far as to write to convents, asking the nuns to pray for its success, suggesting obliquely that a vote for AP was the wish of the bishops and of the Pope himself.[78] The left-wing Christian Democrats, who seem to have assumed that they had the backing of the official Church,[79] suffered a political rout, having received only two per cent of the votes cast. Spain had polled in favour of moderation. On the failure of left-wing Christian Democracy, Preston comments that 'the Church was probably backing the safer options in terms of the future defence of its own interests'.[80] Left-wing Christian Democracy was reduced to Catalonia and the Basque Country, where it had the support of some of the local clergy if not the hierarchy.[81]

Theologians and Church-watchers across the whole political and ecclesial spectrum picked over the professed independence of the episcopate in the 1977 election in what has been called 'the most significant collective act of evaluation on the role played by the hierarchy of the Church during the political transition'.[82] An article in *El País*[83] claimed that, whereas in the 1936 election political unity was imposed on all Catholics in defence of the Church's interests, in 1977 the hierarchy 'did not call for the unity of all Catholics in the election, nor did they attempt to make them form ranks on the right, nor did they condemn nor excommunicate any specific party'. In response, the philosopher José Luis Aranguren[84] alleged that for him there was no doubt that the hierarchy had collaborated effectively in the victory of UCD and in sustaining 'a pseudo-democracy administered by those who were Francoists until the death of Franco and began to cease being Francoists the very next day'. This, he said, had been the strategy of the hierarchy ever since Tarancón's homily on the day of the King's enthronement. Controversy over the issue continued for some time in the press.

What is arguable is that the absence of official Church support for any one political party permitted a delicate sleight-of-hand, denying legitimacy to those parties that did not support Church doctrine, or part of it, or that could be shown to be actively against it. To take an example: official Church pronouncements declared that parties based on marxist ideology were to be shunned by Catholics. This automatically disqualified the PCE and (until 1979) the PSOE, though they were not mentioned by name. At the same time, the bishops vetoed (unnamed) groups for which private property and profit were the sole economic *raison d'être*. Such unbridled capitalism did not feature in the programme of any political party, although UCD and, still more, AP were of course clearly the parties supported by 'capital', and individual capitalists frequently considered profit-maximisation to be the legitimate, sometimes the sole, objective of private business. Insofar as UCD was prepared to back Church influence on society and support Church mandates on 'family matters' – marriage, opposition to abortion, religious education – the government coalition was, in return, likely to have the Church's weight thrown behind it. AP, despite policies in such areas even more in line with the thinking of the hierarchy, was generally too far right of their 'extreme centre' strategy.

With the 1977 election over, political attention centred on devising a new Constitution. The bishops wanted neither a repetition of the traumatic rupture with the State experienced under the Second Republic nor the proclamation of Catholicism as the State-imposed religion, as under Franco's Fundamental Laws. What was at stake was the precise status of the Church as a national institution and, specifically, the maintenance of its role in education and its custody of the nation's morals.

In his opening address to the XXVII Plenary Assembly of the CEE on 21 November 1977, Cardinal Tarancón came out fighting for the 'sociological majority' status of Catholicism in the future sociopolitical organisation of the country. The Catholic Church was a

> social reality... for long years at one with the social realities and most decisive events of our history and as such has an undeniable specific weight.... If politics has to bear in mind and respect the real life of people, it cannot ignore the fact that a large majority of Spaniards belong to the Catholic Church,

and that, since it was not just one Church among others, this fact must be recognised in the Constitution.[85] Earlier in the same address, when discussing the future financing of the Church, he had underlined the weight of Catholic numbers and the Catholic soul of the nation: Catholics would have to make a major contribution but it had to be recognised that, with regard to the State subsidy, 'the State is no more than the administrator of the funds which it receives from a society which is in its majority Catholic'.[86] The Cardinal insisted that he was speaking only for himself, but it was clear that he carried the majority of bishops with him;[87] it was also clear – at least to more progressive Catholics or agnostics in the community – that he was bidding for a 'camouflaged confessionality'[88] of the post-Franco Spanish State.

This was the day before *El País* published part of a leaked draft of the new Constitution which made no explicit reference to the Catholic Church. It also happened that on the following Saturday, 26 November, the bishops issued a document entitled 'Moral and Religious Values and the Constitution'.[89] They argued that it was not enough to affirm the non-confessionality of the State: if the Constitution were worded equivocally and negatively, it might give rise to aggressively secular (*laicistas*) interpretations that would not correspond to the religious reality of Spaniards.[90] Allegations were made by several journals that it was no coincidence that the bishops had brought out their document at that particular time, and that what they had written was coloured by their prior knowledge of what was in the draft. This was strongly denied by the hierarchy and Mgr Iribarren, Secretary to the CEE, said he was prepared to go to the stake ('*Puedo poner la mano en el fuego*') on the matter.[91]

Whatever the role in society determined for it by the forthcoming Constitution, the Church would have to look more carefully at the way in which it was resourced, with a view in the very long run to becoming financially self-supporting. The hierarchy began to rationalise the Church's somewhat anarchic finances and at the same time to make the faithful aware of the need to contribute more to its maintenance. The government also introduced a new system for the public financing of the Church as from 1 January 1978. All secular priests, and members of the religious orders who carried out diocesan work,[92] were henceforth assured of a monthly stipend, and were covered for social security benefits. Furthermore, the State no longer paid subsidies directly to individual organisations, but sent a block grant to the Bishops' Conference for distribution. The approval of this grant by the Cortes was criticised in some lay circles (and by some of the clergy) who opposed the very principle of State subventions. There was talk of introducing a 'religion tax' similar to that which already existed in some other European countries.

When Tarancón was re-elected President of the CEE in February 1978, it appeared that the centrist position of the mainstream of the CEE was being maintained.[93] However, figures on the centre-right of the hierarchy like Mgr Cirarda of Pamplona and Mgr Yanes of Zaragoza, who favoured more direct involvement in the political process, also occupied important posts in the Conference: Mgr Cirarda became Vice-President and Mgr Yanes continued to head the Education Commission, a key post at an important moment.[94]

The majority of bishops continued to fight for the inclusion of an explicit reference to the Church in the Constitution. The political parties were agreed on disestablishment, but differed over whether the Church should nevertheless be favoured by explicit mention. In the end, with the support of the PCE and the Basque and Catalan nationalists, the UCD and AP members[95] of the constitutional drafting committee added to Article 16, which said that 'There shall be no State religion', the sentence: 'The public authorities shall take the religious beliefs of Spanish society into account and shall in consequence maintain appropriate co-operation with the Catholic Church and other confessions'.[96] In including this amendment, the UCD had changed its original position 'because its support for a considerable lessening of the Church's influence could lose it votes to the Right-wing Popular Alliance'.[97] The subtle wording[98] manages to reconcile the irreconcilable – to treat all religions as equal while discriminating in favour of Catholicism – and it does not commit the State to anything. The PSOE representatives walked out of the constitutional Commission of the Congress in March 1978 because the text of Article 16 had already been agreed.

The two other major Church-related issues debated in the Constitution, education and marriage, had already been extensively discussed by the bishops. They were concerned about what they saw as excessive State intrusion (*estatificación*) in education, which they feared might become a State monopoly threatening the very existence of Church schools. There was also the question of the status of religious education in State schools, and of State subsidies for Church schools (which perpetuated the Church's dependence on the State but which the bishops used all manner of arguments to maintain). UCD and AP proposed continuing such subsidies, while the PSOE, which favoured a single, secular, State school system, pressed for an end to them. The PCE, which had kept a low profile throughout the discussion of the constitutional matters which affected the Church,[99] sided with UCD and AP. Behind-doors agreements between UCD and the PSOE, and the application of the guillotine in Congress,[100] avoided a broader debate and confrontation by leaving everything to the future and to whatever government might be in power.

The bishops as a body left the faithful free to make up their own minds on the subsequent referendum to approve the Constitution. There were some reservations about Article 32.2 on marriage which referred to 'dissolution' and also the Articles on education, because, although the Church was permitted to found schools, there was no guarantee that the State would fund them. Despite general episcopal acceptance of the Constitution, nine of the bishops[101] attacked it and wrote hostile pastoral letters to the people of their dioceses.[102] Cardinal González Martín of Toledo, having denounced the Constitution – because it would set up an agnostic State, omitted any reference to God, did not sufficiently safeguard the moral values of the family and failed to put an absolute ban on abortion – then left his flock 'free' to vote according to conscience.[103] Similar repudiation came from Mgr Guerra Campos of Cuenca. The ultra-right Fuerza Nueva deputy Blas Piñar called the other bishops traitors who had done nothing when God was torn out of the Constitution.[104] The President of the integrist *Hermandad Sacerdotal* said that anyone voting in favour of the

Constitution committed a grave sin, and the similarly right-wing lay group *San Antonio María Claret* declared that such people were automatically excommunicated.[105]

Those bishops who considered that Spain should have continued to impose confessionality in God's name as 'the moral duty of societies towards the true religion' might expect to find their views shared in Rome. The new Pope appeared to consider that the majority of the Spanish hierarchy and priests were not up to the historic moment: they had been cowardly in not insisting that the Constitution include the name of God and the special status of the Catholic Church, and so 'the opinion was disseminated that the faith of the people was good but leaders were lacking, that one had to look only to Rome whence came the only true light'.[106]

On 6 December 1978 the Constitution was ratified by national referendum and, at the end of the month, Suárez announced a general election for 1 March 1979. Cracks in the UCD coalition soon became apparent, with the *sector crítico* (right-wing Christian Democrats) feeling outraged by the concessions on divorce and education made behind the scenes to the PSOE.[107] It was then that the Church moved toward a more openly active role in politics. As will be seen in the next chapter, it intervened directly in the March 1979 parliamentary election and later increased pressure on Suárez, whose resignation in January 1981 some blamed in part 'on machinations by Church dignitaries in league with the *sector crítico* of the UCD'.[108]

The papered-over unity of the Franco period had been torn by the pluralism of democratic times extending well beyond the sphere of politics. New times brought home also the fact that ecclesial disarray exceeded even that provoked by the internal conflicts of the 1950s and 1960s. It was not merely that the Spanish Church was being increasingly pushed from the centre stage of public life and had ceased to have an effective monopoly of morality. It was that pluralism was now in and around everything, offering all manner of alternatives. To this extent democratic pluralism hastened the process of secularisation.

6 Learning to Live with Reality (1979 to 1982)

> In modern pluralist States, the Church has lost its old monopoly, with the decline or end of what is known as Christendom... The Church becomes a secondary institution, with diminishing credibility and scant public influence in the ethical, social and political sphere. In this pluralist social context it is not easy to arouse faith, educate it and sustain it, since certain secularised concepts predominate which are alien to Christian tradition and are in opposition to values held as Catholic... The Church's dilemma is dramatic: to become a ghetto of integrist believers on the lines of a sect... or to adapt totally to the secular world by eliminating all that is specifically Christian, since the important thing is to build human reality. What frequently happens is that the integrist is not pluralist and it is difficult for the pluralist to be Christian.[1]

At the end of the Franco period and the beginning of the transition to democracy, the Spanish Church could be described as one of the protagonists shaping post-Franco society. The Church had played a major role in demanding respect for human rights and in supporting the whole democratic process. Cardinal Tarancón's example, and especially his homily at the enthronement of King Juan Carlos barely two days after General Franco's death, had set the tone. But once the foundations of formal democracy had been laid in the country, the Church's role changed; it was now fighting not so much for general freedoms as for what it saw as its own necessary freedoms. This was particularly true after the 1977 elections and the ratification of the 1978 Constitution, both of which pointed to the existence of a whole raft of political and social options in the country. As the political process continued, the Church increasingly focused its energies on the matters that most directly affected its sphere of influence over Spanish society. The bishops did not stop attempting to nudge political events in a particular direction – as the 1979 elections would show most palpably – even though they had been recommended to exercise 'real political abstinence' once the Constitution had been ratified.[2]

The Church's attitudes were conditioned not only by political events in Spain but also by its own internal dynamics and by the influence of the new Pope in Rome. While increasingly critical of the excesses of capitalism, John Paul II was a hardliner in the 'traditional' areas of faith and personal morals. He was already imprinting his authority on the universal Church, on national Churches and on individuals: regressive attitudes were taking over from the hopeful modernising spirit of the Council. Priests and members of the religious orders were summoned to Rome to have their theological knuckles rapped. Permission for priests to return to the lay state was suspended. The Pope's Polish background gave new impetus to the fight against atheistic communism and, whereas Vatican II had marked a period in which the Church felt the need to enter into dialogue with the modern world, including marxism, and to discover its own limitations, the hallmark of the papacy of John Paul II was a return to the theory of the Church as 'perfect society', with an emphasis on relevance and power, on centralised control and on certainty about the rights of the one true Church.[3]

His certainties had to be consolidated in Spain as in the rest of his Catholic world. This became abundantly clear at the beginning of 1979 with the signing at long last of Partial Agreements between the Spanish government and the Holy See which replaced the 1953 Concordat.[4] The main areas covered by the new accords were: (1) the legal status of the Church including the right to exercise its apostolic mission, and recognition of canonical marriage; (2) the right of parents to choose the moral and religious education of their children, the inclusion of (optional) religious instruction at all levels of education in conditions comparable to those of the other core subjects,[5] and the right to State subsidies; (3) religious ministry to the Armed Forces and the military service of priests and members of the religious orders; (4) a State undertaking to collaborate with the Church in appropriate financing, including certain tax exemptions, with a 'religion tax' on personal income to replace the annual State grant within three years, while the Church undertook to achieve self-financing in the long term.

According to Fr Martín Patino SJ who, as Cardinal Tarancón's right-hand man, was in a position to know, the new accords did not suit John Paul II. The Pope was said to be displeased by apparent concessions made by Tarancón and Dadaglio: they had not obliged the Spanish government to give a clear recognition of the jurisdiction of ecclesiastical courts, of the indissolubility of canonical marriage and of freedom for the Church in education. The Vatican did not understand how in a country which, like Poland, was a bastion of Catholicism, the Church had been unable to maintain a more assertive position.[6] Dadaglio and Tarancón were from that moment deemed by Rome to be too acquiescent towards Spanish pluralist democracy in general.

When the agreements came to be ratified by Congress in September 1979, Jordi Solé Tura of the PCE pointed out the problem caused by ratifying such accords before drawing up (national) laws on issues like religious freedom and marriage. He also warned against the danger of going from a Church of privilege to one under protection (*amparada*).[7] The PCE voted against both the economic and education Agreements. The PSOE was to some extent favourably disposed towards the accords, since some of its earlier criticisms had been met satisfactorily as, for example, in an amendment concerning the Church and the media. The original text, which had stated that the media would respect 'the Catholic sentiments of the citizens' was diluted so as to read 'the feelings of Catholics'.[8] The amendment is not without interest, in view of the identification between Spain and Catholicism which the bishops made so often. It was proposed by Gregorio Peces-Barba, the highly regarded constitutional law expert who had drawn up the general lines of the PSOE draft Constitution, and whose open profession of faith as a Catholic made him less suspect as a Socialist to the Spanish hierarchy. In the event, the PSOE voted against the education accord on the grounds that children in Church schools might not be able to opt out of religion classes, and that some powers would be wrongfully delegated from the State to the Church.

Evidently the matters encompassed by the Partial Agreements – which were *international* instruments – were also issues still in dispute at *national* level, at a time when the political scenario was changing in favour of the Socialists. With elections due in March, opinion polls in the first months of 1979 put the PSOE ahead of UCD. In the pre-election period, the behaviour of the hierarchy could be described as direct intervention, as 'the first important instance of a return to pro-conservative political activisim under the new Pope'.[9] Spain's was not the only case. There were other examples suggesting that a pro-active John Paul II was engaged in pushing political affairs in a certain direction: pastoral letters by Cardinal Medeiros of Boston attempted to influence the outcome of the 1980 Democratic primaries; likewise the West German bishops the 1980 Bundestag elections; about the same time, the Pope himself intervened strongly in the controversy raging throughout Italy over divorce and abortion.

On the second day of the election campaign, 8 February 1979, the Standing Commission entered the fray with a document entitled 'The Moral Responsibility of the Vote'.[10] The outcome of the general and local elections, they said, would determine the way people's lives would be run. The Church could not remain neutral 'in the face of possible threats against ethical values or human rights'. After condemning materialistic and totalitarian models of society, and violence as a political weapon, the document addressed the bishops' traditional spheres of interests, at this juncture divorce and abortion specifically.

UCD and AP were able to use the bishops' document to good electoral advantage. All the parties except AP included divorce in their manifestos but, since both the PCE and the PSOE advocated the right to abortion, and to divorce on the grounds of mutual agreement (specifically ruled out in the UCD programme), the bishops' statement could well cause fallout on the electoral chances of the left.

Spaniards went to the polls on 1 March 1979, with the results revealing an almost repeat perfomance of those of June 1977. Whereas AP had probably overplayed its anti-marxist card, Suárez for UCD played it adroitly on television at the end of the election campaign, contrasting the Christian humanism of UCD with the 'materialism' of the parties of the left. He reserved a special petard for the PSOE, which he described as the marxist party of abortion and divorce.

Felipe González continued to foster the PSOE's image of moderation, with evident success. Local elections, held on 4 April 1979, were a triumph for the pact between the parliamentary left parties. The next month, at the XXVIII PSOE Congress (17–20 May 1979), when his proposal to drop the marxist label failed, González resigned. After a summer on the stump convincing the majority of party activists that winning elections and modernising Spain had to take precedence over ideology, he was re-elected as Secretary-General at the Extraordinary Congress of 28–30 September during which marxism was finally dropped from official party ideology.

All the indications were that the Church would soon have to be negotiating its position in society with a Socialist government, which might not prove such a relatively comfortable bedfellow as UCD. Cracks had already appeared within the government coalition which was at the same time in a deepening crisis over its failure to pacify the Basque Country. Terrorist activity, which had been stepped up in the course of the year, raised tension in the army to a new peak, to the extent that rumours grew, later proved well-founded, of plots against democracy being hatched among the military.

It was against this background that on 29 October 1979 a referendum was held in the Basque Country on a statute of autonomy for the region. Ever since the beginning of the transition, recognition and recovery of identity in some of the regions had been a high priority. It was realised that post-Franco democracy had to include devolution of power to the regions (or 'autonomous communities' as they came to be called), because of previous bureaucratic over-centralisation which in certain places amounted to downright repression. The Basque Country and Catalonia had been pushing forcefully for broad self-government powers, and other regions followed suit. The Catalans and Basques voted for their respective statutes, followed by Galicia and subsequently all the remaining regions, until by 1983 all 17 of them had their own specific statute of autonomy and regional government.

The hierarchy as a body had stated in 1977 that the different 'identities proper to the peoples of Spain' had to be respected in the Constitution[11] and, in general, the bishops were supportive of the autonomy process in their regions.[12] With referenda in sight, the Basque bishops published a pastoral letter on the subject,[13] as did the Catalans,[14] both of them emphasising the civic duty to vote. While the 'regional' bishops supported moves to self-government, Cardinal Tarancón expressed his personal reservations about certain aspects of the devolution process being perhaps too precipate. He doubted whether it would be worthwhile unless it helped to reduce socio-economic disparities between the regions. There could also be repercussions in the ecclesial sphere: too much religious autonomy might put additional obstacles in the way of an already difficult unity. The fact, for example, that in some parts there were demands for local-born bishops had its great advantages but might also lead to ecclesial impoverishment.[15] Tarancón's words wounded Basque and Catalan autonomist sensibilities: Cardinal Jubany of Barcelona, speaking for all the Catalan bishops, told journalists that he disagreed with everything Tarancón had said about the regions.[16] On a later occasion, he said that granting autonomy to Catalonia meant recognition by the government of Catalonia's culture, language and history. He also thought that people had the right to expect their bishops to speak their language and know their customs and needs.[17]

The regional issue in all its ramifications did not rest there but it was not the most constant theme of the bishops' deliberations. By now there was a general perception that the CEE had moved from the extreme centre back towards the right,[18] its documents on divorce and education now among the harshest of the many it had issued, and without doubt reflecting robustly traditional views in the Vatican. 'Post-Taranconism' had arrived even before the Cardinal's retirement, in that instead of leading from the front, as he had done in the early days of the transition, he seemed to bend over backwards to patch up unity among the bishops. During the latter part of Nuncio Dadaglio's period in Madrid, there was a 'parallel Nunciature' operating via the chaplain of the Polish colony in Spain, Fr Mariano Valorek. He was close to the reactionary elements in the Spanish hierarchy, who used his frequent visits to Rome to influence Vatican thinking – negatively – on developments in the Spanish Church and society.[19] Dadaglio was recalled from Madrid in October 1980,[20] to be replaced by Mgr Antonio Innocenti. The latter's appointment came at a crucial moment: elections for a new President of the CEE after Tarancón's nine years in office, a papal visit planned for October 1981, and a more liberal divorce Bill were all on the horizon.[21]

The Vatican's view of the Spanish situation seems to have been influenced by Spanish Opus Dei members in Rome. To put the matter at its most neutral, the Opus had over the years created a strong support structure in the Curia, which was valuable in promoting its case for obtaining the status of Personal Prelature (*prelatura nullius*), that is to say, to become canonically the equivalent of a diocese without geographical boundaries, and thus independent of the jurisdiction of a local bishop. Now its time had come. Shortly after his election, John Paul II declared that the legal status of the Opus Dei had to be resolved.

That something was astir became apparent when a special report ('La transformación jurídica del Opus Dei'), on how the Opus had entrenched its position since 1962, was physically removed from the 3 November 1979 issue of *Vida Nueva*, when it had already gone to press, following pressure from the Opus on the publishers.[22] Just over a fortnight later, when the CEE at its XXXII Plenary Assembly discussed the Opus' future legal status, the mood was in general against the creation of a *prelatura nullius*, but this would not be the end of the affair. Thanks to the Pope's favourable attitude, and to their own unremitting tenacity in placing 'their men' in strategic positions in the Curia,[23] in the pursuit of Vatican recognition of the 'uniqueness' of their organisation and of the sanctity of their founder, this was a particularly good period for *opusdeístas*. In 1981 – a mere

15 years after his death – the beatification cause of Mgr Escrivá de Balaguer was initiated in Rome.[24] Furthermore, John Paul, overriding opposition, granted the Opus Dei its *prelatura nullius*; in creating the 'Prelature of the Holy Cross and Opus Dei', he gave it a status in the Catholic Church which was unique, signalling that the winning streak of the conservatives of the Catholic Church, in Spain and throughout the universal Church, was set to continue.

Spain's Opus Dei had its own private conduit to Roman ears via one of its members, Fr Fernando Martínez Loza, whose uncle Mgr Eduardo Martínez Somalo, was considered 'no. 3' at the Vatican.[25] It is not known to what extent the Opus was directly involved in the 'transition' process except insofar as some of its members were AP deputies and others part of the *sector crítico* of UCD. They were certainly involved in an attempt to torpedo the liberal divorce law which was making its way through the Cortes at the beginning of the 1980s.

Encouraged by Rome, the bishops of the conservative sector of the Spanish Church hardened their attitudes during 1980 and 1981. Their support went to the largely like-minded *sector crítico* of UCD, which appeared to be on the verge of forming a right-wing splinter group with an openly Christian Democrat label,[26] and their concerns centred on the Church's role in a forthcoming Schools Statute (*Estatuto de Centros Docentes*), a new law on University Autonomy (*Ley de Autonomía Universitaria*), and the future divorce law. The *Estatuto de Centros Docentes* was a more satisfactory proposition than the previous (1970) Education Act:[27] it clearly encouraged private education and parents' rights and gave proprietors control over the ethos of their schools. For the same reasons it met with strong opposition from the left.[28] After much parliamentary debate and some persuasive talk by Adolfo Suárez with dissidents in his own coalition, it was passed, thanks to support from AP and other smaller parties. The left would have its chance when the PSOE came to power in 1982. Linked to the Schools Statute was the University Autonomy Law, which included a proposal that individuals or institutions should be permitted to found Universities. As far as the Church was concerned, it would be free to establish its own universities in addition to those already existing – Comillas, Deusto, Navarre and Salamanca.[29]

Two further important Bills were on the stocks in 1980. The first, passed into law in July, concerned religious liberty (*Ley Orgánica de Libertad Religiosa*), guaranteeing the right of all citizens to religious freedom and worship. At first UCD had pressed for a specific mention of the Catholic Church in Article 7 of the Law but later withdrew its proposal, since this was already written into the 1978 Constitution. Jordi Solé Tura for the PCE said it was a law that came late, since before Parliament had had the opportunity to debate it, the agreements with the Holy See had been signed, and the *Estatuto de Centros Docentes*, whose provisions were contrary to the principle of religious freedom, had been approved.[30]

The second was a divorce bill, which had a much more tortuous road to travel. The first draft included a harshness clause allowing a judge discretion to refuse a divorce if it was deemed harmful to one or other of the parties or to the children. The clause was dropped when Suárez, whose government was racked with internal dissent, reshuffled his cabinet and gave the Justice portfolio to the Social Democrat Francisco Fernández Ordóñez. The latter liberalised the Bill, allowing divorce by mutual consent, and reducing the time required to obtain a decree. This ran against what the majority of bishops had agreed in accepting a civil divorce law[31] and led the Standing Commission to issue yet another anti-divorce document, this time focused on the mutual agreement clause. The CEE was obviously split on the matter: the Primate of Toledo fulminated that neither the State nor the Pope nor God could dissolve a validly contracted marriage, while bishops such as the new President of the CEE, Díaz Merchán, said more moderately that the CEE documents had a pastoral intention directed fundamentally at the conscience of those who were prepared to listen.[32] It was bruited that the Vatican had threatened to suspend the Pope's visit to Spain, planned for October 1981, to show his displeasure, and that the Nuncio had insinuated the possibility of abrogating the Partial Agreements.[33]

However, in Fernández Ordóñez's view, the State could not impose on all members of society the moral and religious beliefs that affected the conscience of only one sector, nor could the unity of legal norms be broken because of such beliefs.[34] He denied that his Bill accepted 'quickie' divorce, while the PSOE attacked the bishops' document as 'inopportune, immoderate and destabilising'.[35] The PCE warned of the gravity of the issue in a country where 'religious questions have often divided Spaniards, frustrating every plan for democratic harmony', and said there had been a radical shift in the Church's hitherto discreet attitude.[36] Progressive Catholics protested that, as theologians were not of one mind about the intrinsic indissolubility of marriage, the bishops were going too far in pressurising Catholics to reject the divorce law.[37] Some accused the Church of hypocrisy for attacking divorce while trafficking in annulment decrees.[38] The only group to welcome the bishops' latest document was Alianza Popular.[39] An unsuccessful rearguard action fought to reinstate the harshness clause of the divorce Bill ended in failure[40] and the Cortes finally passed the *proyecto Ordóñez* on 22 June 1981. The Secretary to the CEE commented that no fewer than 34 UCD deputies who were at least formally Christian had voted in favour of a divorce law which the bishops had declared unacceptable.[41]

Writing in his capacity as a former spokesman for the Ministry of Justice, José Cavero described the divorce battle as singularly tense, unpleasant and often showing the strength of 'the enemy' whom he identified as the Opus Dei and its press columnists, the Catholic Church and its media, the right and the ultramontane ultra-right – all in a pact, with the Vatican's support, to prevent the 'advance of evil' in Spain being facilitated by Fernández Ordóñez. He claimed that they used arguments of all kinds – the dechristianisation of Spain, Ordóñez's desire to ingratiate himself with the Socialists, even 'friendly warnings' that what he really wanted was an easy formula for separating from his wife.[42]

Adolfo Suárez resigned as Prime Minister on 29 January 1981, and before his successor – Leopoldo Calvo Sotelo – had been elected a month later, the simmering discontent of right-wing elements in the Army had come to a head and Spain had been rocked by an attempted coup d'état. On 23 February members of the Civil Guard under Lieutenant-Colonel Antonio Tejero occupied the Cortes in Madrid and held deputies at gun-point. A state of emergency was declared in Valencia and troop movements were reported in other parts of Spain. However, King Juan Carlos and his close supporters held firm and by midday of 24 February the rebels had surrendered.

While these dramatic events were unfolding, the Spanish bishops were gathered for the first day of their XXXIV Plenary Assembly during which they were to elect a new President to replace Tarancón. Their attitude to the attempted coup, commonly known as the *Tejerazo*, has never been fully clarified. On the evening of the coup they said nothing. Later, rejecting the accusation that their silence was due to an opportunistic desire to await the outcome,[43] there were various not entirely convincing explanations – that there was a lack of information, that they were late in receiving the news, that some had already left for the night, that any statement would be clearly political in character, that there was a leadership vacuum since the new President had not yet been elected.[44] About ten o'clock on the following morning (24 February) the bishops sent a telegram of support to the King. In an interview with *El País*, the newly-elected President, Mgr Díaz Merchán, said that the bishops had not realised that democracy was in danger but thought that a madman had managed to enter Parliament. He added that when he heard the bishops' spokesman (Mgr Montero) say on television that the last prayer of their meeting had been 'for Spain' he was thunderstruck because the sentence was ambiguous and might sound as if the bishops had been praying for Tejero's success.[45] Perhaps the bishops' silence might most charitably be ascribed to typical episcopal prudence. Certainly on this occasion they did not exercise what they regularly claimed to be their right as citizens (that is, to speak), in order to make their positions clear. There is also the presumption, given the differences in their ages and attitudes, that it was psychologically and sociologically impossible for them to speak as one on the night of the 23 February.[46]

In view of rumours about pressures from Rome and the new direction which the CEE was thought to be taking, some commentators and even members of the hierarchy themselves[47] were surprised at the election in Mgr Díaz Merchán of a bishop of the Tarancón line, albeit by the slender margin of three votes.[48] The narrowness of his victory meant that he would have to keep in mind that conservatives in the episcopate were once again strongly positioned. Furthermore, the composition of the Standing Commission – ever a conservative counterweight even in Tarancón's time – remained the same. Shortly after his election, the new President told reporters that he aimed at unity in basics, but not one that was monolithic.[49] He also spoke of relations with radical Christian groups, admitting that the official Church had not always known how to enter into a meaningful dialogue with them.[50]

Meanwhile the bloody war in the Basque Country dragged on. In the face of unremitting ETA attacks on military personnel, and the general feeling in the country that the security forces themselves were increasingly acting as a parallel government, that Spain was living in a democracy under surveillance (*democracia vigilada*), the bishops of the Basque Country, Mgr Larrauri (Vitoria), Mgr Larrea (Bilbao), Mgr Setién (San Sebastián) and Mgr Uriarte (auxiliary Bishop of Bilbao), published a pastoral letter entitled 'Save Freedom so as to Save Peace'.[51]

It opened with a blistering denunciation of ETA for seeking to provoke another coup. It then turned on bunker elements (*sectores inmovilistas*) of Spanish politics, who had not accepted the loss of their hegemony in society and considered democracy to be the cause of its ills. Such groups found support in the Armed Forces, who had their own perception of the unity of Spain and were tempted to listen to siren voices inviting them to take Spain over by pronunciamiento. The proof of this temptation, the bishops said, lay in the attempted coup of 23 February and its subsequent effect on Spanish life. There was also an increasing number of people who yearned for an authoritarian government because they identified peace with a tough law and order policy; there were even more who gazed passively on events that affected everyone's future. Though nothing justified assassinations, threats, kidnappings, 'revolutionary taxes', or attacks on property perpetrated in the name of so-called justice or revolutionary strategy, these did not invalidate the democratic process. The bishops reminded the Armed Forces that their mission was to serve the institutions set up by society, not to 'dictate the legitimacy of the democratic process'. The letter left no-one in doubt that, while condemning ETA, the bishops were this time also denouncing military intervention.

The government overreacted. The situation it created was reminiscent of the way Franco's ministers had mishandled the Añoveros affair of April 1974. Rather than tackling the President of the Bishops' Conference, it pursued the matter at diplomatic level, as one sovereign State to another, since it saw the pastoral letter as a violation, at least in spirit, of the 1979 Agreements. Calvo Sotelo, as Prime Minister, summoned the Nuncio and a formal complaint was presented to the Vatican. Politicians of all persuasions except some of the moderate Basque nationalists (PNV and Euskadiko Ezkerra) were furious. The press on the whole was cautiously receptive to the bishops' arguments though some doubted whether the timing of the letter was opportune,[52] since Spain was being traumatised by an intensification of ETA violence, the UCD government apparently powerless to end it. There was also criticism of the ambiguous attitude towards terrorism on the part of some of the Basque clergy, among whom were known ETA sympathisers sometimes harbouring suspects and providing them with moral and material support. Furthermore, tension was still high after the recent *Tejerazo*. In the following year the Basque bishops again stirred up a political hornets' nest with their pastoral letter 'Respecting Justice and Building Peace'[53] attacking a Bill (*Ley Orgánica de Armonización de los Procesos Autonómicos* – LOAPA) which aimed to rationalise the devolution process. The bishops claimed the LOAPA would devalue the gains made in regional autonomy, undermine justice and peace, and could even lead to increased violence.

Suddenly attention shifted to Rome, with news of an attempt to assassinate John Paul II in St Peter's Square. There were fears for his life and subsequently about whether the visit to Spain which he was scheduled to make in October would actually take place. John Paul made headlines again later in the year with the publication of a major 'social' encyclical, which was published on 15 September. *Laborem Exercens* emphasised the role of the person as being more important than economic systems; both capitalism and collectivism were acceptable provided they fulfilled certain ethical conditions.[54] The Pope appeared to be advocating a 'third way' between capitalism and socialism, as he had done in his address to the Latin American bishops in Puebla (Mexico) in 1979.[55]

In *Laborem Exercens*, John Paul showed that he did not fully agree with capitalism. Yet at the same time he needed the Western – capitalist – powers in his crusade against communism. Similarly, his condemnation of the arms race was always tempered by his need for the support of the United States (and implicitly of NATO) because they provided a powerful bulwark against the Soviet Union.

The new encyclical would in the future be a constant source of reference for the Spanish bishops. For them also the marxist enemy had not disappeared. That could not be expected, in view of international tension between the two major power blocs and the understandably unyielding anti-communism of a Polish Pope, but it no longer figured so prominently in their documents: *Laborem Exercens* seems to mark a point from which the excesses of capitalism took precedence over marxism in their denunciations.

The encyclical was not entirely without critics in Spain. Fr Díez-Alegría questioned it as an expression of the whole approach to what is known as the social doctrine of the Church. Speaking at a Congress on Theology and Poverty in Madrid (21–7 September 1981), he expressed the view that this was neither social nor Catholic, since, he claimed, 'interclass neutrality' was a trap which operated to the benefit of the dominant classes.[56]

Earlier in the year Fr Díez-Alegría had been banned from giving a course at the Catholic Institute of Social Studies in Barcelona. This was not an isolated case of official disapproval at work in Spain: Fr José María Castillo and Fr Juan Estrada were removed from their teaching posts in the Theology Faculty of Granada University.[57] It was part of a wider clampdown in the spirit of orthodoxy exercised with increasing force from the Vatican. The Pope imposed on the Jesuits a papal delegate, 80-year-old Fr Paolo Dezza, a move interpreted as the Pope's wish to see a fundamental change in the direction taken by the Order. The nub of the conflict was the fact that a whole sector of the Society of Jesus was spearheading people's demands for socio-political rights and had a radical commitment to the poor.[58] At the same time, the Pope was demonstrating positive favour towards religious groups whose spiritual life involved little or no commitment to solidarity.

The hierarchy drew extensively on *Laborem Exercens* in its November 1981 document, 'The Grave Unemployment Problem'.[59] It emphasised that work was a fundamental right and that unemployment benefit was an absolute need. There had to be a complete overhaul of the economic order, with overall planning to achieve just and rational co-ordination. The bishops were prompted by the fact that some 14 per cent of the labour force were out of work, two million people, of whom fewer than 40 per cent received unemployment benefit; they pointed to the charitable help offered by Church organisations, especially *Cáritas*, but stated that it was not within the Church's remit to offer solutions. Some of the causes were economic and technical – rising energy costs, technological advance and structural defects both national and international, but in other cases it was the human factor – media manipulation creating new needs, increasing consumerism or, worst of all, loss of awareness of moral values.

This relatively anodyne pronouncement provoked criticism from a group of priests, religious and laity of Andalusia (*Misión del Sur*) during their 1982 Lenten meeting.[60] It claimed that the Church did not seem to take its own documents seriously, since it did not put them into effect. It should demand of its members specific remedies. *Misión del Sur* was practical in its proposals: the bishops should denounce abuses in the workplace such as overtime, holding more than one job (*pluriempleo*), 'legal' but unjust dismissal, absenteeism by bosses and workers, social security fraud and leaving land uncultivated, and deny reception of the sacraments to offenders, since such immorality was no less grave than adultery or divorce. Similar treatment should be accorded to those involved in conspicuous or unnecessary consumption of what rightfully belonged to the poor. Holy Week confraternities should reduce their expenses and give 10 per cent of their budget to *Cáritas* for distribution. The bishops should denounce the government for allowing small and medium-sized businesses to go to the wall, and for cutting off unemployment benefit. During Lent, bishops, priests and religious of Andalusia should give a week's wage and the laity at least one day's wage in solidarity with the unemployed: this obligation was much more binding than the traditional Lenten practice of abstinence from eating meat. The Church must put its institutional power at the service of the unemployed in practical ways, even at the risk of losing prestige and clientèle.

In general the question of how to achieve greater social justice, the capitalism versus anti-capitalism debate, discussed in earlier chapters, was ongoing in ecclesial circles.[61] Some of the bishops were considerably more critical of capitalism than others, wanting a complete socioeconomic change, but their voices were lost in the ecclesiastical wilderness. Mgr Javier Osés of Huesca said in an interview that if the bishops' option for the oppressed and marginalised were clearer, their documents would be different in character and content. But their assumptions did not start from a fundamental option for the poorer strata, but from a position of not opting for anyone nor with anyone, which always left their attitudes fudged. He went on to say that the only objective reality that ought to concern the Church was that 'in Spain we have a capitalist system, the culpable origin of the existence of a great marginalised and exploited mass'.[62]

At the beginning of February 1981, the Diocesan Assembly of Barcelona had declared for a Church that kept itself independent of power, and that did not take refuge in a false neutrality but in a real bias in favour of the poor, justice, freedom and human rights inside and outside the Church.[63] However, a motion presented to the Assembly by CpS asking for respect in temporal matters for any political option, including those of socialism inspired by marxism, was defeated.[64] CpS was one of the groups that spoke out most often against capitalism during the transition; others were HOAC, CCP, Justice and Peace, and various groups of intellectuals and Catholic theologians,[65] but their voices had little or no resonance among the hierarchy except as an irritant. Such progressive groups had no doubts: the Church must not be neutral, it must opt for the poor and marginalised. They claimed, however, that in fact it favoured the better-off members by supporting the centre and right or, as it would say, 'moderate' parties.

Much of the hierarchy's attention during 1982 was taken up with the forthcoming visit of Pope John Paul. In view of the political troubles afflicting UCD and the possiblity of an early election, concern was expressed in both secular and ecclesial circles that a visit that was intended to be pastoral might be manipulated for political ends, with the consequent polarisation of such issues as education and divorce.[66]

A good deal would depend on the political scenario when the Pope actually arrived. Relations between the Church and the UCD government had returned to normal once the diplomatic incident provoked by the Basque bishops' anti-bunker statement had been resolved. However, a lecture given early in 1982 by the UCD Director General of Religious Affairs, Luis Apostúa, on 'Human rights and Religious Freedom',[67] sparked off another conflict. According to Apostúa, the government was minded to handle religious matters within the framework of the Constitution and of the Religious Freedom Law of 1980, and not, as the Church wished, within the framework of the Partial Agreements. The Nuncio insisted that the accords were binding and that neither the State nor the Church could unilaterally abrogate, amend or suspend them. The primacy of the Partial Agreements was an argument which the bishops were to use again in brushes with the next – Socialist – government, in the matter of religious education.

By now the UCD coalition, riven by internal dissension, was imploding. Calvo Sotelo called a general election to be held on 28 October. The PSOE seemed set fair to become the next party of government since Felipe González and his party had been gathering strength and credibility and occupying the middle ground of the political spectrum. To avoid the papal visit being used as a political weapon, and to preserve the 'pastoral' nature of his journey, it was rescheduled for after the election.

Campaigning began in the late summer and was well under way when on 23 September the CEE Standing Commission issued a communiqué on the elections and the likely outcome.[68] Reiterating the ritual declaration that the Church was not partisan, they listed the moral issues at stake and there was a by now *de rigueur* reference to *Laborem Exercens*. At the end came a more eye-catching statement: after the elections, citizens must accept the result, and respect the government which had been elected, and they must continue to cooperate, '*albeit from a position of constructive opposition*', in promoting the good of society. This was the first appeal in an official episcopal document for co-operation from a 'loyal opposition'. It must surely have been, despite Mgr Montero's assurances to the contrary, a tacit acknowledgement of the likelihood of a Socialist victory,[69] and also of a presumption that 'normally' the Catholic vote would not go to the left. It could be interpreted as a signal to the Church's traditional centre-right voting troops that, if democratically elected, even a left-wing government must be accepted.

The PSOE confirmed expectations by winning an absolute majority in the Cortes, having obtained over 47 per cent of the votes cast. Cardinal Tarancón, when asked for his view about the Socialists, declared that 'moderate socialism' was not too bad a thing, adding that there were some twelve bishops who wanted more contacts with the Socialists, another twelve (in which he included himself) who wanted dialogue without any commitment, while twenty others saw the Socialists as the great enemy. The rest had no opinion on the matter.[70] However, on another occasion, Tarancón admitted that it was not easy to collaborate honestly and sincerely with ideological groups which had in the past maintained an overly secular view that was tantamount to anticlericalism,[71] and that in any case his stated preference was for 'Christian humanist' parties.

By contrast, a new, progressive body – the John XXIII Theological Association (*Asociación Juan XXIII*)[72] – issued a document which was highly critical of parties making political capital out of a profession of 'Christian humanism' but, in deference to impartiality in the election campaign and the forthcoming visit by the Pope, they delayed publication until November. To this Association, 'defence of life' – the battle-cry of the political right – meant primarily joining peace movements, and working for nuclear disarmament. The John XXIII theologians also called to aid John Paul II's *Laborem Exercens* to show that the encyclical's social doctrine was hardly compatible with the capitalist doctrine of the right, which claimed to be the representative and guarantor of matters Catholic. Among the variety of political options on offer, socialist proposals, even those advocating the joint ownership of the means of production, could be accepted by Christians, although not uncritically.[73]

This is the kind of message which over the years had been delivered by HOAC and other Catholic activist groups. However, for all the statements made by progressives and radicals during the transition, the impression given was that by now they were in retreat.[74] Their most heroic period, during which, largely under the influence of liberation theology, they made strenuous efforts and sacrifices in an attempt to involve the Church in a real transformation of society, had ended with the end of Francoism. When democracy came, conditions changed and the precise form of a new and more equitable political and social order order divided Catholic activists. In the experience recounted by various HOAC members,[75] which can be taken as representative also of other committed groups, democracy provided a legal space in which to express and organise themselves more effectively in the struggle for social justice. But they also felt that it made them accomplices of the social system by committing them to pacts with the classes in power, the existing and continuing socio-economic structures, the self-perpetuating winners of 'the system'. In this situation the HOAC members shared the general uncertainty concerning a future for what had been a revolutionary ideology; the options ranged from returning to struggle in mass movements to being 'realistic' and to confining themselves to being a 'critical minority'.[76]

Such general uncertainty was not surprising. Spain had gradually converged with a Europe undergoing constant change, coming to grips with the reconstruction of socio-economic models and adjusting to alterations in the balance of social forces. By the time the Second World War had ended, people all over Europe were increasingly disillusioned with and sceptical of a system, its ruling classes and elites, that had possibly engineered, certainly permitted, years of desperation: a deep and long-lasting world economic crisis in the 1930s, mass unemployment and misery leading to fascism, war and – for many – foreign occupation and loss of national independence.

In order to survive, old-style capitalism had to give way to a mixed, managed, new-style capitalism, which Social Democracy and also Christian Democracy had to some extent humanised, providing the working population with at least some of what it had been fighting for – a modicum of job and social security, wider educational opportunities and rising standards of living. This led them to the negotiating table for the purpose of managing conflicts of interest, and some to accept middle-class values of consumerism. By the time they were newly dispossessed by the rising tide of unemployment and the 'new poverty' of the 1980s, they had become locked into the system. For Spain, democracy and improved social rights came in 1975 at a time marked by a series of international economic crises, which, even if the political constellation had been different, would have rendered fundamental socio-economic change difficult, if not impossible.[77]

Even if the left had held the winning cards in 1975 – which evidently it had not – the situation would not have been radically different. By 1982, when the PSOE came to power, they did so with the slogan of 'change' but it was by then too late for fundamental change, even if the political will had been there. In the 1990s, with the collapse in the East of the Soviet model, and the intensification of financial and economic globalism, fissures would become apparent also in the Western model in which the capitalist power groups had successfully regained – partly by market deregulation with the consequent reappearance of national and international mass unemployment – much of what modest ground they had lost to the Social Democrat/Christian Democrat welfare model. Social democracy seemed tainted – even though by improper and undeserved association – by the universal disillusion with Soviet-type 'really existing' socialism. It appeared to lose confidence in itself and to have little further to contribute. To maintain influence, it sacrificed some of its utopian vision of social justice.

Against the background of the transfer of political power from UCD, explicitly pro-capitalist, to the PSOE, in theory pro-socialist, John Paul II made the first official visit of a pontiff to Spain, between 31 October and 9 November 1982. Church representatives were at pains to stress the pastoral nature of his ten days' journeying and preaching round Spain. It was an undoubted personal success, but there is no evidence that the evangelisation effects of John Paul's appeals in Spain for Europe to rediscover its Christian roots[78] were long-lasting.

The Pope's homilies ranged wide, most often likely to gratify the conservative right than the newly elected left, but there was something for everyone: rejection of violence; the respect due to 'the plurality of legitimate options'; the need for restructuring the economy, for agrarian reform, and for improving work prospects; insistence on the stability of the family; the right of the Church to run its own schools; the rejection of the permissive society, of divorce and abortion. It was with regard to these that the incoming Socialist government found, like Don Quixote, that 'friend Sancho, we have run up against the Church', or, rather, that conservative sector of the Spanish Church that was delighted by winds from the Vatican swirling in a pro-Opus climate, and heartened by many of the Pope's homilies. Knowing what was on the PSOE agenda, the hierarchy and some Catholic lay organisations went out of their way to ensure massive popular support for the Pope's stay, in an attempt to demonstrate the strength of Catholic feeling. They responded fervently to the Pope's affirmation that 'the Christian and Catholic faith constitute the identity of the Spanish people'.[79] It was true that some Spaniards still yearned to see their country as a bastion of traditional Catholicism – those who wrote the Pope's addresses for him, or those who bore aloft the ubiquitous Opus Dei-inspired 'Totus Tuus' banners – but to a large extent it was a question of nostalgia, of wishful thinking.

In reality the Pope's was a journey organised for the kind of 'Catholic' country that Spain had ceased to be,[80] or perhaps had not ever been. Most of the signals of the time pointed to a continuous leaching away from the institutional Church. The Friedrich Ebert Foundation published a report showing that while 78 per cent of Spaniards over the age of eighteen saw themselves as Catholics, only 14.4 per cent of the population fully accepted Church guidance on political matters, over 70 per cent favoured the right to abortion, and 72 per cent of PSOE voters and 40 per cent of PCE voters identified themselves as Catholics. The report added that 'Spaniards understand clearly that beliefs are something that affect the personal conscience but that social and political harmony (*convivencia*) are based on pluralism and on the sovereign will of the people'.[81] In a pluralist and democratic social context, the Church had to compete for influence with other sectors and social forces.

Religiosity levels, although high by European standards, were considerably lower than would have been recorded thirty years earlier.[82] Even allowing for social pressure and 'religious inflation' in the statistics of the Franco times, the contrast is significant. The steep decline in religious practice, especially among young people, occurred above all, and not surprisingly, in the large cities. Whereas 91 per cent of young people in 1960 said they were 'practising or not very strongly practising Catholics', in 1982 the figure had dropped to 34 per cent, and the percentage of those who identified themselves as non-practising had risen from 8 per cent to 45 per cent. In the categories 'indifferent' or 'atheist', there were none in 1960, while in 1982 the figure was 17 per cent.[83] On the other hand virulent anticlericalism, both urban and rural, had largely been replaced by impassivity and detachment. Ironically, anticlericalism or even open atheism were most likely to be found among intellectuals educated in Church schools and colleges during the Franco period.[84]

These were indeed significant factors. Perhaps even more ominous for the future of the institutional Church was the fact that indifference to it seemed likely to increase with each coming generation.[85] What remained was a reserve of basic beliefs which still provided points of reference for many of people's values and attitudes. Even so, this reserve might in the future be further dissipated or channelled into other beliefs. The lay theologian Miret Magdalena said he had seen the interest aroused by substitutes for the established religions: there was an increase in 'Eastern and esoteric groups, believers in horoscopes, astrology and the occult',[86] though it was difficult to know how strong their following was. It was a *particular* religious belief as taught by the Church, not necessarily the *capacity for belief*, that was losing ground in Spain. Religion in the institutional sense was giving way to less structured religiosity.

No wonder the Church kept asking itself what its role in society must be and what evangelisation strategy could be used to counteract both its loss of membership in abolute terms and the reluctance of those who remained to accept the full package of its teachings. In the past, pacts had enabled it to occupy its public space and maintain its influence. Now the Church found that its message – certainly in the way it was presented by the hierarchy – was at times diluted, at times contested, but more often than not ignored by an increasing number of Spaniards.

7 The Church and the PSOE Government (1982 to 1996)

> The neoconservative de-privatisation of Catholicism in Spain is marked by the attempt to recover the public role which was obscured or was lost during the transition. It could be said that it is a question of achieving a *repoliticisation of religion and the sphere of private morality* and a *remoralisation of culture and the public sphere*.[1]

It would be tempting to think that the heady days of change in Spain were now over. The election of a PSOE government showed that an alternative political option was possible without provoking traumatic consequences in society. Spaniards had settled into their pluralist way of life. The 'transition to democracy' could *grosso modo* be considered complete. But by no means was everything over in the politics of religion. Interpretation of the spirit of Vatican II remained disputed territory and, despite the hierarchy's protests to the contrary, the PSOE was not far wrong in stating that 'the Church has not altogether found its place in democracy'.[2]

A period of greater mutual distrust in Church–State relations began in 1982, partly because of memories of the PSOE's anticlerical past and the Church's own tradition of anti-socialism. But it was also because the politics of religion must always reckon with the 'Vatican factor'. The dialogue with modernity advocated by John XXIII and the Council was already weaker in the last years of Paul VI and by now had become scarcely audible. Moreover, John Paul II, who had made himself a very visible head of the Catholic Church, was determined that the national churches should also raise their institutional profile. Having fought against what had seemed the ultimate contemporary heresy, atheistic communism, and contributed to its downfall, he inveighed ever more vehemently against the evils of that last – or latest, but intangible – enemy: a secularised society increasingly detached from the Church and from its traditional values.

Deep down, the Church had never abandoned the attempt to play a significant role in Spanish life. By the time of the Pope's visit in the days immediately following the PSOE victory in 1982, the CEE, in tune with the Pope's message, was already shifting well to the right of the relative progressiveness and political neutrality of Tarancón's 'extreme centre'. Its President, Mgr Gabino Díaz Merchán, although basically cast in a 'Taranconian' mould, acted more as a moderator than a leader[3] and was caught between the Vatican juggernaut and the PSOE's secular vision of society, which was increasingly that of Spaniards in general.

Switching from their often bewildered and defensive position during the immediate post-Franco period, the Spanish hierarchy followed the pontiff's own evangelisation strategy for the universal Church: it must keep on restating Catholic truths and, having secured its doctrinal fortress, go on the offensive to reclaim the Church's rightful public place. Catholicism must be 'de-privatised', in the sense that it must not run the risk of suffering the consequences of 'official belligerence in favour of a society which relegates the religious and the moral to the strictly private sphere', as the Spanish bishops announced in a document issued in the wake of the papal visit.[4] Two further documents, 'Witnesses to the Living God' (*Testigos del Dios vivo*) in 1985 and 'Catholics in Public Life' (*Los católicos en la vida pública*) in 1986, also urged Catholics to have greater awareness of what they were and what they had to do, both in general and in the face of what was judged to be government dirigisme verging on 'a totalitarian and state-controlled (*statificado*) running of social life'. 'Catholics in Public Life', an attempt to offer suitable criteria for rebuilding the Catholic social structure, was born of a debate within the CEE in which one sector wanted the Church to endorse a specifically Catholic, Christian Democrat, party, as in some other European countries. Even though the proposal did not prosper, the bishops declared once more in favour of 'associations which are Christian in inspiration'.[5]

For the hierarchy there were two models of society in conflict: one with 'values marked by agnostic humanism', most clearly represented by the Socialists, the other with religious – Catholic – values, which were part of the Spanish people's cultural and moral heritage. They were caught between the need to negotiate with the 'enemy' model and the 'restorationist dynamic which seeks to legitimise itself on the basis of confrontation with the values of secularism and the legislation which it enacts'.[6] The plurality of opinion existing in the Church meant of course that this 'two model' vision of society was not necessarily shared by all the bishops, priests and religious, still less by all Spanish Catholics.

As to the PSOE, its attitude to the Church can be glimpsed in an outline (four-page) assessment which featured in its 1989 'Programme 2000'.[7] It acknowledged the Church's neutrality, even if broken occasionally, during elections in the early transition period. It noted two tendencies current within the hierarchy, the pluralist democracy-accepting 'Taranconian' line, and a faithfully Vatican 'restorationist' line. However, a reference to 'an open Spanish Catholicism with socialist sympathies, liberation theology, and so forth', seemed to recognise that there were some bishops on the episcopal left. Other sections of 'Programme 2000' discussed tendencies among the laity. Just as within the Church, there were within the PSOE ranks different, sometimes overlapping, currents regarding the 'religion factor'. There were those that regarded the Church as a relevant institution (in either a positive or negative sense), those that thought it could be ignored, and those that saw it as an obstacle to Spain's development which should not be allowed to interfere with 'the monopoly of the civil power in the legal ordering of society',[8] since religion was a private matter and must be kept 'privatised'.[9] Clearly, the Spanish bishops regarded the policy of forced privatisation of religion as the one actually being implemented by the Socialist government.

It was a question of overall perception. For the Socialists, the constitution created an a-confessional State, where religion was a private matter, whereas the hierarchy considered that rather than a-confessionality the Socialists were operating a belligerent counter-confessionality (what Mgr Fernando Sebastián, Secretary to the CEE, called 'National Anti-Catholicism'), which ignored the fact that the majority of Spaniards were Catholics. The Church, it has been said, sometimes adopted the role of offended lady and the State that of disdainful knight, possibly because it thought there was no need for a specific policy towards the Church[10] which, in the government's view, was much of the time fighting a unilateral battle: 'the Church has difficulties with Socialist governments'.[11] Relations, never actually broken, remained correct rather than cordial, coloured as they were on the one hand by the PSOE's aim to speed up the laicisation of Spanish society as part of its modernisation project, and on the other by the Church's continuing bid – already clear in UCD times – to maintain its traditional social influence.

The media were a frequent source of indignation to the hierarchy, who protested against the diffuse amorality of some TV programmes and the government's failure to prevent the Catholic religion being ridiculed. Stage, cinema, and press came in for similar criticism. On the other hand, the PSOE was outraged when the radio chain COPE, in which the Church was a major shareholder, made virulent attacks on the government. There were various skirmishes over the PSOE's promotion of sex education and campaigns on contraception geared towards young people. Encouragement of the use of condoms, as much to cut the number of pregnancies among unmarried teenagers as to prevent the spread of sexually transmitted diseases like AIDS, was bitterly contested by the hierarchy and some lay groups.[12]

Announcing 'a hundred years of honesty', a slogan which was to haunt their last years in power, the Socialists had swung in on a platform of change, modernisation and moderation. They were successful in taking Spain into full membership of the European Community (EC) in 1986 (with concomitant economic advantages) and in raising Spain's international standing generally. To their credit in domestic issues stand the consolidation of democracy, including 'civil'-ising the military (a process begun under UCD), the significant extension of welfare in health and social services and the widening of educational opportunities. They won three general elections outright (1982, 1986 and 1989) but after the 1993 poll became dependent on the support of the conservative Christian Democrat Catalan coalition Convergència i Unió (CiU) for their parliamentary majority.

The economy, somewhat neglected under a UCD struggling with pressing political reforms, was modernised and, in line with international trends, alternated between periods of fast and slow growth. Between 1986 and 1991, it expanded more rapidly than that of any other EC member, which led to a spend–spend attitude among those fortunate enough to be part of the two-thirds of society with a secure job and a reasonable income. Easy money, laundered by tax-dodgers, was not infrequently channelled into corrupting public servants. Unemployment, deriving partly from international developments and exacerbated by the legacy of Spain's late industrialisation and the consequent need to pursue an industrial and financial restructuring programme, remained unacceptably high, though it fell sharply between 1985 and 1991. The PSOE failed to achieve a consensual relationship with the trade unions and did not even attempt to pursue joint policies with other left-wing forces.

The Socialists' economic strategy was far from 'socialist' in the sense of seeking to alter the existing socio-economic structures and to redistribute income and wealth in the direction of greater equity. Instead, it paralleled the ever more extreme free-market policies pursued elsewhere in the West. It was therefore not surprising that there was dissent from the trade unions and the left wing of the PSOE over the government's pragmatically 'realistic' approach to economic and social problems. Dissent culminated in two nationwide general strikes (1988 and 1994) against the progressive deregulation of the labour market, which weakened job protection and reduced severance payments for those made redundant. These measures had been taken on the assumption that they would promote greater job creation and lower unemployment, but they failed to do so. The effects of such policies aroused strong criticism right across a wide spectrum of the Spanish people, including the Catholic community. At the same time it was clear that, in the face of an increasingly globalised economy, dominated by triumphant political conservatism and economic liberalism, social democracy had reduced room for manoeuvre; arguably there remained, even so, some margin of discretion which could have been positively exploited.

In the late summer of 1995, the CiU withdrew its support. By then the government was in disarray, burnt out by the long years in office, the swing of the political pendulum was in operation, and disillusion was rife in the country, especially among the young. The political right, now called the Popular Party (PP), which had regrouped around José María Aznar (not tainted, as his predecessor Fraga Iribarne had been, with a Francoist past), was capturing part of the middle ground of politics seized by the PSOE in 1982. Political scandals – allegations of patronage, clientelism, and a 'dirty war' against ETA – threatened the credibility of the government and of Prime Minister Felipe González himself. The PSOE's display of arrogance and the smell of corruption were major factors in bringing the government down in the 1996 election.

Church–PSOE relations had got off to a difficult start. The first full year of the Socialists' mandate, 1983, was sometimes referred to as the 'year of the three wars of religion'. It began with a Bill decriminalising abortion, which was vigorously contested by the CEE itself and by Catholic pressure groups. Mgr Guerra Campos attempted to involve the King, claiming that in the last resort it was the monarch who sanctioned the law of the land.[13] The Popular Alliance, then still headed by Fraga Iribarne, opposed the Bill on the grounds that Article 15 of the Constitution ('Everyone has the right to life') proscribed abortion, and took it before the Constitutional Court. In April 1985 the Bill was declared unconstitutional because the safeguards it provided were inadequate. An amended version eventually passed into law later in the year, decriminalising abortion in the three circumstances specified in the earlier draft: rape, malformation of the foetus and grave danger to the life of the mother.

The next 'war' concerned a catechism of Christian doctrine for the fifth and sixth school grades, which the bishops issued without waiting for the required approval of the Ministry of Education. When the government refused its authorisation, the Church complained that it was a case of 'government intolerance which wanted to control even matters which were nothing to do with them'.[14] In the Ministry's view, the Church had published textbooks deemed to be pedagogically unsound, bearing in mind the age of the children who would be using the catechism, since abortion, terrorism and war were condemned as equally reprehensible in moral terms. In the end a compromise was reached when the Church agreed to add a separate explanatory sheet of 'pedagogical criteria' for the use of teachers.[15]

The third 'war' was also fought over education, on the introduction of the LODE (Organic Law for the Right to Education) which undertook to make education free even in private schools, by granting a 100 per cent subsidy, but with strings attached. The Church, which owned and ran some 90 per cent of private schools, protested. One of the main points at issue was the Catholic ethos (*ideario*) of Church schools, which the hierarchy felt might be undermined because its definition would be subject to ministerial authorisation, because the LODE also affirmed academic freedom, and because the disparate members of the governing body (*Consejo Escolar*) might put constraints on the way the school was run. While filibustering anti-LODE amendments, 4160 in all,[16] were tabled by the parliamentary opposition, various pressure groups of Catholic teachers and parents, particularly the Catholic Parents' Association (CONCAPA), and the Federation of Religious in Education (FERE) organised huge rallies against the Bill but, unlike their French counterparts attacking the '*loi Savary*' in 1984, they were unable to persuade any member of the hierarchy to take part.

Some of the bishops, like Mgr Yanes who headed the CEE Educational Commission, were hardline (*maximalistas*) in their demands; the more moderate (*esencialista*) line pursued by the majority, and by the Christian Schools of Catalonia, was reflected in a statement by Cardinal Jubany of Barcelona that a bad agreement was preferable to a good lawsuit.[17] Such a willingness to compromise was shared by the Catalan Minority Group in Parliament, which succeeded in negotiating with the Socialists a few substantive amendments to the original LODE.

The CEE's stance against PSOE legislation was bolstered by the appointment in July 1985 of a new papal nuncio, Mgr Mario Tagliaferri, fresh from eight years in Peru putting a straightjacket on liberation theology. Tagliaferri set about tilting the balance of the CEE even further towards conservatism. During his ten years at the Madrid nunciature, more than 60 bishops were appointed, and since the Pope's policy worldwide was to ensure that new episcopal appointees were loyally docile, the cumulative effect was one of a grey uniformity. A preponderance of Vaticanly-correct conservative elements in the hierarchy was thus set in place to govern Spain's dioceses for some time to come, with the more progressive bishops reduced to a minority and largely marginalised. Tagliaferri's appointment came just before an Extraordinary Synod in Rome to commemorate the close of the Vatican Council 20 years previously. Though lip-service was paid at the Synod to the spirit of Vatican II, its interpretation was 'corrected'. Emphasis on the prophetic voice of the Church, reading the signs of the times in terms of dialogue and sharing mankind's joys and sorrows, gave way to a more sacralised concept of the Church as 'mystery', the theology of liberation to the theology of the Cross, the concept of the Church as the 'people of God' to identification of the Church with the magisterium.

Tagliaferri was known to operate at times over the head of the CEE as a body, using a network of private informants in the different dioceses and sending detailed reports to Rome denouncing perceived deviations on the part of some theologians and members of the clergy or too relaxed an atmosphere in the seminaries. The decision of two bishops – Mgr Buxarrais of Málaga and Mgr Castellanos of Palencia – to resign well before retirement age, one to go as a missionary to Bolivia and the other to work among the poor in Ceuta, may well have been influenced by Tagliaferri's interfering and humiliating way of operating. Cardinal Tarancón, who had retired in 1983 and could therefore express his opinions more freely, was heard to say on one occasion that the Nuncio was behaving with the Church in Spain as if it were the Church of a banana republic.

Tarancón was succeeded as Archbishop of Madrid by Mgr Angel Suquía, who was elevated to the cardinalate in 1985 and was among the Pope's 20 personal nominees to the Rome Synod. Elected President of the CEE in 1987, Suquía, who strongly empathised with the Opus Dei and other conservative groups, showed during his two terms of office that he was very much in tune with the recommendations and activities of the Nuncio, just as Tarancón in his time had worked closely with Luigi Dadaglio, but from a different perspective. The appointment Suquía made in 1985 of three new auxiliary bishops to the Madrid diocese drew a critical letter from 300 priests, protesting that it was yet another signal of a move to the right.[18] Mgr Suquía, who said that he would like to be remembered as the Archbishop under whose mandate the Almudena cathedral in Madrid was completed, had his wish fulfilled and the satisfaction of seeing Pope John Paul consecrate the new cathedral during his fourth visit to Spain in 1993. Suquía remained in charge of the See of Madrid for three years after reaching the official retirement age of 75. It had not been so with Cardinal Tarancón whose resignation had been accepted by the Vatican with almost indecent haste in 1983.

With the introduction in 1990 of a new law, the LOGSE (Organic Law for the General Regulation of the Educational System) the education issue flared up again. The bishops claimed that the LOGSE contravened the 1979 Education and Cultural Matters Agreement with the Vatican, which declared that the teaching of the Catholic religion would be included at all levels and in all schools, in conditions on a par with those of other 'core' subjects. Such teaching was not obligatory for pupils but it had to be on offer and under UCD the alternative subject had been ethics, whereas none was envisaged in the LOGSE. The PSOE came to decree a series of different options, all of which threatened to downgrade the status of religion as a core subject. Cardinal Suquía urged Catholics to 'fight, to demand your fundamental rights even against the established power'[19] and the hierarchy appealed successfully to the Supreme Court.

The issue would continue to smoulder, unresolved, beyond the PSOE government's election defeat in March 1996. The communist-led United Left (IU) wanted religion taken out of schools and called for a revision of the 1979 accords.[20] Nor did all Catholics believe that the school was the appropriate place for instilling the Catholic faith. Some grass-roots Christian communities, for example, as well as representatives of the Christian Schools of Catalonia, maintained that, while schools should be free to offer religious education – as a cultural subject and not as indoctrination – the rightful place for transmitting the faith was within the community of believers.[21]

Mgr Suquía's presidency of the CEE marked a low-water mark in post-Franco Church–State relations. At the CEE Plenary Assembly of November 1990, he claimed that the Socialist government was guilty of abuse of power in attempting to impose an aggressively secular culture on society. Hard on the heels of his accusation came a pronouncement – the most hostile and catch-all of those made by the CEE during the PSOE years – denouncing the growing moral decadence of Spanish society. This long document, 'The Truth Shall Set You Free' (*La verdad os hará libres*) reminded the faithful of the ongoing validity of Catholic ethical and moral values, and painted an almost apocalyptic vision of a morally sick society, for which religion alone could provide the authentic cure. It lambasted legislation allowing abortion, the Socialists' 'cultural and moral dirigisme', influence peddling, fraud and other corrupt practices, and the displacement of valid ethical criteria 'by the dialectic of majorities and the force of votes'.[22] When the Spanish bishops began their *ad limina* visits to Rome in the following year, the Pope echoed their criticisms, ascribing the 'neopaganism' of Spanish society to a 'misunderstood progressiveness' which sought to identify the Church with 'rigid (*inmovilistas*) attitudes from the past'.[23]

The timing of Suquía's speech, of 'The Truth Shall Set You Free' and of the Pope's comments, is not without significance, coming as they did so soon after the fall of international communism. John Paul's constant call for a more pro-active Christian presence in society and culture and a return to the 'old certainties' of Christendom, with an emphasis on traditional 'Catholic values' particularly in marriage, sexual morality and religious education, accorded well with similar concepts associated with the American (mainly Protestant) 'moral majority' which during the 1980s had been making attempts to use Christianity as an indirect legitimiser of capitalism.[24] His third 'social' encyclical, on the triumph of capitalism after the fall of communism, was shortly to be published; in 1991 *Centesimus Annus* made it clear that the Catholic Church was not going to propose a 'third' socio-economic way, once seemingly under consideration, between capitalism and socialism. The technical and economic validity of the capitalist system was recognised, but would be given an ethical foundation:[25] the moral vacuum left by the collapse of the great left-wing dreams must be filled by a return to God, with the Church as His instrument.

Reactions to 'The Truth Shall Set You Free' were predictably varied. A (centre-right) Popular Party spokesman gave full support, declaring that it deserved to be the subject of meditation by society and all political forces. Among those who defended the right of the bishops to express their opinion freely about the state of Spanish society was the President of the Employers' Association. The PSOE response was that it contained 'anti-democratic elements', that it was 'harsh and unjust towards society' and that 'we cannot allow the Catholic Church to set itself up as the Court of public life'. The IU said that there was indeed evidence of corruption and abuse of power in some PSOE activities, but that the bishops had not issued such documents against the much worse corruption of Franco's time.[26]

Others, including some base-community Christians, objected to the recriminatory and authoritarian tone[27] of the bishops' document. They also pointed out that, whereas the diagnosis of the existence of evils, ranging from the idolatry of money to political corruption, was entirely accurate, it was not justifiable to put the whole blame on the PSOE. Neither was it true that the Church alone had the authentic remedy. The bishops were reminded that believers did not have a monopoly in defending humanistic values, since many non-believers also abhorred the competitiveness and emptiness of society[28] as it was being shaped by capitalism. In any case, said one agnostic Socialist activist, the claim made by the bishops that modernity's values of liberty, solidarity and equality could not survive without the support of the Church and a return to 'Christian roots' rang rather hollow in a Church whose pre-Vatican II record could hardly be said to have underpinned them.[29] Furthermore, the bishops were attempting to roll back the dialogue with modernity by pointing to an intra-ecclesial danger of Catholics absorbing, as they put it, 'points of view and thought patterns of secular culture', which 'breaks the unity of the personal conscience of Catholics and threatens the visible unity of the Church'. The autonomy of the individual conscience as proclaimed by Vatican II and emancipation from religious tutelage had receded.[30]

The hierarchy's sometimes heavy-handed endeavours to preserve the 'visible unity of the Church' continued to be brought to bear. Teachers and theologians who were not considered sufficiently docile vis-à-vis the magisterium or whose explorations of the faith were deemed suspect faced sanctions; Pedro Miguel Lamet was dismissed as editor of *Vida Nueva* in 1987, and Benjamín Forcano of *Misión Abierta* in 1988; in 1993 the Vatican vetoed the election of José Ramón Busto SJ as Rector of the Pontifical University of Comillas. Joan Bada was not permitted to become Dean of the Faculty of Theology of Barcelona, and Juan de Dios Martín Velasco was dismissed as Rector of the Madrid Seminary, both because of problems with their local archbishop. Seminarians were now attracted to studies of dogmatic rather than of pastoral theology, and were directed towards a spirituality with little or no social dimension. In 'pioneer versus settler' terms, the theological settlers were in the ascendant.

The hierarchy as a body tended to speak as if it represented the mind of the Church at all levels, disqualifying those who disagreed, whereas there were clearly differentiated voices and ways of operating within the ecclesial body. There was little room for the precept of the *'sensus fidelium'* (that of the whole people of God, set out in the Council's *Lumen Gentium*) to find expression. Division was inevitable and visible, given the differences between bishops of rural dioceses and bishops of urban dioceses, between bishops and theologians, between bishops and some religious orders, between the less 'pastoral' bishops and their grass-roots communities. A fresh symptom of dissatisfaction with the status quo and of desire for renewal was the setting-up in Spain in 1996 of the 'We are Church' movement which had spread from Austria across Europe and which looked towards a 'Church more in accordance with the gospel and with the signs of the times'.[31]

Since the CEE was divided and yet committed to giving the impression of unity, its documents were often clear only when they defended the Church's traditional vested interests or served as a stick to beat the PSOE. As the far-from-radical *Vida Nueva* pointed out, there was a need for a plurality of voices to be heard, for more prophetic, more adventurous, gospel-based opinions. The CEE lagged behind those in the vanguard – religious, theologians, committed lay people, grass-roots Christian communities.[32] In socio-economic matters, hard-hitting pronouncements were sometimes shunted off to one of its Commissions that did not have the full weight of the CEE imprimatur behind them. At the November 1993 Plenary Assembly, the CEE was due to centre its discussion on an important ninety-page document, 'Charity in the Life of the Church' (*La caridad en la vida de la Iglesia*) on organising services for the poor but also creating new social conditions, a See–Judge–Act document drawn up by groups working directly in the field. In the event, the significance of the 'Charity' document was largely overshadowed, for in his opening speech Mgr Yanes chose to lead on criticism of the government's intention to liberalise the abortion law.[33] Furthermore, the conservative members of the CEE did not wish to put their names to the first two parts of the document (analysis of the situation and theological reflection) because they did not share the underlying critique of capitalism,[34] and the CEE confined itself to issuing a press release on 'The Church in the Face of the Socio-economic Crisis' (*La Iglesia ante la crisis actual*) which was sound but said nothing new. The third part of the document, proposing what action should be taken, was published in a watered-down version in February 1994.

The analytical and reflective body of the text (the first two sections) was published the same month by the Social Pastoral Commission of the CEE (CEPS)[35] – not under the aegis of the CEE as a body – under the title 'The Church and the Poor' (*La Iglesia y los pobres*). This strongly worded document (in which, according to the CEPS President, Mgr Guix, 'one can even see Karl Marx's beard'),[36] attacked the injustice of the development model that increased the gap between rich and poor. It referred to Spain's two-thirds society, divided between the 'haves' and the 'new poor' – temporary workers, the unemployed and pensioners – as well as the marginalised homeless, alcoholics, prostitutes and drug addicts. It criticised the Socialist government's 'total free market' economic policy, although recognising that this was a consequence of the existing international economic order, and of Spain's wish to be in the first cohort to enter European Monetary Union, embracing economic laws that generated poverty and marginalisation. It blamed transnational corporations for encouraging insecure job and work patterns in order to reduce labour costs and put pressure on EU governments to deregulate the labour market in accordance with their profit criteria. During a press conference to present 'The Church and the Poor', Mgr Guix attributed responsibility for Spain's economic and social ills first to the government, and then to entrepreneurs and trade unionists. It was, in his view, very probable that the financial elites and the transnationals were aiming to supplant democratically elected governments in drawing up policies.[37]

Echoes of papal encyclicals emphasising the conceptual priority of labour over capital, and recognition, as a fact, of the globalisation of the economy informed pronouncements, both individual and collective, by the bishops. Mgr Echarren of the Canary Islands questioned whether deregulation of the labour market would actually create more jobs.[38] The Bishop of Jaén denounced the possible closure of the factory Suzuki-Santana in Linares for making the firm's social commitment to its workers dependent on profit as the decisive factor.[39] A little later, the CEPS, recalling *Centesimus Annus*, reminded entrepreneurs that investment was a moral duty especially when the minimum welfare of so many families was at stake, and asked them not to yield to the temptation to look for (cheaper) locations abroad.[40] The Bishop of Huesca, Mgr Osés, asked for 0.7 per cent of Spain's GDP to be given to aid the Third World.[41]

In November 1994, the bishops presented another statement, this time in the name of the CEE itself. Possibly for that reason, and because it was primarily concerned with the role of Catholic workers in the Church (*La pastoral obrera de toda la Iglesia*), its criticism of government policy was less searching than the CEPS' in-depth document 'The Church and the Poor'. Nevertheless, with resonances of *Labor Exercens*, it denounced the PSOE's recent labour reform package 'as incompatible with the dignity of the human person and with respect for human rights'. The economy, it affirmed, had to be at the service of people and society, work was more important than capital and what was needed was a culture of solidarity. The document was seen as vigorous support for Christian Workers' movements like HOAC and JOC. The HOAC President welcomed the document's explicit recognition of their work but, in a reference to the Catholic Action crisis of earlier years, he added 'We would have liked the document to come sooner. Many Christian activists left because they felt they were not given support [by the bishops]. At the present time no trade union is understandable without Christian activists and this fact is not very well known'.[42]

An editorial in the conservative Catalan newspaper *La Vanguardia* criticised the document as relating more to nineteenth-century England than to current economic realities in Spain;[43] *El País* denounced it as an interference in what was, in the final analysis, Parliament's business[44]. The Minister of Labour and Social Security asked why 'the Church' had kept silent about the situation of workers during the Franco period when the situation was worse. This of course raises the question of who is 'the Church' since it was the Church as HOAC and JOC activists that had been in at the birth of the left-wing clandestine trade union activity which worked against Francoism, while it was the Church as hierarchy that had not supported them.

Bishops were not alone in denouncing economic strategies over which 'the Catholic consciousness of the need for solidarity is going to come up against increasing and rampant neo-liberalism, and not merely in Spain'.[45] HOAC accused business and the government of introducing measures to reduce salary costs, deregulate the labour market and reduce social protection, placing the burden on the weakest while those with the greatest economic and political power and responsibility made few sacrifices.[46] *Cáritas*, the semi-independent charity arm of the Church, was equally trenchant in stating that recent measures, instead of creating jobs via reindustrialisation and social welfare, had harmed the most vulnerable social groups, and, in the name of the competitiveness demanded by economic convergence with Europe, restricted labour and social rights that had been hard won over many decades.[47] The John XXIII Association debated the subject of 'Marginalisation and Christianity' over five days at its XIV Congress in September 1994. This was attended by some two thousand people but with no Spanish bishop present.[48]

Mgr Tagliaferri's departure from Spain in 1995 was greeted with relief by a good number of bishops, who were disturbed by the stifling ecclesiastical atmosphere he had generated.[49] One of his last acts was to attend the Catalan Council, held in 1995, which had been set up to examine intra-ecclesial and Church–society relations in Catalonia, draw conclusions for evangelisation and explore greater interdiocesan co-ordination. The controversial issue of whether or not the Catalan Church should have its own Bishops' Conference, independent of the CEE – a matter first broached openly by Mgr Deig of Solsona in 1991 – was, after some intense debate, left in the hands of the Catalan bishops.[50] Tagliaferri's closing speech included an admonition to avoid 'exacerbated nationalisms' and to note that 'Catalan pastoral unity could not have a political, but only a strictly ecclesial meaning'.[51] Although his words were set in the context of the Pope's views on the generality of nationalisms, they were badly received in Catalonia's political and intellectual as well as ecclesiastical circles, since they implied a criticism of its very strong sense of sub-State national identity.

Tagliaferri's successor as Nuncio, Mgr Lajos Kada, also found himself in trouble in Catalonia. During a visit to the monastery of Montserrrat (the spiritual heartland of Catalan patriotism) Kada made a remark which caused consternation among the monks: 'Poor Aznar – how dearly he is paying for this pact with the nationalists'.[52] His comment was made against the background of the 1996 general election won by the Partido Popular but without an overall majority. José María Aznar's government (like that of the PSOE before him in 1993) needed the support of Catalan (CiU) nationalist deputies, and so was forced – in sharp contrast to its long-standing policies – to make concessions to Catalan autonomy. Ten Catalan intellectuals wrote to the Nuncio, reminding him that Catalonia was a nation and therefore to be treated in accordance with its 'differential factor'. They also reminded him of the mistake made during the last two dictatorships – of General Primo de Rivera and General Franco – of imposing non-native bishops, against ecclesial tradition and the will of the people, in pursuit of de-Catalanisation.

Perhaps conditioned by his Hungarian background and by the experience of the Hungarian minority in Slovakia, Mgr Kada did nothing diplomatic to hide his hostility towards what he perceived as the dangerous *catalanismo* of the Church in Catalonia.[53] His indignation knew no bounds when the parish bulletin of the dioceses of Vic, Tarragona and Solsona protested about attack on Catalans from both civil and ecclesiastical quarters, and charged Spanish (Castilian) speakers living in Catalonia to respect Catalan identity and to learn 'to speak and write – correctly – Catalan, the language proper to Catalonia'.[54] The bulletin was clearly supportive of a new language law which was being debated in the Catalan Parliament.

The issue of non-native bishops had also arisen in the Basque Country, that other strongly nationalist region, when Mgr Ricardo Blázquez became Bishop of Bilbao in 1993. His appointment was strongly criticised by nationalist groups, including the Basque Nationalist Party (PNV), and it was thought that his appointment might have been made to counterbalance the 'Basqueness' of Mgr José María Setién, of the neighbouring diocese of San Sebastián. However, a year later Mgr Blázquez's positive comments on the mediating role the Church might have in the event of negotiations between ETA and the Spanish government were welcomed by a PNV spokesman who declared that 'he is now more our Blázquez'.[55] Mgr Blázquez supported the stance of Mgr Setién who was frequently criticised for not condemning ETA with sufficient vehemence. In fact, he had not only constantly denounced ETA's barbarous terrorist activities, but also, when occasion demanded, the brutality of the security forces and the 'dirty war' that they waged against ETA. The offers made by the bishops of the Basque Country to mediate so as to bring about peace and reconciliation by dialogue were not always understood by the politicians and some of the media (especially the Right-wing daily *ABC*).

With abortion, education and corruption issues providing ammunition for Church attacks on the Socialists, the spasmodic skirmishes must have played a part in Felipe González's refusal to receive Mgr Suquía during the last four years of his CEE presidency: clearly the Prime Minister found the attitude of the Church under his mandate unacceptable. At a seminar in Moscow, González commented that, whereas in the early stages of the 'transition' the Catholic Church did not interfere in people's freedom of choice as to strictly political options, he 'would not be so sure that the situation today is the same'.[56] This view was echoed two days later by Cardinal Tarancón, who went on to refer to a 'climate of conflict' in which 'Let us not deceive ourselves, things have changed now, both here and in Rome'.[57]

In 1993, Mgr Suquía's term of office came to an end. In his final speech as CEE President he remained true to form, describing Spain as riddled with moral corruption and despairing of the possibility 'that one day the world may be a pleasant and merciful place'.[58] The bishop seen by many as the Nuncio's candidate to succeed him, Mgr Ricard Maria Carles of Barcelona, was defeated by Mgr Yanes of Zaragoza. Circumstances, it must be said, condition perceptions: in 1981, when Yanes was defeated by Mgr Díaz Merchán, he had been considered to be a hardline conservative, particularly on his own (education) patch; by 1993 he was called a 'liberal'. The new CEE President and a like-minded Vice-President (Mgr Fernando Sebastián) and Secretary (Mgr Sánchez) formed a troika whose atttitude promised to be more open and responsive. The change was not fundamental, but the accent was on a more media-friendly approach and especially on dialogue with the government. This had some tangible results, including an increase in the State's block grant to the Church, which, during Suquía's mandate, had remained frozen between 1990 and 1993.[59] The grant (approaching 19 billion pesetas in the mid-1990s) remains the major component of the total receipts of the Church, whose financial dependence on the State is likely to continue for the foreseeable future, even though the 1979 Agreement on Economic Matters envisaged eventual self-financing.

Since 1988 the composition of the block grant has been related to the wishes of taxpayers who can choose whether a fixed share of their payment (currently 0.5 per cent but the hierarchy has pressed for a higher proportion) is earmarked for the Church or for 'other social purposes'. In fact their choice does not affect the Church's actual income, since any shortfall in the amount it receives via income tax is then made up by the State. In addition, beneficiaries under the heading of 'other social purposes' include some Church-related groups. Tensions sometimes arose with the PSOE over their allocation of funds to *Cáritas*, because it did not mince words in criticising government economic and social policies when occasion demanded. At the end of the 1980s it issued a controversial report on the plight of eight million people living in poverty; it was also critical of legislation on immigration, housing policy, and what it saw as the inadequacy of pensions and government measures to reduce youth unemployment and to integrate gypsies into society.[60]

Mgr Yanes trod a careful path between fidelity to the Vatican and improving relations with the Socialist government. In November 1994 a misunderstanding arose when, on the occasion of the LXII Plenary Assembly, he told journalists in answer to the question 'Would you be in favour of limiting the mandates of public posts?'[61] that he would be pleased to see a change (*'A mí personalmente me agrada que haya un cambio'*). Indignant PSOE and gratified PP politicians as well as the media took the statement to refer to his wanting a change of government but Mgr Yanes explained later that it had been a reference to an ethical change and a change in political attitudes so as to combat corruption.[62] Referring to Mgr Yanes' preference for limiting mandates, Felipe González suggested that the Church should 'preach by example'[63] while Víctor Urrutia, the (Catholic) Director for Religious Affairs in the Ministry of Justice, commented that the Church had a serious difficulty in expressing its plurality as the process for choosing bishops was not democratic but monarchist. He was referring to the lack of consultation with priests and people over such appointments, and to the way the Church authorities tended to ignore any recommendations that were made.[64]

Church pronouncements about elections were almost inevitably coloured by the hierarchy's ongoing political agenda and by the stance of conservative bishops clearly favouring the right, together with the failings and shortcomings of the PSOE government, their long years in power, and the general climate of corruption which generated widespread disillusion and distrust. Before the country went to the polls in June 1993, the Church was widely expected to take sides officially, as the Catholic establishment did in Italy and Germany: the circumstances were such that it was difficult to be prophetic and yet remain non-partisan. However, before the election itself, the more moderate Mgr Yanes had replaced Suquía as CEE President, and the Standing Commission's pre-election guidelines for the Catholic conscience could be considered balanced, stating that 'We do not wish to disqualify anybody or support any specific party'.[65] Several members of the hierarchy nonetheless maintained that the Church had the right to recommend a particular political option.[66] The bishop of Mondoñedo-Ferrol, Mgr Gea, was unashamedly partisan; his pastoral letters[67] condemning the PSOE for decriminalising abortion, for quasi-dictatorial procedures and for responsibility for Spain's decadence once again reflected the views of the ultra-conservative wing of the Church.

The moderation of the Church's official stance seemed to have been somewhat dissipated by the time of the March 1996 general election. The bishops as a body felt it necessary to deny that they were campaigning for the centre-right PP. Mgr Yanes (recently re-elected as CEE President) was careful to say that they had kept to the rule they had followed ever since the advent of democracy of not specifying which party people should vote for.[68] However, the constant anti-abortion and anti-corruption pronouncements were seen, and not only by the PSOE, as blatant electioneering. The guidelines laid before the voters could be considered – depending on the perspective – an unbiased enumeration of criteria to enable the Catholic electorate to make an informed choice, or a line-up of factors that largely disqualified the PSOE and the IU, and thus tantamount to backing for the PP.

In the run-up to the polls came a document from the bishops of the South entitled 'By Their Fruits Shall You Know Them' (*Por sus frutos los conoceréis*),[69] another from the Standing Commission,[70] and, with the polls less than a month away, the CEE in a plenary session published 'Morality and Democratic Society' (*Moral y sociedad democrática*) which carried on from 'The Truth Shall Make You Free' which had aroused such controversy in 1990. Drawing on two recent papal encyclicals, the 1993 *Veritatis Splendor* and the 1995 *Evangelium Vitae*, the bishops commented on the consequences of freedom and of democracy 'when erroneously interpreted', and the breakdown of public confidence in some politicians. By now they had gone some cautious way – as they had done in 'The Truth Shall Set You Free' – towards accepting the possibility that a civil ethic could exist, but carefully hedged round its definition as being 'the recognition of some authentic common values which, rooted in man's truth, beyond mere... consensus and majority decisions, deserve the name of values and serve as a basis for harmonious living in justice and peace'.[71] Mgr Gea once again counselled Catholics to vote neither for the PSOE nor for IU, both of which favoured liberalising the abortion law.[72] The Bishop of Jérez de la Frontera told his people not to vote for Carmen Romero, Socialist MP and wife of the Prime Minister, because of her similar stance.[73]

Of course the PSOE had left itself wide open to criticism from civil society as well as from all levels of the Church, especially over the political scandals and what has been called a certain 'PSOEisation of the State'.[74] The hierarchy attempted to be what Cardinal Tarancón had some years earlier called 'the critical conscience in an unjust society denouncing injustices prophetically even though it might have to confront the powerful',[75] but the impact of their words was blunted insofar as they tended to impute to the Socialists in power much if not most of the responsibility for Spanish society's ills. Yet these ills were prevalent throughout the West, and were in no way less evident in countries governed by conservative, including Christian Democrat, parties. Also a (centre-right) PP government could hardly be expected to be more clearly committed than the PSOE to policies that would make socio-economic structures less unjust and reduce the glaring inequalities in Spanish society. Perhaps for these reasons the hierarchy's statements appeared not to make much impact on the Catholic electorate: 30 per cent of IU voters and 60 per cent of PSOE voters said they were Catholics, all practising to some extent; PP's share was 76 per cent. The number of practising Catholics voting PSOE was actually on the increase, the number voting PP declining.[76]

The Church's changing self-perception and its relationship with society over past decades have been described as a kind of drama in several acts: in the 1930s it saw itself as martyr and militant; in the 1940s and 1950s it was triumphalist, allied to earthly powers; the mid-fifties to the end of the sixties were years of disquiet following the Second Vatican Council, the 1970s years of moderate euphoria because the Church was a co-protagonist in the succesful introduction of democracy. In the 1980s it found itself largely reduced to the status of just another pressure group, having to adapt to laws which it only half supported or with which it disagreed altogether, with very limited influence on the political class and, above all, an increasingly tenuous influence on society generally.[77] In the 1990s it can be said to have manoeuvred between hostility towards the PSOE and the need to negotiate with it,[78] and subsequently, following the advent to power of the centre-right PP, to be expecting more favourable political treatment.

There was some speculation that the Opus Dei had been involved in an attempt to unite the forces of the political right, in a bid to reassert its own influence and to push for a strong conservative stand in the government on moral issues that would match that of the bishops. Such speculation came to the fore with the PP winning the 1996 general election but, as indicated above, without an overall majority. To obtain the support it needed from CiU deputies, the PP, which had been consistently hostile to what it saw as the excessive self-determination demands of the Catalans, had to undergo a Damascene conversion and to make far-reaching concessions. The pact between

PP and CiU was said to have been brokered by members of the Opus Dei.[79] In the event, although there were members and sympathisers of the Opus in the first PP administration, the government did not abolish the abortion law passed under the Socialists, nor did it rush to satisfy the bishops' demands over religious education. Even the appointment in May 1997 of a highly conservative *opusdeísta*, Jesús Cardenal, as the new State Attorney-General did not of itself presage a return to 'traditional values'. The fact was that 'Spain's conservatives have ceased to be religious crusaders'[80] and even if they were, that would not enable the Church to recapture let alone extend its moral constituency.

The many sociological surveys covering this period[81] confirmed a continuation of the slide into indifference – not necessarily towards any kind of religiosity, but towards institutionalised religion – that has been charted earlier. Mainstream Spanish Catholicism has been described as 'socially tenuous, culturally anodyne and religiously routine',[82] in line with that of much of the Western world. According to the Church's own statistics, although 90 per cent of Spaniards continued to be Catholic, only 30 per cent went to Mass relatively often, and about 40 per cent never or hardly ever, with the figure for young people even lower.[83] Between 1985 and 1995 there was a slight drop in the number of seminarians (from 2022 to 1917) which meant that there were not enough future priests to meet Spain's replacement needs.[84]

The reasons for the progressive 'de-catholicising' of Spaniards are, as has been seen, highly complex and their relative weight has shifted according to circumstance. In engaging with modernity and the plurality which characterised it, the Church found in Spain, as elsewhere in the Catholic world, that acceptance of plurality also affected its members, particularly since Vatican II had also sanctioned freedom for the individual conscience.

The post-conciliar Church found that its openness to the world did not provide an answer to dechristianisation, for modern man increasingly passed it by, and the modern Spaniard was no exception. By the end of the 1960s, a 'new' heresy had appeared. Postmodernity, seen by some to have been triggered by the upheavals of 1968, had started to underscore the general crisis of ideas in the West, with its questioning of authority in general and its absence of absolute points of reference. Postmodernity is fragmented, having none of the absolute scientific certainties entertained by earlier post-Enlightenment generations, and it does not create values of its own.

The enemy without – postmodern secularisation – and the enemy within – an increasingly disaffected and pluralised membership – threatened the relevance of the institutional Church as it then was and acted. For the Church could not be said to be effective if the 'actual effectiveness of a specific organisation is determined by the degree to which it realises its goals',[85] since it was not really achieving its goals of reaching and influencing people in spiritual and temporal affairs. Its effectiveness was largely confined to conserving an institutional presence in society. In the past, the Church had formed and developed its doctrines as an answer to heresy, but it could not pit its own 'superior' truth, ideology and teaching against a heresy that professed no truth, ideology or teaching.

Nor in this dilemma could allies and patrons be of assistance in the struggle to halt secularisation, if indeed any were still to be found. Pacts with the politically or socio-economically powerful have always been anti-evangelical and in recent times have also been shown to be ineffective, if not actually counterproductive. The 'power game' which the Church used to play in league with the dominant elites, and the attempt to invoke the old certainties and to raise the 'visibility' of Catholicism which Pope John Paul II demanded as part of an evangelisation crusade, had failed. If 'de-secularisation' and real evangelisation were to be achieved, it would have to be by another route, or other routes.

Such routes would lead the Church to make yet another appraisal – as it has done constantly – of how to carry out the twin imperative to love God and to love one's neighbour in the way that is most appropriate to the particular moment in history. Some fulfil this command in generous and unobtrusive service. To others fulfilment involves the equally generous but active service in commitment to social justice and striving after what one might call a 'three-thirds' society. Such commitment is a *sine qua non* of their faith and includes an awareness of the need to essay in the present time a fresh rapprochement with the secular left, much of which has still to be persuaded that Christianity – or religion in general – can make a positive contribution to society's values. In Spain, as in other countries, tentative moves are being made again on both sides. The common objective is to create a new model of society that is a credible alternative to the current ubiquitous forms of capitalism, which in our times are becoming increasingly both ultra-conservative politically and ultra-liberal economically, and which flourish at huge human and ecological cost.

There are no *a priori* answers, but surely eyes must remain turned towards Utopia,[86] in Christian terms the Kingdom of God, a new world to be built in the here and now. Participation in the task of building the Kingdom, in our times grounded on Vatican II's expression of the Church's self-understanding (*Lumen Gentium*) and dialogue with the modern world (*Gaudium et Spes*), is at heart of the Church's mission. In this context, fulfilment of Christ's two-fold command can be found to be at work in all manner of ordinary as well as extraordinary people and situations, since the Spirit, like the wind, 'bloweth where it listeth'. In order to feel and respond to the breath of the Spirit, perhaps it is time for the Church in Spain – and indeed worldwide – to be less 'institution' and more 'community of believers', the pilgrim, tatterdemalion, people of God struggling towards Vatican III, in prophetic witness, the 'leaven in the mass', working alongside others, in search and dialogue, service and solidarity.

Notes

INTRODUCTION

1. Díaz-Salazar and Giner, 1993, XIII.
2. Berger, 1969, 107.
3. Fitzgerald, 1988, 3.
4. *Vida Nueva*, No. 1.565, 1987, 194.
5. Easton, 1965, passim.
6. Ruiz Rico, 1977, passim.
7. A. Knoll, 'La acción católica y la acción de los católicos', in Daim et al., 1964, 81–113.

1 THE SPANISH CHURCH AND THE SECOND VATICAN COUNCIL

1. Enrique y Tarancón, 1996, 115.
2. After consultations with the Spanish government, the papal nuncio in Madrid sent the names of at least six bishops to the Vatican. The Pope returned the names of three, from which Franco made the final choice.
3. C. Martí, '*La Iglesia en la vida política*' in Belda et al., 1977, 155.
4. *Incunable* was less radical than *El Ciervo* but had a positive influence in broadening the outlook of the clergy. There was also *Abside,* published by a group of young priest-theologians. An even earlier progressive Catholic journal, *Cruz y Raya,* had been founded in the 1930s by the poet José Bergamín.
5. Laín Entralgo, 1989, 432.
6. See 'Sobre campo y fueros del magisterio de la Iglesia', in J. Iribarren (ed.), *Documentos colectivos del episcopado español 1870–1974,* BAC, Madrid, 1984, 283–4, and 'Sobre la misión de los intelectuales católicos', ibid., 286–91 (henceforth *Docs I*).
7. Cited in Muntanyola, 1974, 422.
8. Lannon, 1987, 212.
9. Cited in P. Castón Boyer, 'La religión en una sociedad secularizada', in *Pastoral Misionera,* No. 168, 1990, 48.
10. Cited in Díaz-Salazar, 1988, 48.
11. Cardinal Basil Hume, cited in *The Tablet,* 20 April 1991, 463.
12. 'Pope John ... saw the world in imminent danger of self-destruction. He saw a steady drift away from the Christian religion'. Moorman, 1967, 12.
13. Franco complained to his cousin that *Pacem in Terris* was being used as a weapon against the regime, distorting the pontiff's real meaning when he used the term 'freedom'. Franco Salgado-Araujo, 1976, 399, 404.

14. 'The Pastoral Constitution on the Church in the Modern World' (65), more commonly referred to as *'Gaudium et Spes'*, in Abbott, 1967, 273.
15. A. Comín, 'La evangelización de los pobres, conversión de la Iglesia', in *Iglesia Viva*, No. 5, 1966, 33–47. See also J. M. González Ruiz, 'Problemas del postconcilio', in *Cuadernos*, X, Special Issue, October 1968, 39–40.
16. Comín, 'La evangelización', 43, citing *Lettre*, Paris, December 1964.
17. 'Sobre el próximo concilio Vaticano II', February 1961, *Docs I*, 339–49.
18. 'Sobre la elevación de la conciencia social', 13 July 1962, *Docs I*, 349–58.
19. Ibid., 355.
20. E. Vilanova, 'Los "vota" de los obispos españoles', in *Revista Catalana de Teología*, XV/2, 1990, 389.
21. J. M. Laboa, 'Marco histórico y recepción del Concilio', in Laboa (ed.), 1988, 13.
22. Quoted in López Rodó, 1990, 573.
23. Franco Salgado-Araujo, 1976, 433.
24. Preston, 1993, 707.
25. O. González de Cardedal, 'La Iglesia española: desde 1940 a 1990', in *Ecclesia*, Nos. 2509–10, 1991, 33.
26. Cited in Tusell, 1993, 288. This was in 1962, before the Council declarations on religious freedom, and Carrero never changed his attitude. Ibid., 290. He did not believe that the Pope would sign them. Fraga Iribarne, 1980, 116.
27. Franco Salgado-Araujo, 1976, 405.
28. Rynne, Vol. I, 1968, 183.
29. 'Sobre libertad religiosa', 22 January 1968, *Docs I*, 417.
30. Cardinal Arriba y Castro, cited in F. Anderson (ed.), *Council Day Book*, 3 Vols., National Catholic Welfare Conference, Washington, 1965, Vol. II, 172. (henceforth *CD*).
31. Archbishop Segundo de Sierra y Méndez of Burgos, *CD III*, 89.
32. Cardinal Arriba y Castro, *CD III*, 89.
33. Mgr Antonio Pildaín, *CD II*, 222.
34. Rynne, Vol. IV, 1968, 100.
35. *CD III*, 94.
36. Blázquez, 1991, 155. Tierno Galván, 1981, 335–6.
37. Estruch, 1994, 347. Moncada, 1987, 27, claims that Montini refused the Opus permission to open a residence in Milan.
38. López Rodó, 1987, 41.
39. 'Sobre la acción en la etapa posconciliar', 8 December 1965, *Docs I*, 359–70.
40. *La Vanguardia*, 20 February 1993. Blázquez, 1991, 169.
41. See Joan Crexell, 1987, passim. Domínguez, 1985, 150–61.
42. Franco Salgado-Araujo, 1976, 472.
43. 'La Iglesia y el orden temporal a la luz del Concilio', 29 June 1966, *Docs I*, 370–403.
44. Ibid., 401.
45. *Cuadernos*, No. 37, 1966, 7–10.
46. *Cuadernos*, No. 66, 1966, 733.

47. *Docs I*, 384.
48. For a background analysis of the Catholic Action movements see F. Urbina, 'Reflexión histórico-teológica sobre los movimientos especializados de Acción Católica', in *Pastoral Misionera*, Nos. 3–4, 1972, 268–364.
49. C. Martí, 'La Iglesia en la vida política', in Belda et al., 1977, 159.
50. Tierno Galván, 1981, 357–8. M. Tuñón de Lara, 'La Iglesia y el movimiento obrero en España', in *El País*, 6 November 1982.
51. Romero, 1986, 201.
52. *Cuadernos*, No. 31, 1966, 2.
53. Domínguez, 1985, 213. See also D. Nicholl, 'Religious liberty in Spain: a survey to 1968', in *Iberian Studies*, Vol. 1 No. 1, Spring 1972, 4–14.
54. *Docs I*, 6 December 1966, 403.
55. 'Actualización del apostolado seglar en España', 4 March 1967, *Docs I*, 404–11.
56. Ibid., 406.
57. Interview with José María Arizmendi-Arrieta, founder of the Mondragón co-operatives, in *Palabra*, No. 65, 1971, 19.
58. Tuñón de Lara, 1968, 170.
59. Ibid., 172–3.
60. Dadaglio had previously been Nuncio in Venezuela. Franco noted suspiciously, 'Nuncios in Latin America usually meddle in politics. We ought to find out more about Mgr Dadaglio'. López Rodó, 1987, 48.
61. Mgr Antonio Montero, interviewed in *Ecclesia* special issue, Nos. 2509–10, 1991, 77.
62. Montini spoke in these terms to the Spanish Ambassador, Antonio Garrigues, who reported them to Franco.
63. J. M. Laboa, 'Pablo VI, el régimen político y la sociedad española' in *XX Siglos*, No. 20, 1994, 9.
64. Text of both letters in *Iglesia-Mundo*, Year 1, No. 1, April 1971.
65. Examples in Angulo Uribarri, 1972, passim, under various headings: The Church and the Poor, The Church and Political Social and Economic Reality, The Church and the Workers, and so forth.
66. *Ecclesia*, 2 November 1968, 1643.
67. Comín, 'La evangelización', 33–47.
68. R. Belda, 'Obstáculos a la penetración del Concilio en España', in *Iglesia Viva*, No. 5, 1966, 79–87.
69. *Cuadernos*, No. 2, 1963, 5.
70. *Vida Nueva*, Nos. 740–1, 1970, 1059.
71. Fundación FOESSA, 1970, 461–5. It was not fully comprehensive: because of censorship, Chapter 5, on politics, was not included.

2 AGGIORNAMENTO MA NON TROPPO

1. J. Tusell. 'El impacto del Concilio Vaticano II en la política y en la sociedad española', in Laboa (ed.), 1988, 379.

2. According to Antonio Garrigues, Spanish Ambassador to the Vatican. López Rodó, 1991, 398. See also Laboa, 'Pablo VI', 8.
3. Franco Salgado-Araujo, 1976, 538.
4. In 1970 Cirarda suspended the customary *Te Deum* commemorating the entry of Franco's troops into Bilbao.
5. Franco Salgado-Araujo, 1976, 539.
6. Mgr Díaz Merchán, then bishop of Guádix-Baza, told the Granada daily paper *Patria* that there was a diversity of opinions but denied that there was a division into integrists and progressives: any conservative element there might be was not enough to satisfy many Spanish Catholics whose clock had stopped at Trent, while any progressive element would not upset a cloistered nun. *Ecclesia*, 1 March 1969, 307.
7. *Cuadernos*, No. 66, March 1969, 31–3.
8. López Rodó stated that the Basque priests' involvement was well known ('*notoria*'); he recalled how Franco jested with his Minister of the Interior, General Vega, who pursued them relentlessly: 'Don't eat priests, Camilo – their flesh is indigestible'. López Rodó, 1987, 40.
9. Angulo Uribarri, 1972, 53–69.
10. *Ecclesia*, 5 July 1969, 919–20.
11. *The Times*, 24 October 1969.
12. *Ecclesia*, 16 May 1970, 676–7.
13. In Spain 1 May was celebrated by Church and regime as the feast of 'St Joseph the Worker' to undermine its usual socialist overtones.
14. *Informaciones*, 13 April 1971.
15. Text in *Ecclesia*, 1 August 1970.
16. *Vida Nueva*, No 766, 1971, 114.
17. *Vida Nueva*, No. 731, 1970, 747–52.
18. The text of the part of Pope Paul's speech referring to Spain is transcribed in *Cuadernos*, No. 69, June 1969, 10.
19. *Ecclesia*, 4 October 1969, 1345–7.
20. Fundación FOESSA, 1970, 465.
21. Gómez Pérez, 1976, 163.
22. López Rodó, 1977, 327.
23. The Matesa scandal involved financial irregularities in obtaining export credits.
24. Text in *Vida Nueva,* No. 706, 1969, I–VIII.
25. Martí, 'La Iglesia', 161.
26. Tarancón's words. Enrique y Tarancón, 1996, 263.
27. López Martínez, 1970. He was a member of the Opus Dei.
28. Lecture delivered in San Isidro Church, Madrid. *Ya*, 1 April 1971. Similar ideas were expressed by Franco's former minister, Manuel Fraga: 'The Spanish Church went into obvious crisis; and not only because of grave political events, but also because of the paucity and uncertainty of vocations, the hierarchy's loss of authority, [and] the growing desacralisation of sectors of social life, which automatically started to become politicised'. Fraga Iribarne, 1980, 236.
29. Blázquez, 1991, 194. To Franco, Spain's 'familiar demons' were a spirit of anarchy, negative criticism, divisions between men, extremism and mutual enmity.

30. J. Iribarren (ed.), *Documentos de la Conferencia Episcopal Española, 1965–1983*, BAC, Madrid, 1984, 281–4 (henceforth *Docs II*).
31. *Ecclesia*, 1 March 1969, 307.
32. The first comprehensive educational legislation in Spain since the 1857 *Ley Moyano*.
33. Over 90% of private schools were in Church hands.
34. 'Sobre la vida moral de nuestro pueblo', 18 June 1971, *Docs I*, 472–80.
35. Reprinted in *Ecclesia*, 18 October 1969, 1415–16.
36. *Ecclesia*, 31 October 1970, 2017.
37. Enrique y Tarancón, 1996, 290ff.
38. *The Economist*, 20 March 1971. J. M. Santiago Castelo, 'Concordato 1971', in *Avanzada*, No. 24, 1 March 1971.
39. *The Times*, 21 February 1971.
40. Enrique y Tarancón, 1996, 298.
41. Ibid., 320.
42. *El Ciervo*, February 1971, No. 204, 1.
43. 'La Iglesia y los pobres', 11 July 1970, *Docs I*, 455–63.
44. The key figures of the state holding company INI created to industrialise the country were army men. Moya, 1975, 111.
45. 'The financial oligarchy which controls private banking, industry and big business is another of the most influential sectors [the armed forces had already been mentioned] into which, at the beginning of these 1970s, there has been grafted a highly professionalised group of people who also belong to Opus Dei'. J. Cortezo, 'Los grupos sociales y políticos ante los años 70', *Cuadernos*, XVII Extraordinario, 1971, 18.
46. Moya, 1975, 173. See also Cortezo, 'Los grupos sociales', 18.
47. Romero, 1986, 207. Hélder Câmara was the Archbishop of Olinda-Recife, Brazil, famous for his statement: If I give food to the poor I am called a saint; if I ask why they are poor I am called a communist.
48. Interview with Alfonso Comín, *Cuadernos*, No. 75, 1969, 41.
49. *ABC*, 17 September 1970.
50. *Docs I*, 425.
51. Mgr Javier Osés, in *Ecclesia*, 4 July 1970, 947.

3 THE VICTORY OF THE 'EXTREME CENTRE'

1. Gómez Pérez, 1986, 279.
2. The expression was first used to describe the position adopted by Mgr Léon-Joseph Suenens of Belgium in the post-conciliar Church. See Hebblethwaite, 1993, 533. Mgr Ramón Echarren speaks of the temptation to take up a position of 'extreme centre' against the extreme right as well as the extreme left, a balanced attitude expressive of *in medio virtus*. 'Evolución del episcopado y clero españoles desde el Concilio hasta nuestros días', in Suquía Goicoechea et al., 1984, 61–75. J. M. Rovira Belloso uses this term in a related way to describe one set of interpretations of the Council (as against two other approaches, the

'traditionalist', which seeks to ignore it altogether, and the 'subjectively utopian', which goes beyond conciliar teaching) 'which look like common sense because they risk nothing, since they play with formulae or opportunism instead of scratching below the surface of words to see what the real problems and tendencies are'. 'Significación histórica del Vaticano II', in Floristán and Tamayo (eds), 1985, 36. Ruiz Rico, 1977, 262, refers to the 'centrist or reformist position' of the Spanish Church. See also Sáez Alba, 1974, LXXV.

3. The first to be held since the dissolution of the Junta of Metropolitan Bishops in the wake of the Council.
4. Martín Descalzo, 1982, 96.
5. Pope Paul said to Tarancón that 'This is a very difficult moment for the Spanish Church. You are going to be elected President of the Bishops' Conference... There will soon be important changes in Spain and for this moment of the transition I need a fully trustworthy man in Madrid'. Martín Descalzo, 1982, 99.
6. Membership claimed by its organ *Dios lo quiere*, *Criba*, 25 September 1971. By 1976, it was over 7000, according to its Secretary, Fr Venancio Marcos, in *Sábado Gráfico*, 18 September 1976.
7. For the whole background to the Joint Assembly, and the speeches, proposals and conclusions, see Secretariado Nacional del Clero, *Asamblea Conjunta obispos-sacerdotes*, BAC, Madrid, 1971 (henceforth *Asamblea Conjunta*).
8. J. A. Novais, 'Les Plans de Développement ont renforcé les inégalites sociales', *Le Monde*, 7 May 1971.
9. *Asamblea Conjunta*, 170–1. The resolution was then amended, and went to a second vote with a similar result: 123 in favour, 113 against and 10 blank papers.
10. *New York Times*, 17 September 1972.
11. Noted for his authoritative work on the persecution of the Spanish Church during the Civil War. Montero, 1961.
12. In conversation with the author.
13. In conversation with the author.
14. In conversation with the author.
15. *Asamblea Conjunta*, 688, 707.
16. For example, 'La Asamblea conjunta, un signo de los tiempos', Editorial, *Pastoral Misionera*, November–December 1971, 580–9. *Iglesia Viva* devoted a whole issue to the subject and its aftermath, 'La clave del proceso a la Asamblea conjunta', No. 38, March–April 1972. *Cuadernos*, October 1971, No. 97, 5, under an editorial headline 'A historic Assembly', said that it meant such a qualitative leap in the religious dimension that it could well be considered one of the key moments in the modern history of Spain. The January 1972 editorial (No. 100, 12) stated that it had 'changed the centre of gravity on which the Christian mission in Spain was based', from the 'vertex of the pyramid of power... to the popular base'.
17. *The Tablet*, 18 March 1972.
18. Martí, 'La Iglesia', 162.
19. Text in *Vida Nueva*, No. 811, 1971, 1712.

Notes

20. The original term used by the Joint Assembly was 'confirm', but it was watered down to 'assume' by the CEE following opposition from some of its members.
21. Blázquez, 1991, 201–3.
22. Vázquez et al., 1973, 364–70.
23. M. Walsh, 'Spain on the move', in *The Month*, June 1972, 167.
24. Reported in *The Times*, 30 October 1971.
25. Mgr Jubany, bishop of Girona, replaced Mgr González Martín in Barcelona; Mgr Méndez went from Tarazona to Pamplona, Mgr Añoveros from Cádiz to Bilbao, Mgr Del Val, auxiliary in Seville, to Santander, Mgr Cirarda from Santander to Córdoba. Mgr Peinado became bishop of Jaén, Mgr Gea and Mgr Pla auxiliaries in Valencia.
26. Chao Rego, 1976, 222.
27. *Vida Nueva*, No. 878, 1973, 537.
28. *The Times*, 1 May 1973.
29. *The Times*, 10 May 1973.
30. Cardinal Tarancón spoke of 'the first of May...when Blas Piñar's people invented "Tarancón to the firing squad"'. Rodríguez, 1991, 116.
31. For details of the bunker, its rivalry with the technocrats, and its sympathisers in Franco's family circle, see Preston, 1993, 748–60.
32. R. Matthews in *Financial Times*, 11 May 1973.
33. J. L. Aranguren, interviewed in *Criba*, 1 July 1972.
34. *Si quieres la paz trabaja por la justicia*. Typescript given to the author in 1974 by the then General Secretary.
35. *The Economist*, 25 December 1971. *Vida Nueva*, No. 813, 1972, 6–7, gives an extended summary and background to the controversy surrounding the document.
36. *Cuadernos*, in which it was published, was seized by the police.
37. Walsh, 'Spain on the move', 165.
38. *Vida Nueva*, No. 813, 1972, 7. *Nuevo Diario*, 20 August 1972, referred to the December 1971 appointments as 'a new gesture of tolerance on the part of the Spanish government towards the game played by Vatican diplomacy on the Spanish chess-board'. Cited in *Vida Nueva*, No. 846, 1972, 1458.
39. In conversation with the author.
40. M. Tuininga, 'La Grande Mutation de l'Eglise en Espagne', *Informations Catholiques Internationales*, 1 May 1972, 14–17.
41. Cited in *Vida Nueva*, Nos. 806–7, 1971, 1585. The Society of Jesus made this text the basis for a rethinking of its entire work at its 32nd General Congregation in 1975. P. Hebblethwaite, 'The popes and politics: shifting patterns in "Catholic social doctrine"', in *Daedalus*, Winter 1982, 91.
42. Editorial in *El Alcázar*, 22 December 1971, quoted in *Vida Nueva*, No. 813, 1976. *El Alcázar* reflected the views of the die-hard nationalist forces.
43. López Martínez, 1972, 42–3.
44. *Criba*, No. 81, 24 December 1971.
45. Cited in *Criba*, No. 83, 8 January 1972.
46. *Vida Nueva*, Nos. 824–5, 1972, 564, and No. 826, 1972, 575.

47. Alvaro del Portillo and Julián Herranza, according to Enrique y Tarancón, 1996, 512.
48. Enrique y Tarancón, 1996, 497. Walsh, 'Spain on the move', 163–75. Ruiz Rico, 1977, 223–4. Chao Rego, 1976, 219.
49. Martín Descalzo, 1982, 179–80. Enrique y Tarancón, 1996, 498.
50. He obtained 52 of the total of 76 votes.
51. *The Tablet*, 15 April 1972.
52. The retired bishop Mgr Luis Almarcha Hernández was also a nominee in the Cortes.
53. *Cuadernos*, editorial, No. 109, October 1972. He was appointed to the television slot by the Ministry of Information, not by the other members of the hierarchy. For a eulogy of Guerra Campos, see *¿Qué Pasa?*, No. 558, 7 September 1974.
54. Tarancón said that Franco 'was obsessed' by the issue. Martín Descalzo, 1982, 77. In a round-table discussion with the Spanish Ambassador to the Holy See, Antonio Garrigues, the economist Prados Arrarte, and the lay theologian Enrique Miret Magdalena, Joaquín Ruiz Giménez stated that, in the period prior to the original Concordat negotiations, he – at that time himself Ambassador to the Vatican – had put to Franco the need to renounce the privilege of being involved in the appointment of bishops. Franco replied that he was right, adding 'it would amount to the Holy See wanting to interfere in the appointment of my ministers'. Ruiz Giménez wondered what happened afterwards. 'I think that the Spanish hierarchy wanted to maintain the *status quo*, and furthermore that Pius XII did not at the time feel himself very much affected by the problem. Whatever the case, there is no certainty about the matter'. *Criba*, 24 November 1973, 6–7. See also *Vida Nueva*, No. 826, 1972, 576, for a less detailed version but ending with two unanswered questions from the journal: 'This was going on in 1951. What happened afterwards? How is it that after twenty-five years and with a Council somewhere in between what seemed so clear then is still so unclear?'
55. Gómez Pérez, 1986, 169, 171.
56. In 1969, following a Vatican suggestion, an attempt had been made by Cardinal Bueno y Monreal to change the rules, but it was defeated by 42 votes to 32 with 2 abstentions. By the beginning of 1971, the number of retired bishops was 22, more than 20 per cent of the total membership. See letter to *Vida Nueva*, No. 765, 1971, 75.
57. *Vida Nueva*, No. 810, 1971, 1675. At the time there were 18 retired and 17 auxiliary bishops.
58. *Vida Nueva*, No. 765, 1971, 78, cites an attack by the journal *Resurrexit*, and No. 770, 1971, 272, cites an editorial from the Opus-controlled *Nuevo Diario*, couched in similar terms.
59. Enrique y Tarancón, 1996, 528.
60. A. de la Hera, 'Iglesia y Estado en España, (1953–1974)', in Gallego et al., 1979, 365.
61. Ibid., 366.
62. Cited in *Vida Nueva*, No. 861, 1972, 2156. The Admiral's indignant comments were widely reported in the press. See Iribarren, 1992, 336–8.

Notes 149

They echoed an address given by Franco before the National Council of the Falange in November 1971, where he declared that the Church had regarded the Civil War as a Crusade and that those who now questioned this were endangering the peace of the nation. See also *The Tablet*, 13 November 1971.

63. J. M. Laboa, 'De la Asamblea Conjunta al Documento Iglesia Comunidad Política', in *XX Siglos*, No. 4, 1993, 83.
64. Tusell, 1993, 407–8.
65. Enrique y Tarancón, 1996, 576.
66. *Pueblo*, 8 December 1972.
67. Cited in *Criba*, 6 January 1973. The quotation comes from the CEE Conference of 29 June 1966.
68. *Vida Nueva*, No. 863, 1972, 2212.
69. *The Economist*, 30 December 1972.
70. *Vida Nueva*, No. 959, 1974, 2097.
71. 'Sobre la Iglesia y la comunidad política', 23 January 1973, *Docs II*, 245–79.
72. For the full background, including the document itself, secrecy, delays, other similar documents published in 1972, the different Church committees involved, the draft document's four times' change of name: Church–State Relations, Church–Political Community Relations, Church and Political Order, The Church and the Political Community, see *Vida Nueva*, Nos. 867–8, 1973, 65–112.
73. *Iglesia-Mundo* carried an attack on the unpublished draft on 20 December 1972. *Europa-Press* stated that the voting had been against nearly all the contents, whereas the oppposite was true. On 8 January, the final version of the text was sent to all bishops but also leaked to *Europa Press*. *Vida Nueva*, No. 866, 1973, 93.
74. Requiring a two-thirds majority in favour for acceptance, the document was passed by 59 votes to 20, with 4 abstentions.
75. Tarancón said in his opening address, referring to the divisions between the bishops: 'Something has to be done so that disunity in the Spanish Church is not institutionalised'. *Vida Nueva*, No. 860, 1972, 2073.
76. See *Vida Nueva*, No. 867–8, 1973, 22–9 for details of its difficult passage.
77. Alvarez Bolado, 1976, 17.
78. *Docs II*, 274–5.
79. José María Totosaus, 'Presencia de la Iglesia en el sector escolar', in Belda et al., 1977, 270.
80. *Docs II*, 276.
81. Totosaus, 'Presencia de la Iglesia', 271. He refers in a footnote to a similar document issued by religious education authorities in Barcelona in May 1974.
82. J. Ruiz Giménez, participating in Mesa Redonda – 'La Iglesia y la Comunidad Política', in *Cuadernos*, No. 113, February 1973, 80 (henceforth *Mesa Redonda*)
83. Alvarez Bolado, 1976, 17. J. Ruiz Giménez made a parallel point when he said that it looked like three, sometimes overlapping, documents. *Mesa Redonda*, 69.

84. Alvarez Bolado, 1976, 140–1.
85. V. Martínez Conde, *Mesa Redonda*, 75.
86. E. Nasarre, *Mesa Redonda*, 72. J. Ruiz Giménez, *Mesa Redonda*, 78, said that the Church was the only institution in Spain to have taken a real step towards social and political pluralism.
87. J. M. Gil-Robles, *Mesa Redonda*, 70. J. León, *Mesa Redonda*, 70. J. Ruiz Giménez, *Mesa Redonda*, 71.
88. Martí, 'La Iglesia en la vida política', 163.
89. *Octogesima Adveniens*, apostolic letter addressed to Cardinal Maurice Roy, international President of the Justice and Peace Commission, marking the eightieth anniversary of *Rerum Novarum*, in Walsh and Davies (eds), 1991.
90. Martí, 'La Iglesia en la vida política', 163.
91. Alvarez Bolado, 1976, 162–3. Full text (in Spanish) of the French bishops' document 'Para una práctica cristiana de la política. Política, Iglesia y fe' (30 October 1972), in Martín (ed.), 1975, 128–56.
92. J. Ruiz Giménez, *Mesa Redonda*, 71.
93. There were tax exemptions for churches, chapels and their annexes; residences of bishops, canons and parish priests, when the building was owned by the Church; buildings used by diocesan Curia and by parishes, Church universities, seminaries, schools and other education centres. A. Greco, *Criba*, 2 October 1971.
94. 'L'Eglise a décroché tous les wagons... sauf le wagon restaurant'. *Le Monde*, 3 May 1972. During a debate with J. Ruiz-Giménez and Ambassador Antonio Garrigues, E. Miret Magdalena said he thought that there would be a Concordat because the bishops feared that the 'State subsidies tap would be turned off'. *Criba*, 24 November 1973.
95. Alfredo Fierro suggested that 'revolution' could be in radical changes like the common ownership (*socialización*) of urban land, agrarian reform, the gradual replacement of military service by a civil service of national reconstruction and international co-operation, the abolition of bank secrecy, effective equality of opportunities for all in access to education at every level, freedom of expression in the press and TV, the control of the means of production neither by individuals nor the State, but by the community of producers. 'What is revolutionary does not consist of one isolated measure but in the methodical and rapid application of measures aimed at achieving a global change which will generate new relations in work, in public order and even friendship and love'. A. Fierro, 'De la conversión a la revolución', in *Cuadernos*, No. 95, August 1971, 36.
96. *Docs II*, 27 November 1972, 218–43.
97. See Alvarez Bolado, 1976, 137–71.
98. J. Guichard, 'La estrategia política de la Iglesia católica', in *Indice*, Nos. 350–1, 1 and 15 April 1974, 48–9.
99. A notable exception was the Catalan bishops' 'Paschal Mystery and Liberating Action', 1974. See Chapter 4.
100. Hebblethwaite, 1993, 594.

Notes 151

101. On the occasion of a Eucharistic Congress in Valencia in May 1972, Pope Paul stated that 'No argument, no ideal, no diversity can justify dividing ecclesial unity'. Text in *Vida Nueva*, No. 851, 1972, 977.
102. Casiano Floristán, Juan Llopis and Evangelista Vilanova.
103. Text in *Vida Nueva*, No. 827, 1972, 627–9.
104. Cited in *Mundo*, No. 1.681, 22 July 1972, 57.
105. Ibid. In the same address the Pope states in connection with his responsibilities: 'We wish therefore to be able, more than ever, to exercise the function which God conferred on Peter: you must confirm your brothers in the faith'.
106. 'Orientaciones pastorales sobre apostolado seglar', 27 November 1972, *Docs II*, 218–44.
107. Pope Paul lamented in a general audience on 11 September of the following year: 'Yes, the Church is in difficulties. So we find that even some of her sons have sworn love and fidelity and yet leave her; so we find that no small number of seminaries are almost empty, religious congregations which can scarcely find new members; and so we find faithful who are no longer afraid to be unfaithful... The list of these calamities which afflict the Church of God today, despite the Council, could go on, until we find that a vast number of these calamities do not assault the Church from outside, but afflict her, weaken her from inside'. *Ecclesia*, No. 1.709, 1974, 1487–8.
108. Ibid
109. Vázquez et al., 1973, 464–5.
110. See Tarancón's comments in *Vida Nueva*, No. 804, 1971, 1469.

4 PREPARING FOR A FUTURE WITHOUT FRANCO

1. A. Duato, 'Retos a la Iglesia española', in Floristán and Tamayo, 1985, 395. His quotation is from the editorial 'Afirmaciones para un tiempo de crisis', in *Iglesia Viva*, No. 109, 1984, 72.
2. Preston, 1986, 17.
3. Enrique y Tarancón, 1996, 538, 547.
4. Ibid., 548.
5. Ibid., 558–60.
6. Typescript documents supplied to the author.
7. *Vida Nueva*, No. 907, 1973, 1807.
8. These were base Church communities. After 1974 they tended to be known as the Popular Christian Communities (*Comunidades Cristianas Populares*-CCP).
9. Chao Rego, 1976, 230–1, says that Estepa let the police in. Tarancón, 1996, 564, speculates that the demonstrators themselves tipped off journalists and even the police.
10. Typescript documents supplied to the author.
11. Enrique y Tarancón, 1996, 606–14.
12. Rodríguez, 1991, 116–17.

152 Notes

13. J. M. Díez-Alegría, 'Espoirs et craintes de l'Eglise', in *Le Monde Diplomatique*, February 1974, 9.
14. *The Times*, 20 November 1973. Blázquez, 1991, 210.
15. Full text of Arias' speech in *ABC*, 13 February 1974.
16. Text of speech in *ABC*, 12 May 1974.
17. Alvarez Bolado, 1976, 11, 113, calls it 'neo-gallicanism', by which he means the attempt by the political establishment to manipulate and control the Church so that the Church itself chooses to be and do what is wanted by the political establishment, and co-operates in maintaining the social order.
18. Ibid., 13.
19. *Informaciones*, quoted in De las Heras and Villarín, 1975, 89.
20. López Rodó, 1993, 25.
21. *ABC*, 30 January 1974.
22. *Sunday Times*, 10 March 1974.
23. *El cristianismo mensaje de salvación para los pueblos*, Obispado de Bilbao. Read in the churches of the diocese on 24 February 1974.
24. In a letter of 28 January 1974, Ubieta indicated that it 'must be read in full'.
25. Lannon, 1987, 254–5.
26. *Financial Times*, 9 March 1974.
27. Martín Descalzo, 1982, 205.
28. Rodríguez, 1991, 116.
29. Martín Descalzo, 1982, 209. Enrique y Tarancón, 1996, 628.
30. Enrique y Tarancón, 1996, 627–701.
31. *The Times*, 11 March 1974.
32. Cited in *ABC*, 11 May 1974.
33. Rodríguez, 1991, 115.
34. Cited in *Vida Nueva*, No. 964, 1975, 6.
35. Areilza, 1977, 73.
36. J. M. García Escudero, 'Presencia de la Iglesia en la política', in Suquía Goicoecha et al., 1984, 244.
37. Hera, 'Iglesia y Estado' in Gallego et al., 1979, 364.
38. Martín Descalzo, 1982, 159.
39. Full text in *Vida Nueva*, No. 959, 1974.
40. Tarancón's expression is 'some historical events'. In recent months, right-wing activity had been particularly violent, with Blas Piñar avowing that 'the Civil War is not over'.
41. This did not prevent the creation of fledgling political parties of different persuasions.
42. The Civil Guard and other police bodies would attend Mass armed with tape-recorders.
43. *Vida Nueva*, No. 972, 1975, 360–2, lists some 110 fines for sermons over the preceding three years.
44. *Vida Nueva*, No. 983, 1975, 850; No. 991, 1975, 1231. Fr Félix Iraurgui, Fr. Tomín Arteche and others were also tortured and beaten by police during interrogation. N. Cooper, 'The Church: From Crusade to Christianity', in Preston, 1976, 80.
45. Chao Rego, 1976, 252.
46. Enrique y Tarancón, 1996, 157.

Notes 153

47. Enrique y Tarancón, 1996, 751–801. *Vida Nueva*, No. 974, 1974, 446–9.
48. *Vida Nueva*, No. 982, 1975, 806–9.
49. *Vida Nueva*, No. 992, 1975, 1251.
50. *The Tablet*, 31 May 1975.
51. So called because of the grey (*gris*) colour of their uniforms and the brutality of their methods.
52. *Vida Nueva*, No. 998, 1975, 1510–11.
53. Text in *Vida Nueva*, No. 999, 1975, 1553.
54. *The Times*, 29 September 1975.
55. *The Times*, 15 October 1975.
56. [Catalan Bishops], *Misterio pascual y acción liberadora*, 1974.
57. Ibid., 29 and 54, footnote 13 bis.
58. 'Actitudes cristianas ante la situación económica', *Docs II*, 322–32.
59. Text in special 16-page supplement, *Vida Nueva*, No. 949, 1974. Almost all of its authors were recognised as being on the progressive wing of the hierarchy. They were Mgr Díaz Merchán, Archbishop of Oviedo, Mgr Infantes Florido of the Canary Islands, Mgr Guix Ferreres, Auxiliary Bishop of Barcelona, Mgr Montero Moreno, Auxiliary Bishop of Seville, Mgr Osés Flamarique, Apostolic Administrator of Huesca, and Mgr Setién Alberto, Auxiliary Bishop of San Sebastián.
60. Alvarez Bolado, 1976, 64–6.
61. 'La reconciliación en la Iglesia y en la sociedad', 17 April 1975, *Docs II*, 342–63.
62. F. Miret Magdalena, interviewed in *Criba*, 10 October 1970.
63. *Boletín HOAC* (Extra) July–August, 1974, 33.
64. Ibid., 29.
65. Text in *Vida Nueva*, No. 959, 2091–7.
66. 'With a few exceptions the hierarchy remains tied to a centre – prudent, conciliar, but centre.' J. Llimonera, 'Cambios en la Iglesia española', in *Cuadernos*, Extraordinario No. XXXVIII, December 1973, 489.
67. In conversation with the author in September 1974, the then General-Secretary said 'The State is gunning for us. There are conversations between the Nuncio and Cortina about domesticating or suppressing us'.
68. The Justice and Peace Commission's connection with the hierarchy was via the bishops' Social Apostolate Commission; its declarations were a halfway house between official and pastoral pronouncements and private expressions of opinion.
69. To commemorate the tenth anniversary of *Pacem in Terris*, and in anticipation of the twenty-fifth anniversary of the UN Declaration of Human Rights, the Justice and Peace Commission organised in May 1973 a meeting which included an address by Professor Vittorino Verone, President of the Peace Commission of the Pontifical 'Justitia et Pax' Commission, in which he urged: 'Against the appropriation of the means of production by a minority and the unjust distribution of national income, the equal right of all to sufficient property, to a just participation in the goods produced and to a gradual socialisation of the means of production for the benefit of the common good'. *Paz y Derechos Humanos*, 1973, 28.

70. This was the personal opinion of Fr Rodríguez Ugarte in conversation with the author. The Commission President, Joaquín Ruíz Giménez, was in favour of 'democratic socialism' which was difficult to achieve because Spain started 'from a society which is capitalist in the economic field and autocratic in the political, so the change is a big one and too big for some. For that reason, those in power do not want to hear or talk about evolution... My attitude is socialist as regards the technique of radically changing collective structures'. *The Tablet*, 4 August 1973, 723. See also the interview with Ruiz Giménez in *Criba*, 8 January 1972.

71. An attempt was made to frustrate the amnesty petition by circulating a letter, on Justice and Peace notepaper, purporting to be a message from the Commission denying that they were organising an amnesty campaign. (Photocopies given to the author by Fr Ugarte.) Cardinal Tarancón was somewhat reluctant to deliver the amnesty petition though he did in the end agree; the bishops presented their own petition, which was confined to asking for 'clemency'. *Vida Nueva*, No. 969, 1975, 219–20; No. 970, 1975, 273.

72. *Vida Nueva*, No. 990, 1975, 1161.

73. See special report by Antonio Matabosch, 'Cristianos por el Socialismo', in *Vida Nueva*, No. 945, 1974, 1487–92; Chao Rego, 1976, 223–4.

74. According to Fr J. M. Díez-Alegría, writing in *Le Monde Diplomatique* in February 1974, Christians for Socialism wanted their political option to be accepted explicitly within the spectrum of political options that the official Church recognised as possible. He said that this would be a decisive step towards freeing the Spanish Church from past alliances that still compromised the validity of its evangelical witness.

75. See the condemnation of the marxist option for Christians by Mgr Infantes Florido, in response to the CpS 'Avila' document. Abbreviated text in *Vida Nueva*, No. 899, 1973, 1458–60.

76. Chao Rego, 1976, 224.

77. Mgr Iniesta, interviewed in *Posible*, No. 5, 1975, 21.

78. E. Mujal-León, 'The left and the Catholic Question in Spain', in *West European Politics*, Vol. 5, No. 2, April 1982, 45. The word 'curious' is in itself a criticism.

79. Tuñón de Lara, 1968, 163–4. Ruiz Rico, 1977, 169.

80. 'I am sympathetic towards the Yugoslav-style workers' ownership and control of enterprises co-operatively [*autogestión*]. A [kind of] socialism. Where labour is the owner of the enterprises and capital a tool of labour and not the other way round... I fear the triumph of capitalism, that it will win people over. The opulent society with feet of clay, as in North America. I fear capitalism will corrupt the people and make them accomplices of its system'. Interview in *Criba*, 11 July 1970. See also 'Charlie, Charlie', interview in *Arriba* (Sunday supplement), 11 April 1971.

81. 'The doctrine of the New Testament does not give us a socio-economic or juridico-political formula for organising the ownership of goods and in particular the means of production. But at the present stage of the evolution of history, the "socialist road" (leaving open all the problems

	which have to be left open) shows a possibility of organising the "human city" in a way which is not in contradiction with the great evangelical virtues...Capitalism (with all its chameleon-like 'neos') does not provide such a possibility'. J. M. Díez-Alegría, 1972, 103.
82.	Asked whether he would find a capitalist acceptable within the Church, he replied, 'I would lay down two conditions. First that he recognised that the capitalist structure in which he lives is in itself sinful and anti-evangelical, and that he should not attempt to adduce Christian motives to justify it. And second that he should in future adopt a suicidal attitude. I mean: that he should use the very means of the capitalist world to fight against that structure'. Interview in *Criba*, 19 May 1973.
83.	J. M. González Ruiz, '¿Seré yo otro?' in *Sábado Gráfico*, 16 April 1977.
84.	'Espiritualismo dualista, temporalismo, filomarxismo'. Address delivered 11 October 1974. Text in *Vida Nueva*, Nos. 954–5, 1974, 1892–3.
85.	E. Martínez Lozano, 'La Iglesia ante la evolución socioeconómica', in Belda et al., 1977, 198.
86.	A. Alvarez Bolado, 'Algunos procesos de crisis de fe', in *Iglesia Viva*, No. 37, 1972, 30.
87.	J. M. Díez-Alegría, 'Espoirs et craintes de l'Eglise'. Interview in *Criba*, 7 April 1973.
88.	De Miguel, 1976, 204–26, charts the secularisation process from the 1940s to the end of the Franco regime, including the decline in religious practice and belief and the drop in vocations to the priesthood.
89.	Cited in *Vida Nueva*, No. 910, 1973, 1945.
90.	*Vida Nueva*, No. 997, 1975, 1482–91.
91.	S. Lorente in ibid., 1485.
92.	Fernando Robles, 'Juventud española 75', special report in *Vida Nueva*, No. 990, 1975, 1174–83.
93.	J. L. Aranguren, 'Cambios culturales en la juventud con respecto a la religión', in Almerich et al., 1975, 165–78.
94.	*Vida Nueva*, No. 990, 1975, 1177–8.
95.	'Orientaciones sobre pastoral vocacional', 19 September 1974, *Docs II*, 321.
96.	'On the Church and the Political Community', 23 January 1973, *Docs II*, 257.
97.	'Creencias y vivencias de la mujer trabajadora', in *HOACF* (Encuentro Nacional Cuenca), July 1972, 1–11.
98.	See J. Dalmau, 'Problemas de fondo de la Iglesia católica', in *Cuadernos*, May 1972, 337–41.

5 THE CHURCH AND THE COMING OF DEMOCRACY

1. Ruiz Rico, 1977, 232.
2. *The Times*, 6 March 1976.
3. *Vida Nueva*, No. 1.009, 1975, 2090.
4. Ibid.

5. See *Vida Nueva*, No. 1.015, 1976, 189 and No. 1.018, 1976, 335.
6. *Vida Nueva*, No. 1.012, 1976, 52–3.
7. *Vida Nueva*, No. 1.018, 1976, 334.
8. *Vida Nueva*, No. 1.025, 1976, 698.
9. See *Vida Nueva*, No. 1.034, 12 June 1976, 1166. Text of the letter, 1171.
10. 'El momento del país', 27 November 1976, *Docs II*, 401–2.
11. Cited in *Vida Nueva*, No. 1.019, 1976, 390.
12. In one of his series of letters ('Cartas Cristianas') to the people of the Madrid diocese the Cardinal wrote (27 December 1976): 'In Spain... even those who are non-practising feel impelled by Christian sentiments almost without realizing it, by virtue of a centuries-old tradition'. Enrique y Tarancón, 1977, 116.
13. Joaquín Ortega, 'La España del posconcilio', in *Vida Nueva*, No. 1.000, 1975, 1657.
14. Martín Descalzo, 1982, 248. See also comments by Mgr Díaz Merchán, by then President of the Bishops' Conference. *Vida Nueva*, No. 1.317, 1982, 383–9.
15. J. Jiménez Lozano, 'Iglesia y democracia', in *Tiempo de Historia*, No. 72, 1980, 127.
16. 'Postura de la Hermandad Sacerdotal española en este instante de España', extract published in *Vida Nueva*, No. 1.017, 1976, 285–6. They would later call the Spanish bishops heretics and attack Paul VI for his political blindness in temporising with communism. *Vida Nueva*, No. 1.139, 1978, 1422.
17. Cited in *Vida Nueva*, No. 1.136, 1978, 1259–62.
18. Statement made at the First Meeting of Christian Communities of the Spanish State, Madrid 19–21 March 1976, quoted in *Vida Nueva*, No. 1.023, 1976, 10–13.
19. See Jiménez Lozano, 'Iglesia y democracia', 128–9.
20. G. Chiarante, 'From Pius XII to John Paul II', in Mulazzi Giammanco, 1989, 84. See also J. Fontecha Inyesto, 'El conservadurismo eclesial', in *Iglesia Viva*, Nos 134–5, 1988, 183.
21. Tarancón, opening address to the XXIII Plenary Assembly of the CEE, in *Vida Nueva*, Nos 1.009, 1975, 2095.
22. The majority of the issues listed are found in *'Christians and the Elections'* ('El cristiano ante las elecciones'), 7 May 1977, issued by the General Secretariat of the Episcopate, *Docs II*, 425–35. This document is largely a compilation of texts from previous CEE or papal pronouncements, including 'The Church and the Present Moment' ('La Iglesia ante el momento actual') *Docs II*, 19 December 1975, issued at the XXIII Plenary, which was based on a document prepared for the Standing Commission by Mgr Yanes, then Secretary to the CEE – see *Vida Nueva*, No. 1.010, 1975, 2136–7. Díaz Salazar, 1981, 316, considers the latter a key text for understanding the attitude of the hierarchy during the transition to democracy, because it sets out official attitudes to capitalism, socialism, Church–State relations, civil rights, and so on. See also 'Comunicado final: ante las próximas elecciones', 22 April 1977, *Docs II*, 407–8, and Cardinal Tarancón's pastoral letters on politics to the people of his Madrid diocese, especially 'La participa-

Notes 157

23. ción', and 'Partidos de inspiración cristiana' in Enrique y Tarancón, 1977, 95, 117.
24. Text in *Vida Nueva*, No. 1.007, 1975.
24. On the theocratic element, see Jiménez Lozano, 'Iglesia y democracia', 126. He likens the scene to that of Bishop Remi of Rheims instructing King Clovis in the fifth century.
25. Tarancón said shortly afterwards, at the XXIII Plenary Assembly of the CEE, that although he spoke strictly for himself, he knew that his words at the enthronement Mass 'would be interpreted as showing the attitude of the Church'. Cited in *Vida Nueva*, No. 1.009, 1975, 2093.
26. There was also a tendency to use the terms 'Catholic' and 'Christian' interchangeably, as if the non-Catholic Christian minorities did not exist.
27. Díaz-Salazar, 1981, 353.
28. Martín Descalzo, 1982, 303–22, quotes a wide spread of opinion from newspapers, journals and letters, both those in praise of the homily (the majority) and those either against or with reservations (right-wing Francoists and Catholic progressives, for obviously different reasons).
29. *Vida Nueva*, No. 1.009, 1975, 2092–7.
30. In a highly critical evaluation of Tarancón's address, Casimir Martí says the Cardinal gives the impression of trying to justify all the attitudes of the hierarchy however irreconcilable they may seem, and to imply – wrongly – the religious and political unanimity of Catholics forty years earlier. 'La Iglesia de Cataluña en el cambio de la sociedad', in *Iglesia Viva*, No. 61, 1976, 30–1.
31. *Vida Nueva*, No. 1.020, 1976, 440–1. The questionnaire was drawn up by five bishops: Díaz Merchán, Cirarda, González Moralejo, Montero and Setién.
32. There was a collective response from the ecclesiastical provinces of Andalusia (Granada and Seville) Tarragona and Oviedo. The number of individual respondents was small, according to *Vida Nueva*, No. 1.020, 1976, 441.
33. Equipo Común, 'La tercera vía o la cuadratura del círculo', *Posible*, No. 82, 5–11 August 1976, 26–8.
34. This criticism of CpS is summarised in *Vida Nueva*, No. 1.020, 1976, 441.
35. Rafael Alberdi, Rafael Belda, Olegario González de Cardedal, Juan Martín Velasco, Antonio Palenzuela, Fernando Sebastián, José María Setién, 'Afirmaciones para un tiempo de búsqueda', in *Iglesia Viva*, No. 62, March–April 1976, 177–88.
36. *Vida Nueva*, No. 1.034, 1976, 1169–70.
37. See 'Las tentaciones del neocapitalismo', *Ecclesia*, No. 1.816, 1976, 1694–5. *Vida Nueva*, No. 1.058, 1976, 2366.
38. See 'La Iglesia ante el momento actual', 19 December 1975, *Docs II*, 371–5.
39. Martín Descalzo, 1982, 248.
40. '¿Partidos políticos cristianos?', in Enrique y Tarancón, 1977, 114.
41. This is what he seems to hint at in his *Carta cristiana* of 12 December 1976. Enrique y Tarancón, 1977, 106–7.

42. 'Partidos de inspiración cristiana', in Enrique y Tarancón, 1977, 118–9.
43. Preston, 1987, 93.
44. J. M. González Ruiz, '¿La Iglesia "caballo de Troya" del centro?', in *El País*, 16 July 1977.
45. The '*Tácitos*' were a group of conservative Christian Democrats in the Franco administration who wrote articles in the early 1970s in favour of political reform, in the Catholic daily paper *Ya*, under the collective pseudonym *Tácito*. Some went on to join UCD.
46. Preston, 1987, 113–14.
47. Gunther et al., 1988, 111.
48. R. López Pintor, 'Francoist reformers in democratic Spain: the Popular Alliance and the Democratic Coalition', in Penniman and Mujal-León, 1985, 191.
49. Tarancón, cited in Martín Descalzo, 1982, 271.
50. Díaz-Salazar, 1988, 79.
51. Preston, 1987, 114.
52. Díaz-Salazar, 1988, 83.
53. 'The bishops feel the weariness of repeating what they have already said a thousand times', comments Mgr Iribarren in his introduction to the Standing Commission's 'Final Communiqué: on the forthcoming elections', 22 April 1977, *Docs II*, 407. Between 1976 and 1982, quite apart from directives included in other individual or collective statements, at least three specific documents on education and five on marriage and divorce were published either by the bishops in plenary session or by one of the various episcopal commissions.
54. Ibid., 403. Mgr Díaz Merchán, Tarancón's successor as CEE President, spoke in very similar terms in 1982: 'There are certain sectors of public opinion which are offended by everything the Church does. If the Church speaks, they are offended because it speaks. If the Church remains silent, then they are offended because it remains silent'. *Vida Nueva*, No. 1.317, 1982, 385.
55. Episcopal Commission for the Doctrine of the Faith, 'La estabilidad del matrimonio', 7 May 1977, *Docs II*, 408–21.
56. *Vida Nueva*, No. 1.082, 1977, 1052.
57. *Vida Nueva*, No. 1.109, 1977, 2453.
58. Declaration published in *Vida Nueva*, No. 1.087, 1977, 1314–15.
59. Text in *Vida Nueva*, No. 1.096, 1977, 1783–6.
60. *Vida Nueva*, No. 1.109, 1977, 2458–9.
61. *Vida Nueva*, No. 1.083, 1977, 1104.
62. Martín Descalzo, 1982, 257–8.
63. Interviewed in *Blanco y Negro*, 27 February 1980, 4–11.
64. CEE Standing Commission, 'Nota sobre la participación política', 2 February 1977, *Docs II*, 403–5.
65. They were Gabriel Urralburu and Lluis Maria Xirinachs as deputies to the Congress, Celso Montero and Martínez Fuertes to the Senate, three of them on the left and one on the right wing of UCD. *Vida Nueva*, No. 1.086, 1977, 1262.
66. Gunther et al., 1988, 110.
67. Card no. 14.747, according to *Vida Nueva*, No. 1.055, 1976, 2223.

Notes 159

68. *Vida Nueva*, No. 1.083, 1977, 1104.
69. Archbishop García de Sierra (Burgos) and Bishops Peralta (Vitoria) Granados (Palencia) and Cardenal (Osma-Soria).
70. *Vida Nueva*, No. 1.079, 1977, 896.
71. Ibid.
72. López Camps, 1989, 47.
73. Ibid, 50.
74. *Vida Nueva*, No. 1.085, 1977, 1209.
75. *Vida Nueva*, No. 1.079, 1977, 899.
76. *Vida Nueva*, No. 1.084, 1977, 1162–3.
77. *Vida Nueva*, No. 1.085, 1977, 1209.
78. Text in *Vida Nueva*, No. 1.081, 1977, 1007.
79. See interview with J. Ruiz Giménez, in *Vida Nueva*, No. 1.112, 1978, 39–42.
80. Preston, 1987, 110.
81. J. Bécarud, 'Eglise et politique dans l'après-franquisme (1975–1978)', in *Pouvoirs*, No. 8, 1978, 42.
82. Díaz-Salazar, 1981, 353–4. Calleja, 1988, 258.
83. A. Marzal, 'La Iglesia y las elecciones', in *El País*, 24 June 1977.
84. J. L. Aranguren, 'Suplantaciones políticas', in *El País*, 29 June 1977.
85. Address cited in *Vida Nueva*, No. 1.106, 1977, 2283.
86. Ibid., 2281.
87. Comment in *Vida Nueva*, No. 1.107, 1977, 2332.
88. Díaz Salazar, 1981, 363. Similarly, *Diario 16*, quoted in *Vida Nueva*, No. 1.107, 1977, 2333: 'The attitude expressed by Tarancón... implies a new confessionality which is more subtle than the traditional one, but no less effective'. See also *El País*, 8 July 1978. Mujal-León, 'The left and the Catholic question', 50.
89. 'Los valores morales y religiosos ante la Constitución', 26 November 1977, *Docs II*, 439–45.
90. Mgr Yanes spoke in similar vein at the Club Siglo XXI on 25 November. De la Cuadra and Gallego-Díaz, 1981, 75.
91. Iribarren, 'Episcopado y Conferencia Episcopal', 238–41. De la Cuadra and Gallego-Díaz, 1981, 75, speak of 'prior knowledge' or at least 'extraordinary intuition', adding that some clerics may have acted as consultants on particular issues affecting the Church and so would have been aware in any case of the content of the draft.
92. At the time there were 24 500 diocesan priests (both active and retired) and religious holding diocesan posts. *Informations Catholiques Internationales*, No. 522, 1978, 11. See also L. de Echeverría, 'La Iglesia española reorganiza su economía', in *Vida Nueva*, No. 1.289, 1981, 1529–40.
93. As this was his third and, according to the statutes, his last possible term, Tarancón needed to obtain two-thirds of the votes, which he did in the second round. He received 50, his closest rival, the highly conservative Primate of Toledo, Mgr González Martín, only 13; six years previously the Primate had received some 20 votes.
94. Bécarud, 'Eglise et politique', 44.
95. Gunther et al., 1988, 468, footnote 3.

160   *Notes*

96. The *opusdeísta* deputy for AP, López Rodó, had wanted the formulation to include the word 'majority' before 'religious beliefs'. López Rodó, 1993, 360.
97. *The Times*, 5 December 1977.
98. 'So subtle that it almost seems drawn up by an ecclesiastical hand'. Ramón Cotarelo, 'El sistema de partidos', in Tezanos et al., 1989, 366.
99. Mujal-León, 'The left and the Catholic question', 51, attributes this PCE attitude during the constitutional debate to their aim of defusing the Catholic issue and strengthening their own democratic credentials.
100. See López Rodó, 1993, 389–95, for the AP protest against the UCD–PSOE pact and the guillotine measure, and his proposed amendments to the articles on marriage and education, all favourable to the Church's interests.
101. The Cardinal Primate of Toledo, the Bishops of Cuenca, Burgos, Alicante, Tenerife, Ciudad Rodrigo, Sigüenza, Orense, and the Apostolic Administrator of Vitoria.
102. *Vida Nueva*, No. 1.157, 1978, 2428.
103. Text in *Vida Nueva*, No. 1.157, 1978, 2439–40.
104. Ibid., 2386.
105. See *Vida Nueva*, No. 1.157, 1978, 2427.
106. O. González de Cardedal, 'Teología en España 1965–1987', in Laboa (ed.), 1988, 71, footnote 5.
107. Preston, 1987, 161.
108. Mujal-León, 'The left and the Catholic question', 49.

6 LEARNING TO LIVE WITH REALITY

1. C. Floristán, 'La tensión unidad-pluralismo', in *Iglesia Viva*, No. 127, 1987, 7.
2. O. González de Cardedal, 'Iglesia y política en España', in González de Cardedal (ed.), 1980, 23–60.
3. 'John Paul II has clearly made it understood that, although tensions and difficulties persist, the postconciliar crisis ought to be considered surmounted. It is no longer a time of self-criticism, but of consolidation: the internal vigour of the Church ought to be strengthened so as to gain credibility in the eyes of the world'. Editorial, 'El papado en el momento presente', in *Iglesia Viva*, No. 83, 1979, 476.
4. The King had already renounced his *derecho de presentación* in 1976.
5. This became a bone of contention between Church and State in the 1980s and 1990s when the PSOE was in power.
6. J. M. Martín Patino, 'La Iglesia en la sociedad española', in Linz et al., Vol. 1, 1984, 173.
7. *El País*, 14 September 1979.
8. Ibid.
9. Gunther et al., 1988, 468, footnote 8.
10. 'La responsabilidad moral del voto', 8 February 1979, *Docs II*, 517–20.

Notes 161

11. 'Diversidad de los pueblos de España', in 'Valores morales y religiosos ante la Constitución', 26 November 1977, *Docs II*, 439–45.
12. For example, the bishops of Andalusia wrote in support of the autonomy process. *Vida Nueva*, No. 1.217, 1980, 2901. The bishops of Galicia asked for responsible participation in the regional referendum. *Vida Nueva*, No. 1.257, 1980, 4955.
13. 'Responsabilidad cívica y conciencia cristiana ante el referéndum sobre el estatuto de autonomía'. *Vida Nueva*, No. 1.196, 1979, 1832.
14. 'Reflexiones ante el referéndum sobre el Estatuto', *Vida Nueva*, No. 1.198, 1979, 1936.
15. Opinion cited in *Vida Nueva*, No. 1.204, 1979, 2251. This was not an isolated utterance. As he was leaving the presidency of the CEE, Tarancón made a similar, stronger, statement in an interview with *Diario 16*, 11 February 1981.
16. Reported in *Vida Nueva*, No. 1.204, 1979, 2299.
17. See *Vida Nueva*, No. 1.293, 1981, 1728.
18. Felipe González said of the Church in this period that 'lately there has been another regression. I do not know whether it is because of the education problem or because of a general problem of the Church'. Interview in *Blanco y Negro*, 27 February 1980, 11.
19. Lamet, 1995, 308.
20. Dadaglio left Madrid without being given a red hat, which was traditional for nuncios departing from Spain. He received it five years later.
21. *Vida Nueva*, No. 1.247, 1980, 4419.
22. Editorial in *Vida Nueva*, No. 1.202, 1979, 2143.
23. In 1984 a (Spanish) member of the Opus Dei, Joaquín Navarro Valls, was appointed to the influential position of Director of the Holy See's Press Office.
24. He was beatified in 1992.
25. Hernández, 1984, 40–1
26. Meliá, 1981, 31–2.
27. The ambiguous wording of the 1970 Education Act might be interpreted as discouraging private schools, and control of the ethos of a Church school might be put at risk under an unsympathetic government. See McNair, 1984, 144–5.
28. According to former UCD minister Emilio Attard, 1983, 124, debate on the 1980 Education Bill was one of the longest in the history of the Cortes, and filled over a thousand pages of the official parliamentary record (*Trabajos Parlamentarios*).
29. This is the interpretation of the Agreements by Urbano Valero, the Chancellor of the Pontifical University of Comillas. *Vida Nueva*, No. 1.212, 1980, 2628–9.
30. *El País*, 26 March 1980.
31. Attard, 1983, 230. He claims this information came from Miguel Herrero, the UCD spokesman. Fernández Ordóñez, 1982, 76, similarly quotes Herrero as saying the bishops had agreed it 'point by point and comma by comma'. Cavero, 1990, 418, speaks of 'the agreed and "authorised"' draft.
32. *El País*, 20 March 1981.

33. Chamorro, 1981, 29.
34. *Vida Nueva*, No. 1.272, 1981, 636.
35. *Vida Nueva*, No. 1.265, 1981, 271.
36. *El País*, 5 February 1981.
37. These were some of the views expressed at a meeting of several hundred Christians meeting in Madrid, including Fr Díez-Alegría and Enrique Miret Magdalena. *El País*, 19 October 1980.
38. *El País*, 25 January 1981. Fernández Ordóñez, 1982, 76, said Cardinal Felici had told him the number of Church annulments had increased by 5000 per cent in the previous ten years, that is since 1970–1. Apart from the accusation often made against ecclesiastical marriage tribunals that annulments could be bought and false evidence concocted, charges were being levied about this time that there was a trade in Zaire tribunals in false annulment documents for Spanish citizens. See *Vida Nueva*, No. 1.251, 1980, 4650–2.
39. *El País*, 5 Feburary 1981.
40. Chamorro, 1981, 299.
41. *Docs II*, 622.
42. Cavero, 1990, 418–19. See also Fernández Ordóñez, 1982, 79–80.
43. J. Iribarren, Introduction to *Docs II*, 36–7.
44. For comments on the bishops' silence and later statements, see Calleja, 1988, 118–19, footnote 266.
45. *El País*, 15 March 1981.
46. J. M. González Ruiz, '¿Políticos con escapularios?', in *El País*, 18 March 1981.
47. According to *Vida Nueva*'s review of 1981, Nos 1.308–9, 26 December 1981–2 January 1982, 2503.
48. Mgr Díaz Merchán received 34 votes, Mgr Yanes of Zaragoza 31, Mgr Delicado Baeza of Valladolid 4.
49. *Vida Nueva*, No. 1.268, 1981, 428.
50. *El País*, 15 March 1981.
51. 'Salvar la libertad para salvar la paz', in *Vida Nueva*, Nos. 1.273–4, 1981, 690–1.
52. Ibid. for comments by politicians and leading articles from the main Spanish daily papers, 687–9, 692–9.
53. 'Respetar la justicia y construir la paz', in *Vida Nueva*, No. 1.340, 1982, 1571–2.
54. Text in Walsh and Davies, 1991.
55. Editorial, *Vida Nueva*, No. 1.294, 1981, 1179.
56. Reported in *Vida Nueva*, No. 1.296, 1981, 1885.
57. *Vida Nueva*, No. 1.275, 1981, 784.
58. *Vida Nueva*, No. 1.300, 1981, 2093.
59. 'El grave problema del paro', 27 November 1981, *Docs II*, 659–65.
60. See *Vida Nueva*, No. 1.319, 1982, 492–3.
61. One of the best-known examples is the controversy sparked off by Enrique Ureña, 1981, countered by González Faus, 1983. Ureña attacked again in 1984.
62. Interviewed by Calzada, 1979, 60–1.
63. Calleja, 1988, 126.

Notes 163

64. *Vida Nueva*, No. 1.265, 1981, 276.
65. See *Informe FOESSA*, 1983, 582–3.
66. *Diario 16*, cited in *Vida Nueva*, No. 1.315, 1982, 273. *Vida Nueva*, No. 1.331, 1982, 1068.
67. 'Derechos humanos en el ámbito de la libertad religiosa', in *Vida Nueva*, No. 1.314, 1982, 231–4.
68. 'La conciencia cristiana ante las próximas elecciones', 23 September 1982, *Docs II*, 702–6.
69. *The Guardian*, 25 September 1982.
70. Martín Descalzo, 1982, 264–5.
71. Enrique y Tarancón, 'Perspectivas de la Iglesia en España', in Suquía Goicoechea et al., 1984, 301.
72. Set up in January 1982, its name is redolent of the hope within the Church for its future, which John XXIII inspired by his encyclicals and by summoning Vatican II.
73. *Vida Nueva*, No. 1.354, 1982, 2304–5.
74. Calleja, 1988, 147.
75. Pereda et al., 1983, 108.
76. Ibid. See also J. L. Aranguren, 'El postcristianismo', in *El País*, 18 October 1981. Alfredo Fierro, 'La religiosidad extraeclesiástica', whose main points are outlined in *Vida Nueva*, No. 1.298, 1981, 1992.
77. Díaz-Salazar, 1990, 291–7.
78. 'Discurso sobre las raíces cristianas de Europa'. Text in *El País*, 10 November 1982.
79. Ibid.
80. See J. Gomis, 'El viaje de Juan Pablo II a España', *El Ciervo*, No. 381, November 1982.
81. Fundación Friedrich Ebert, 1983, 8.
82. Orizo, 1983, 158.
83. Beltrán Villalba et al., 1984, 122 (table).
84. F. Urbina and J. Sánchez, 'Religion et société dans l'histoire de l'Espagne', in *Social Compass*, XXXIII/4, Louvain, 1986, 349.
85. See J. Martínez Cortés, 'La demanda social de enseñanza religiosa en la Escuela Pública ("Documento Gómez")', in *Sal Terrae*, March 1987, 219–28.
86. E. Miret Magdalena, 'Religión y juventud en España', in Ministerio de Cultura, Madrid, 1985, 98.

7 THE CHURCH AND THE PSOE GOVERNMENT

1. Mardones, 1991, 256.
2. PSOE, 1988, 138.
3. Hernández, 1995, 222.
4. 'La visita del Papa y la fe de nuestro pueblo', *Docs II*, 25 June 1983, 750.
5. A. Alvarez Bolado, 'La Iglesia en el Programa 2000', in *Iglesia Viva*, Nos. 140–1, 1989, 259.

6. J. López Camps, 'L'església catòlica, entre la necessitat i l'hostilitat', in *Correspondència Socialista*, No. 18, March–April 1993, 14–21.
7. PSOE, 1988, 135–9.
8. PSOE declaration on the Divorce Law, in *Ecclesia*, No. 2.018, 1981, 24.
9. Recio et al., 1990, 53. Alvarez Bolado, 'La Iglesia en el Programa 2000', 251–2. R. Díaz-Salazar, 'Sociología socialista de la Iglesia', in *Noticias Obreras*, No. 1.015, 1989, 2.
10. J. L. Ortega, 'Iglesia, estado y sociedad en el decenio socialista', in J. Rupérez and C. Moro (eds), 1992, 108–9.
11. Rosa Conde, PSOE spokesperson quoted in *ABC*, 14 December 1991.
12. J. Hooper in *The Guardian*, 21 December 1990.
13. *El País*, 27 February 1983.
14. J. M. Laboa, 'La religiosidad de los españoles', in Laboa et al., 1986, 86.
15. Hernández, 1995, 214.
16. Almost four times as many as had been lodged during the constitutional debates. *El País*, 11 February 1984.
17. *La Vanguardia*, 11 March 1994.
18. Text in *Vida Nueva*, No. 1.475, 1985, 708.
19. Homily reported in *El Independiente*, 31 December 1990.
20. *El País*, 1 March 1994.
21. *El País*, 16 April, 5 December 1990.
22. Conferencia Episcopal Española, 1990.
23. Text in Cárcel Ortí, 1991, 257–63.
24. J. M. Mardones, 'Cristianismo e izquierdas en España', in Fundación Friedrich Ebert, 1991, 6–7.
25. G. Girardi, interviewed in *El País*, 18 February 1993.
26. Opinions reported in *La Vanguardia*, 24 November 1990.
27. Mgr Ioan Martí Alanis, President of the Episcopal Commission for the Media, said that he agreed 'with the lyrics but not the tune' of the document. He went on to say that the main cause of 'demoralisation' stemmed from the influence of the culture imported from the United States rather than from the action of the Socialist government. *El País*, 30 November 1990.
28. J. Lorés in *La Vanguardia*, 22 November 1990. Editorial, *El País*, 24 November 1990. C. Martí in *La Vanguardia*, 3 December 1990.
29. A. García Santesmases, 'La izquierda española ante el Cristianismo de izquierda', in Fundación Friedrich Ebert, 1991, 75–89.
30. Ibid.
31. *Vida Nueva*, No. 2.046, 1996, 12–13.
32. Editorial in *Vida Nueva*, No. 1.934, 1994, 5.
33. *Vida Nueva*, No. 1.922, 1993, 12–14.
34. P. M. Lamet, 'La Iglesia en el corazón de la crisis' in *Iglesia Viva*, No. 168, 1993, 565; 'El primer año de Monseñor Yanes', in *Iglesia Viva*, No. 169, 1994, 84–5.
35. Mgr Guix explained that CEPS could be 'a litttle more daring than the Plenary'. *Vida Nueva*, No. 1.933, 1994, 12.
36. *El País*, 22 February 1994.

Notes 165

37. Summary of text in *Vida Nueva*, No. 1.934, 1994, 23–30. *El País*, 22 February 1994.
38. *El País*, 23 January 1994.
39. *Vida Nueva*, No. 1.935, 1994, 6.
40. *El País*, 29 May 1994.
41. *ABC*, 21 September 1994.
42. *Vida Nueva*, No. 1.970, 1994, 13.
43. *La Vanguardia*, 21 November 1994.
44. *El País*, 19 November 1994.
45. A. Alvarez Bolado, 'Aprender de los muertos', in *El País*, 11 April 1991.
46. *El País*, 23 January 1994.
47. Ibid.
48. *El País*, 21 September 1994. Present at the Congress were the progressive bishops Samuel Ruiz of Chiapas (Mexico) and Pedro Casaldáliga of São Félix do Araguaia (Brazil).
49. Tagliaferri's move was to France where his attitude was much more moderate. His conduct in Spain may have been influenced by the fact that the majority of the Spanish bishops already had what Tarancón called a crick in the neck (*tortícolis*) from over-zealously keeping their faces turned towards Rome.
50. Mgr Yanes (when CEE President) thought that the idea of a separate Catalan Bishops' Conference lacked a 'pastoral basis' and could only be motivated by 'political symbolism'. *La Vanguardia*, 12 September 1994.
51. *La Vanguardia*, 23 June 1995.
52. *La Vanguardia*, 11 May 1996.
53. 'El nuncio exacerbado', *El Periódico*, 11 May 1997. See also *Vida Nueva*, No. 2.085, 1997, 13, for other comments by Mgr Kada.
54. Full Parroquial, 'No prendràs el nom de Déu en va', 20 April 1997.
55. *Ecclesia*, No. 2.813, 2 November 1996, 1618.
56. *La Vanguardia*, 9 July 1991.
57. *El País*, 10 July 1991.
58. *La Vanguardia*, 16 February 1993.
59. *El País*, 21 October 1993.
60. S. Giner and S. Sarasa, 'Religión y modernidad en España', in Díaz-Salazar and Giner (eds), 1993, 70.
61. *El País*, 20 November 1994.
62. *El País*, 16, 18 November 1994.
63. *La Vanguardia*, 20 November 1994.
64. *El País*, 20 November 1994.
65. 'Votar como un pueblo responsable de su futuro', *Vida Nueva*, No. 1.892, 1993, 18–19.
66. *ABC,* 12 January 1993.
67. 'Iglesia, Gobierno y elecciones', 'El hombre, especie no protegido' and 'Todavía estamos a tiempo'.
68. *Vida Nueva*, No. 2.029, 1996, 10.
69. *Ecclesia*, No. 2.772, 1996, 61.
70. *Vida Nueva*, No. 2.026, 1996, 14–15.

71. *Vida Nueva*, No. 2.030, 1996, 12–13.
72. *Vida Nueva*, No. 2.025, 1996, 12–13.
73. A. Gooch, in *The Guardian*, 22 February 1996.
74. Alvarez Bolado, 'La Iglesia en el Programa 2000', 261.
75. 'Búsqueda de nuevos modos de estar y de actuar en la sociedad española', in *XX Siglos*, No. 8, 1991, 71.
76. Extrapolated from J. R. Montero, 'Las dimensiones de la secularización' in Díaz-Salazar and Giner (eds), 1993, 238–9.
77. Pérez Díaz, 1993, 161–2.
78. López Camps, 'L'església católica', 14.
79. J. Ynfante, 'Resurrección del Opus Dei', in *Le Monde Diplomatique* (Spanish edition), Year 1, No. 9, 1996, 4–5. Martínez Reverte, 'El Opus milita en el Partido Popular', cited in Vázquez Montalbán, 1996, 203–5.
80. T. Burns, in *The Tablet*, 27 July 1996.
81. Examples are: González Blasco and González-Anleo, 1992. Tornos and Aparicio, 1995. Orizo, 1996.
82. J. L. Ortega, in J. Rupérez and C. Moro (eds), 1992, 123.
83. OESI, 1995, 180.
84. *Vida Nueva*, No. 2.034, 1996, 12.
85. Etzioni, 1964, 8.
86. For examples from both the Christian and the secular left, see R. Díaz-Salazar, 'Las masas y la religión. ¿Requiem o realimentación del nacionalcatolicismo?', in *Sal Terrae*, Vol. 70, No. 84, November 1982, 793–807. F. J. Vitoria Cormenzana, 'Cristianismo y socialismo en el horizonte 2000' (267–81) and J. García Roca, 'Laicidad y factor religioso en el Programa 2000' (219–30), in *Iglesia Viva*, Nos. 140–1, 1989. R. Obiols, 'Socialismo y mundo cristiano', in *La Vanguardia*, 26 November 1990. *Qüestions de Vida Cristiana*, No. 172, 1994, passim. *Pastoral Misionera*, No. 193–4, 1994, passim. J. López Camps, 'Diálogos para un amigo neoliberal', in Rojo et al., 1993, 113–47, and *Cristianismo y socialismo: un diálogo a retomar* (April 1994), lecture manuscript given to the author. Fundación Friedrich Ebert, 1991, passim. Riera et al., 1996, passim. *Iglesia Viva*, No. 187, 1997, passim.

Bibliography

I PRIMARY SOURCES

(a) Church-Related Material

(Various unpublished documents are referred to in the notes.)
Abbott, Walter M., SJ (ed.), *The Documents of Vatican II*, Geoffrey Chapman, London, 1967.
Angulo Uribarri, Javier, *Documentos socio-políticos de obispos españoles (1968–1972)*, PPC, Madrid, 1972.
Añoveros, Antonio, *Pastorales*, Taurus, Madrid, 1970.
Batllori, M. and Arbeloa, V. M. (eds), *Arxiu Vidal y Barraquer, Església i estat durant la segona república espanyola 1931–1936*, 3 vols., Monestir de Montserrat, 1971–7.
Bernárdez Cantón, A., *Legislación eclesiástica del Estado*, Tecnos, Madrid, 1965.
Carvajal, José G. M. de and Corral, Carlos (eds), *Iglesia y Estado en España: régimen jurídico de sus relaciones*, Rioduero, Madrid, 1980.
[Catalan Bishops], *Misterio pascual y acción liberadora*, PPC, Madrid, 1974.
Comisión Episcopal de Apostolado Social, *Declaración Pastoral sobre el Plan de Apostolado Social y el Orden Económico*, Madrid, 1965.
Comisión 'Justitia et Pax', *Paz y derechos humanos*, PPC, Madrid, 1973.
Comisión 'Justitia et Pax', *Todo hombre es mi hermano*, PPC, Madrid, 1971.
Conferencia Episcopal Española, *La verdad os hará libres*, PPC, Madrid, 1990.
Corral, Carlos and Echeverría, Lamberto de (eds), *Los acuerdos entre la Iglesia y España*, BAC, Madrid, 1980.
Enrique y Tarancón, Vicente, *Los cristianos y la política: cartas cristianas del Cardenal Tarancón*, Editorial del Arzobispado de Madrid Alcalá, Madrid, 1977.
Fitzgerald, Garret, *Christianity and Contemporary Political Theory*, Maurice Bennington Centenary Lecture, Lambeth Palace, Lancaster University, 19 May 1988.
Gomá y Tomás, Isidro, *Por Dios y por España 1936–1939*, Balmes, Barcelona, 1940.
Guerra Campos, José (ed.), *Crisis y conflicto en la Acción Católica Española y otros órganos nacionales de apostolado seglar desde 1964*, Ediciones Adue, Madrid, 1989.
Iribarren, Jesús (ed.), *Documentos colectivos del episcopado español 1870–1974*, BAC, Madrid, 1974.
Iribarren, Jesús (ed.), *Documentos de la Conferencia Episcopal Española 1965–1983*, BAC, Madrid, 1984.
John XXIII, Pope, *New Light on Social Problems*, Catholic Truth Society, London, 1961.

John XXIII, Pope, *Peace on Earth*, Catholic Truth Society, London, 1963.
López Camps, Jordi (ed.), *Diálogo 14–15, 17 años de compromiso a través de 38 documentos*, Secretariado Cristianos por el Socialismo, Barcelona, 1989.
Martín, Isidoro (ed.), *Concordato de 1953 entre España y la Santa Sede (textos y documentos anejos)*, Facultad de Derecho, Madrid University, 1961.
Martín, Isidoro, *La revisión del Concordato de 1953 en la perspectiva del episcopado español*, Fundación Universitaria Española, Madrid, 1974.
Martín, Isidoro (ed.), *La Iglesia y la comunidad política: documentos colectivos de los episcopados católicos de todo el mundo 1965–1975*, BAC, Madrid, 1975.
Ministerio de Justicia, *Ley de regulación del ejercicio del derecho civil a la libertad religiosa*, Madrid, 1967.
Ministerio de Justicia, *Resoluciones sobre reconocimiento legal de asociaciones confesionales no católicas*, Madrid, 1970.
OESI (Oficina de Estadística y Sociología de la Iglesia), *Estadísticas de la Iglesia Católica en España 1995*, Madrid, 1995.
Secretariado Nacional del Clero, *Asamblea Conjunta obispos-sacerdotes*, BAC, Madrid, 1971.
Walsh, Michael and Davis, Brian (eds), *Proclaiming Justice and Peace: One Hundred Years of Catholic Social Teaching*, CAFOD/Collins, London, 1991.
Pastoral letters in diocesan bulletins or as published in *Ecclesia* and *Vida Nueva*.

(b) Memoirs and speeches

Areilza, José María, *Diario de un ministro de la monarquía*, Planeta, Barcelona, 1977.
Areilza, José María, *Crónica de libertad*, Planeta, Barcelona, 1985.
Díez-Alegría, José María, *¡Yo creo en la esperanza...!*, Desclée de Brouwer, Bilbao, 1972.
Enrique y Tarancón, Vicente, *Recuerdos de juventud*, Grijalbo, Barcelona, 1984.
Enrique y Tarancón, Vicente, *Confesiones*, PPC, Madrid, 1996.
Fernández Ordóñez, Francisco, *Palabras en libertad*, Argos Vergara, Barcelona, 1982.
Fraga Iribarne, Manuel, *Memoria breve de una vida pública*, Espejo de España, Barcelona, 1980.
Franco, Francisco, *Discursos y mensajes del Jefe del Estado 1964–1967*, Publicaciones Españolas, Madrid, 1968.
Franco Salgado-Araujo, Francisco, *Mis conversaciones privadas con Franco*, Planeta, Barcelona, 1976.
Iribarren, Jesús, *Papeles y memorias*, BAC, Madrid, 1992.
Laín Entralgo, Pedro, *Descargo de conciencia (1930–1960)*, Alianza, Madrid, 1989.
López Martínez, Alfredo, *Iglesia y Estado*, Ilustre Colegio de abogados de Valencia, Valencia, 1970.

López Rodó, Laureano, *La larga marcha hacia la monarquía*, Noguer, Barcelona, 1977.
López Rodó, Laureano, *Testimonio de una política de Estado*, Espejo de España, Planeta, Barcelona, 1987.
López Rodó, Laureano, *Memorias*, Plaza y Janés, Esplugues de Llobregat, 1990.
López Rodó, Laureano, *Memorias: años decisivos*, Plaza y Janés, Esplugues de Llobregat, 1991.
López Rodó, Laureano, *Claves de la transición, Memorias IV*, Plaza y Janés, Barcelona, 1993.
Romero, Emilio, *Papeles Reservados II*, Plaza y Janés, Esplugues de Llobregat, 1986.
Tierno Galván, Enrique, *Cabos sueltos*, Bruguera, Barcelona, 1981.

II SECONDARY SOURCES

Aguirre, Jesús, et al., *Cristianos y marxistas: los problemas de un diálogo*, Alianza, Madrid, 1969.
Almerich, P., et al., *Cambio social y religión en España*, Fontanella, Barcelona, 1975.
Alvarez Bolado, Alfonso, *El experimento del nacional catolicismo 1939–1975*, Edicusa, Madrid, 1976.
Amoveri, Francesco, *Stato cattolico e chiesa fascista in Spagna: analisi critiche ed esperienze alternativa*, Celuc, Milan, 1973.
Anderson, Floyd (ed.), *Council Day Book*, 3 vols., National Catholic Welfare Conference, Washington, 1965.
Aradillas, Antonio, *Piedra de escándalo: la Iglesia en el cambio*, Plaza y Janés, Esplugues de Llobregat, 1986.
Aranguren, José Luis, *La juventud y otros ensayos*, Seix Barral, Barcelona, 1961.
Arias, Juan, *El enigma Wojtyla*, Ediciones El País, Madrid, 1985.
Armero, José Mario, *La política exterior de Franco*, Planeta, Barcelona, 1978.
Artigues, Daniel, *El Opus Dei en España 1928–1962: su evolución ideológica y política de los orígenes al intento de dominio*, Ruedo Ibérico, Paris, 1971.
Attard, Emilio, *Vida y muerte de UCD*, Planeta, Barcelona, 1983.
Barker, David, Halman, Loek and Vloet, Astrid, *The European Values Study 1981–1990: Summary Report*, Gordon Cook Foundation, London, 1992.
Belda, R., et al., *Iglesia y sociedad en España 1939–1975*, Editorial Popular, Madrid, 1977.
Beltrán Villalba, Miguel, García Fernando, Manuel, et al., *Informe sociológico sobre la juventud española 1960/82*, Fundación Santa María, Madrid, 1984.
Ben-Ami, Shlomo, *The Origins of the Second Republic in Spain*, Oxford University Press, 1978.
Benavides, Domingo, *El fracaso social del catolicismo español, 1870–1951*, Nova Terra, Barcelona, 1973.
Berger, Peter, *The Social Reality of Religion*, Faber and Faber, London, 1969.

Blanshard, Paul, *Communism, Democracy and Catholic Power*, Jonathan Cape, London, 1952.
Blanshard, Paul, *Paul Blanshard on Vatican II*, Allen and Unwin, London, 1967.
Blázquez, Feliciano, *La traición de los clérigos en la España de Franco: crónica de una intolerancia*, Trotta, Madrid, 1991.
Botti, Alfonso, *Cielo y dinero: el nacionalcatolicismo en España (1881–1975)*, Alianza, Madrid, 1992.
Brenan, Gerald, *The Spanish Labyrinth*, Cambridge University Press, Cambridge, 1976.
Brey, María Luisa, *Conversaciones con el Cardenal Tarancón*, Mensajero, Bilbao, 1994.
Butler, Christopher, *The Theology of Vatican II*, Darton, Longman and Todd, London, 1967.
Callahan, William J., *Church, Politics and Society in Spain, 1750–1874*, Harvard University Press, Cambridge, Mass., 1984.
Calleja, José Ignacio, *Discurso eclesial para la transición democrática (1975–1982)*, Editorial Eset, Vitoria, 1988.
Calzada, J. Manuel, *Diálogos con la mitra*, Sal Terrae, Santander, 1979.
Campo Vidal, Manuel, *La España que hereda Felipe González*, Argos Vergara, Barcelona, 1982.
Cárcel Ortí, Vicente, *¿España neopagana?*, Edicep, Valencia, 1991.
Carr, Raymond, *Modern Spain 1875–1980*, Oxford University Press, Oxford 1980.
Carrillo, Santiago, *Problems of Socialism Today*, Lawrence and Wishart, London, 1970.
Castaño Colomer, José, *La JOC en España (1946–1970)*, Ediciones Sígueme, Salamanca, 1978.
Castro Zafra, Antonio, *Los círculos del poder: apparat vaticano*, Editorial Popular, Madrid, 1987.
Cavero, José, *Poderes fácticos en la democracia*, Espasa Calpe, Madrid, 1990.
Chamorro, Eduardo, *Viaje al centro de UCD*, Plaza y Janés, Barcelona, 1981.
Chao, Pepe, *La Iglesia que Franco quiso*, Mañana, Madrid, 1977.
Chao Rego, José, *La Iglesia en el franquismo*, Felmar, Madrid, 1976.
Cierva, Ricardo de la, *Historia del franquismo: aislamiento, transformación, agonía, 1945–1975*, Planeta, Barcelona, 1978.
Codina, Víctor, Pereda, Carlos and Prada, Miguel Angel de, *Analizar la Iglesia*, HOAC, Madrid, 1981.
Comas, Ramón, *Gomá-Vidal i Barraquer: dues visions antagòniques de l'Església del 1939*, Laia, Barcelona, 1974.
Comín, Alfonso C., *España ¿país de misión?*, Nova Terra, Barcelona, 1966.
Comisión General de la HOAC, *Cristianos y revolucionarios: programa militante de la HOAC*, HOAC, Fuenlabrada, 1979.
Comisión General de la HOAC, *Cristianos en la lucha obrera*, HOAC, Madrid, 1981.
Cooper, Norman, *Catholicism and the Franco Regime*, Sage Research Papers in the Social Sciences, Vol. 3, Beverly Hills, London, 1975.
Crexell, Joan, *La caputxinada*, Edicions 62, Barcelona, 1987.
Cuadernos de Ruedo Ibérico, *Horizonte español 1972*, 3 vols., Paris, 1972.

Bibliography

Daim, W., Heer, F. and Knoll, A., *Iglesia y tiempos nuevos*, Ediciones Paulinas, Madrid, 1964.
De Esteban, Jorge and López Guerra, Luis, *La crisis del Estado franquista*, Labor, Barcelona, 1977.
De la Cuadra, Bonifacio and Gallego-Díaz, Soledad, *Del consenso al desencanto*, Editorial Saltés, Madrid, 1981.
De las Heras, Jesús and Villarín, Juan, *El año Arias*, Sedmay, Madrid, 1975.
De Miguel, Amando, *40 millones de españoles 40 años después*, Grijalbo, Barcelona, 1976.
Díaz Mozaz, José María, *La Iglesia de España en la encrucijada*, Ediciones Paulinas, Madrid, 1973.
Díaz-Salazar, Rafael, *Iglesia dictadura y democracia: catolicismo y sociedad en España (1953-1979)*, Ediciones HOAC, Madrid, 1981.
Díaz-Salazar, Rafael, *El capital simbólico: estructura social, política y religión en España*, HOAC, Madrid, 1988.
Díaz-Salazar, Rafael, *¿Todavía la clase obrera?*, HOAC, Madrid, 1990.
Díaz-Salazar, Rafael and Giner, Salvador, *Religión y sociedad en España*, CIS, Madrid, 1993.
Domínguez, Javier, *Organizaciones obreras cristianas en la oposición al franquismo, 1951-1955*, Ediciones Mensajero, Bilbao, 1985.
Easton, David, *A Systems Analysis of Political Life*, John Wiley, New York, 1965.
Editorial Cuadernos para el Diálogo, *España: realidad y política*, Colección los suplementos, Edicusa, Madrid, 1969.
Equipo para la Investigación de Cuestiones Actuales, *Comunidades de base y nueva Iglesia*, Ediciones Acción Católica, Madrid, 1971.
Estruch, Joan, *Santos y pillos: el Opus Dei y sus paradojas*, Herder, Barcelona, 1994.
Etzioni, Amitai, *Modern Organizations*, Prentice-Hall, New Jersey, 1964.
Fernández de Castro, Ignacio, *De las Cortes de Cádiz al posfranquismo*, 2 vols., El Viejo Topo, Barcelona, 1981.
Floristán, Casiano, *Vaticano II, un 'concilio pastoral'*, Sígueme, Salamanca, 1990.
Floristán, Casiano and Tamayo, Juan-José (eds), *El Vaticano II, veinte años después*, Ediciones Cristiandad, Madrid, 1985.
Fraga, Manuel, et al., *La España de los años 70*, Vol. III/1, Editorial Moneda y Crédito, Madrid, 1972.
Fundación FOESSA, *Informe sociológico sobre la situación social de España*, Euramérica, Madrid, 1970, 1976, 1983, 1984.
Fundación Friedrich Ebert, *Elecciones generales 1982: opiniones y actitudes políticas de los españoles*, Madrid, 1983.
Fundación Friedrich Ebert, *Euroizquierda y cristianismo: presente y futuro de un diálogo*, Madrid, 1991.
Gallego, J. Andrés, et al., *Estudios históricos sobre la Iglesia española contemporánea*, III Semana de Historia Eclesiástica de España Contemporánea, Biblioteca 'La Ciudad de Dios', El Escorial, 1979.
García Villoslada, Ricardo (ed.), *Historia de la Iglesia en España*, Vol. 5, BAC, Madrid, 1979.

Gil Novales, Alberto (ed.), *La revolución burguesa en España*, Universidad Complutense, Madrid, 1985.
Gómez Pérez, Rafael, *Política y religión en el régimen de Franco*, Dopesa, Barcelona, 1976.
Gómez Pérez, Rafael, *El franquismo y la Iglesia*, Rialp, Madrid, 1986.
González Blasco, Pedro and González-Anleo, Juan, *Religión y sociedad en la España de los 90*, Fundación Santa María, Madrid, 1992.
González de Cardedal, Olegario (ed.), *Iglesia y política en la España de hoy*, Sígueme, Salamanca, 1980.
González Faus, José Ignacio, *El engaño de un capitalismo aceptable*, Sal Terrae, 1983.
González Ruiz, José-María, *El cristianismo no es un humanismo*, Ediciones Península, Madrid, 1966.
Graham, R. A., SJ, *Vatican Diplomacy*, Princeton University Press, 1959.
Gunther, Richard, Sani, Giacomo and Shabad, Goldie, *Spain after Franco: The Making of a Competitive Party System*, University of California Press, 1988.
Gurian, Waldemar and Fitzsimmons, Matthew Anthony (eds), *The Catholic Church in World Affairs*, University of Notre Dame Press, Notre Dame, Ind., 1954.
Hales, E. E. Y., *The Catholic Church in the Modern World*, Image Books, New York, 1960.
Hales, E. E .Y., *Pope John and His Revolution*, Eyre and Spottiswoode, London, 1965.
Hebblethwaite, Peter, *Paul VI. The First Modern Pope*, HarperCollins, London, 1993.
Hermet, Guy, *Los católicos en la España franquista: I, los actores del juego político*, CIS, Madrid, 1985.
Hernández, Abel, *Crónica de la cruz y de la rosa*, Argos Vergara, Barcelona, 1984.
Hernández, Abel, *El quinto poder*, Temas de Hoy, Madrid, 1995.
Heywood, Paul, *Marxism and the Failure of Organised Socialism in Spain, 1879–1936*, Cambridge University Press, Cambridge, 1990.
Hills, George, *Franco, the Man and his Nation*, Hale, London, 1967.
Hills, George, *Spain*, Ernest Benn, London, 1970.
Iniesta, Alberto, *La Iglesia en una sociedad pluralista y democrática*, Fundación Santa María, Madrid, 1983.
Juliá, Santos, *Manuel Azaña, una biografía política*, Alianza, Madrid, 1990.
Kaiser, Robert, *Inside the Council*, Burns and Oates, London, 1963.
Keogh, Dermot, *The Vatican, the Bishops and Irish Politics 1919–1930*, Cambridge University Press, Cambridge, 1986.
Laboa, Juan M. (ed.), *El postconcilio en España*, Ediciones Encuentro, Madrid, 1988.
Laboa, Juan M. et al., *Diez años en la vida de los españoles*, Plaza y Janés, Esplugues de Llobregat, 1986.
Lamet, Pedro Miguel, *Hombre y Papa*, Espasa Calpe, Madrid, 1995.
Lannon, Frances, *Privilege, Persecution and Prophecy: The Catholic Church in Spain 1875–1975*, Clarendon, Oxford, 1987.
Linz, J. et al., *España: un presente para el futuro*, 2 vols., IEE, Madrid, 1984.

Bibliography

López Martínez, Alfredo, *La Iglesia desde el Estado*, Editora Nacional, Madrid, 1972.
Mardones, José María, *Postmodernidad y cristianismo: el desafío del fragmento*, Sal Terrae, Santander, 1988.
Mardones, José María, *Capitalismo y religión*, Sal Terrae, Santander, 1991.
Marías, Julián, *Innovación y arcaísmo*, Ediciones de la Revista de Occidente, Madrid, 1973.
Marquina Barrio, Antonio, *La diplomacia vaticana y la España de Franco (1936–1945)*, CSIC, Madrid, 1982.
Martín Descalzo, José Luis (ed.), *Todo sobre el Concordato*, PPC, Madrid, 1971.
Martín Descalzo, José Luis, *Tarancón, el cardenal del cambio*, Planeta, 1982.
McNair, John, *Education for a Changing Spain*, Manchester University Press, Manchester, 1984.
McSweeney, Bill, *Roman Catholicism, the Search for Relevance*, Blackwell, Oxford, 1980.
Medhurst, Kenneth and Moyser, George, *Church and Politics in a Secular Age*, Clarendon, Oxford, 1988.
Meliá, Josep, *Así cayó Adolfo Suárez*, Planeta, Barcelona, 1981.
Ministerio de Cultura, *Crónicas de Juventud: los jóvenes en España 1940–1985*, Madrid, 1985.
Miret Magdalena, Enrique, *Los nuevos católicos*, Nova Terra, Barcelona, 1967.
Moncada, Alberto, *Historia oral del Opus Dei*, Plaza and Janés, Esplugues de Llobregat, 1987.
Montero Moreno, Antonio, *Historia de la persecución religiosa en España 1936–1939*, BAC, Madrid, 1961.
Moorman, John, *Vatican Observed: An Anglican Impression of Vatican II*, Darton, Longman and Todd, London, 1967.
Moya, Carlos, *El poder económico en España*, Tucar, Madrid, 1975.
Mujal-León, Eusebio, *Communism and Political Change in Spain*, Indiana University Press, 1983.
Mulazzi Giammanco, Rosanna, *The Catholic–Communist Dialogue in Italy*, Praeger, New York, 1989.
Muntanyola, Ramón, *Vidal i Barraquer, el cardenal de la paz*, Laia, Barcelona, 1974.
Orizo, Francisco Andrés, *España, entre la apatía y el cambio social*, Mapfre, Madrid, 1983.
Orizo, Francisco Andrés, *Sistemas de valores en la España de los 90*, CIS, Madrid, 1996.
Payne, Stanley G., *El catolicismo español*, Planeta, Barcelona, 1984.
Penniman, Howard R. and Mujal-León, Eusebio (eds), *Spain at the Polls, 1977, 1979 and 1982*, Duke University Press, North Carolina, 1985.
Pereda, C., Urbina, F. and de Prada, M. A., *Cambio de actitudes religiosas y secularización de comportamientos en la situación española actual*, Colectivo IOE, Madrid, 1983.
Pereña Vicente, Luciano, *La objeción de conciencia en España*, Colección Justicia y Paz, PPC, Madrid, 1971.
Pérez Díaz, Víctor, *La primacía de la sociedad civil*, Alianza, Madrid, 1993.

Preston, Paul (ed.), *Spain in Crisis*, Harvester, Sussex, 1976.
Preston, Paul, *The Coming of the Spanish Civil War*, Methuen, London, 1983.
Preston, Paul (ed.), *Revolution and War in Spain*, Methuen, London, 1984.
Preston, Paul, *The Triumph of Democracy in Spain*, Methuen, London, 1987.
Preston, Paul, *Franco*, HarperCollins, London, 1993.
Pro Vita Mundi, *La actualidad social y religiosa en España*, Brussels, 1979.
PSOE, *La sociedad española en transformación: escenarios para el año 2000*, Siglo XXI, Madrid, 1988.
Raguer, Hilari, *La espada y la cruz (la Iglesia 1936–1939)*, Bruguera, Barcelona, 1977.
Ravitch, Norman, *The Catholic Church and the French Nation*, Routledge, London, 1990.
Recio, Juan-Luis, Uña, Octavio and Díaz-Salazar, Rafael, *Para comprender la transición española: religión y política*, Verbo Divino, Estella, 1990.
Rhodes, Anthony, *The Vatican in the Age of The Cold War 1945–1980*, Michael Russell, London, 1992.
Riera, Ignasi, et al., *De la fe a la utopía social: miscelánea Juan N. García-Nieto París*, Sal Terrae, Santander, 1996.
Rodríguez, Pedro, *Vicente Enrique y Tarancón ¿Yo soy así?*, Grupo Libro 88, Madrid, 1991.
Rodríguez Aisa, María Luisa, *El Cardenal Gomá y la guerra de España: aspectos de la gestión pública del Primado 1936–1939*, Instituto Enrique Flórez, CSIC, Madrid, 1981.
Rojo, Eduardo, et al., *El neoliberalismo en cuestión*, Sal Terrae, Santander, 1993.
Romero, Emilio, *Papeles Reservados II*, Plaza y Janés, Esplugues de Llobregat, 1986.
Ruiz Giménez, Joaquín (ed.), *Iglesia, Estado y Sociedad en España, 1930–1982*, Argos Vergara, Barcelona, 1984.
Ruiz Giménez, Joaquín and Bellosillo, Pilar (eds), *El concilio del siglo XXI: reflexiones sobre el Vaticano II*, PPC, Madrid, 1987.
Ruiz Rico, Juan José, *El papel político de la Iglesia católica en la España de Franco 1936–1971*, Tecnos, Madrid, 1977.
Rupérez, Javier, *Estado confesional y libertad religiosa*, Edicusa, Madrid, 1970.
Rupérez, J. and Moro, C. (eds), *El decenio socialista*, Ediciones Encuentro, Madrid, 1992.
Rynne, Xavier, *Letters from Vatican City*, 4 vols., Faber and Faber, London, 1968.
Sáez Alba, A., *La asociación católica de propagandistas*, Ruedo Ibérico, Paris, 1974.
Sebastián, Fernando and González de Cardedal, Olegario, *Iglesia y enseñanza: variaciones sobre un tema*, Ediciones SM, Madrid, 1977.
Secretariado Diocesano de Catequesis, *Comunidades plurales en la Iglesia*, Ediciones Paulinas, Madrid, 1981.
Southworth, H. R., *El mito de la cruzada de Franco*, Ruedo Ibérico, Paris, 1963.
Squires, Judith (ed.), *Principled Positions: Postmodernism and the Rediscovery of Value*, Lawrence and Wishart, London, 1993.

Bibliography 175

Suquía Goicoechea, Angel, et al., *Al servicio de la Iglesia y del pueblo: homenaje al Cardenal Tarancón en su 75 aniversario*, Narcea, Madrid, 1984.
Tamames, Ramón, *La República: la era de Franco*, Historia de España, Vol. 7, Alfaguara, Madrid, 1975.
Tezanos, José Félix, Cotarelo, Ramón and Blas, Andrés de (eds), *La transición democrática española*, Sistema, Madrid, 1989.
Tornos, Andrés and Aparicio, Rosa, *¿Quién es creyente en España?*, PPC, Madrid, 1995.
Tuñón de Lara, Manuel, *El hecho religioso en España*, Librairie du Globe, Paris, 1968.
Tuñón de Lara, Manuel (ed.), *Historiografía española contemporánea*, Siglo XXI, Madrid, 1980.
Turner, Bryan S. (ed.), *Theories of Modernity and Postmodernity*, Sage, London, 1990.
Tusell, Javier, *Carrero, la eminencia gris del régimen de Franco*, Temas de Hoy, Madrid, 1993.
Tusell, Javier, *Franco y los católicos – la política interior española entre 1945 y 1957*, Alianza, Madrid, 1984.
Ubieto, Antonio, Reglá, Juan, Jover, José María and Seco, Carlos, *Introducción a la historia de España*, Editorial Teide, Barcelona, 1970.
Ureña, Enrique, *El mito del cristianismo socialista*, Unión Editorial, Madrid, 1981.
Ureña, Enrique, *El neoclericalismo de izquierda*, Unión Editorial, Madrid, 1984.
Vázquez, Jesús M., et al., *La Iglesia española contemporánea*, Editora Nacional, Madrid, 1973.
Vázquez Montalbán, Manuel, *Un polaco en la corte del Rey Juan Carlos*, Alfaguara, Madrid, 1996.
Vorgrimler, Herbert (ed.), *Commentary on the Documents of Vatican II*, 5 vols., Burns and Oates, London, 1969.
Welles, Benjamin, *Spain, the Gentle Anarchy*, Pall Mall Press, London, 1965.
Ynfante, Jesús, *La prodigiosa aventura del Opus Dei*, Ruedo Ibérico, Paris, 1970.
Zahn, George C., *German Catholics and Hitler's Wars – A Study of Social Control*, Sheed & Ward, New York, 1962.

Index

ABC, 133
Acción Católica Obrera, 8
aggiornamento, 12, 16, 25
agnosticism, 10, 40, 60, 89, 95, 97, 120
Alfonso XIII, 30
Alianza Popular (AP), 89, 90, 91, 93, 94, 96, 97, 102, 105, 107; attitude of hierarchy to, 90, 94; woos the Catholic vote, 93; *see also* Partido Popular
Almarcha, Luis, 20
Alvear, Carmen, 91
Añoveros, Antonio, 16, 23, 63, 66, 67, 68, 69, 109; 1974 pastoral letter, 66-8
anticlericalism, 7, 11, 40, 50, 53, 71, 90, 114, 117, 119
Antoniutti, Ildebrando, 22
Apostúa, Luis, 113
Aranguren, José Luis López, 9, 77, 94
Araujo, Miguel Angel, 51
Arboleya, Maximiliano, 11, 23
Areilza, José María, 68
Argaya, Jacinto, 27, 31, 81
Argüello, Kiko (Francisco), 76
Arias Navarro, Carlos, 65, 66, 69, 80, 81, 89
Aristotle, 78
atheism, 2, 5, 10, 14, 18, 21, 40, 41, 60, 73, 78, 84, 93, 100, 117, 119
Augustine, St, 78
Aznar, José María, 123, 132
Azpiazu, Joaquín, 11

Bada, Joan, 128
Barcelona Theology Faculty, 27, 128
base (grass-roots) communities, 9, 63, 64, 70, 73, 89, 126, 128, 129; *see also* Comunidades Cristianas Populares; Iglesia Popular
Basque Country, 6, 8, 21, 26, 27, 53, 63, 66, 69, 70, 80, 94, 102, 103, 108-10, 133; bishops of and regional autonomy, 103; pastoral letters, 27, 31, 66-7, 81, 103, 108-10, 113; priests and ETA, 28, 31, 69, 109
Basque Nationalist Party *see* Partido Nacionalista Vasco
Benavent, Emilio, 28
Blázquez, Ricardo, 133
Brezhnev, Leonid, 84
Bueno y Monreal, José María, 16
bunker, 25, 48, 65, 108-9, 113
Burgos trial, 31, 47, 63
Busto, José Ramón, 128
Buxarrais, Ramón, 125

Calvo Sotelo, Leopoldo, 107, 109, 113
Câmara, Hélder, 39
Camprodón, Jaume, 65
Cantero, Pedro, 15, 20, 34, 52
capitalism, 1, 2, 3, 6, 8, 10, 13, 16, 19, 21, 23, 36, 37, 38, 39, 42, 44, 50, 57, 58, 60, 71, 72, 73, 75-6, 84, 85, 86, 87, 88, 89, 94, 100, 110, 112, 114, 115, 116, 122, 123, 127, 128, 129, 130, 131, 139
Caputxinada, 18
Cardenal, Jesús, 138
Cardijn, Joseph, 8
Cáritas, 37, 111, 131, 134
Carles, Ricard Maria, 134
Carrero Blanco, Luis, 15, 38, 53, 61, 62, 64, 65, 66; relations with Tarancón, 53
Carrillo, Santiago, 92
Casaroli, Agostino, 35, 36, 62, 63, 68
Castán Lacoma, Laureano, 14
Castellanos, Nicolás, 125
Castillo, Jose María, 110
Catalonia, 6, 8, 26, 67, 94, 103, 132, 133; Assembly of, 65; bishops of and regional autonomy, 103; Catalan Council, 132; Christian Schools of, 124, 126

Index 177

Catholic Action, 7–8, 9, 14, 15, 18, 19–20, 21–2, 30, 34, 46, 131; crisis of, 9, 21–2, 131; *see also* Movimiento Católico de Empleados; Acción Católica Obrera; FLP; HOAC; JOC; VOJ; VOS
Catholic Church: models of, 1; system-regime alliance strategy of, 5, 12, 13, 139; *see also* Spanish Church
Catholic Employees' Movement *see* Movimiento Católico de Empleados
Catholic Parents' Association *see* CONCAPA
Catholic Workers' Action *see* Acción Católica Obrera
Cavero, José, 107
CEE – *see* Conferencia Episcopal Española
Charismatic Renewal Communities, 76
Christian Democracy Federation (FDC), 89, 93–4; failure of in 1977 elections, 93
Christians for Socialism *see* Cristianos por el Socialismo (CpS)
Cicognani, Gaetano, 22
Girarda, José María, 26, 27, 28, 31, 96
clergy: and the *Caputxinada*, 18; 'charter' of 28, 35, 53, 68; crisis and laicisation of, 22–3, 24, 32, 42, 59; fined and imprisoned, 26–27, 39, 43–4, 69; Hermandad Sacerdotal *see* separate entry; progressive and radical, 2, 9, 18, 19, 26, 28, 29, 39, 45, 46, 47, 73, 75, 80, 92; Zamora prison for, 28, 53, 62, 63
Cold War, 7, 12
Comín, Alfonso, 9, 13, 39, 90
Comisiones Obreras (CCOO), 9, 19, 47, 63, 64, 129
communism, 2, 5, 7, 12, 14, 16, 19, 58, 75, 84, 93, 100, 110, 119, 127
Comunidades Cristianas Populares (CCP), 76, 93, 112

CONCAPA, 91, 124
Concordat, 7, 9, 16, 28, 35–6, 44, 47, 52, 53, 55, 56, 62, 63, 64, 66, 67–8, 69, 85, 100; *see also* derecho de presentación
Confederación Nacional del Trabajo (CNT), 8
Conferencia Episcopal Española (CEE): set up, 16; Social Pastoral Commission (CEPS) of, 130, 131
Constitution (1978), 95–6, 97–8, 99, 101, 103, 106, 113, 123
Convergència i Unió (CiU), 122, 123, 132, 137, 138
Conversations of Gredos, 9–10
COPE, 122
Cortina, Pedro, 66, 68
Council of Trent, 12
Cortes (Spanish Parliament), 15, 20, 23, 33, 50, 52, 67, 81, 96, 105, 106, 107, 108, 114, 124, 131
Cristianos por el Socialismo (CpS), 9, 74, 75, 76, 87, 93, 112
Cuadernos para el Diálogo, 17, 19, 24, 46
Cubillo, Jesús, 80

Dadaglio, Luigi, 22, 32, 43, 44, 50, 52, 62, 100–1, 104, 126
Deig, Antonio, 132
derecho de presentación, 7, 22–3, 35, 52–3, 55, 67, 68
Dezza, Paolo, 111
Díaz Merchán, Gabino, 28–9, 33, 74, 106, 108, 120, 134
Díez-Alegría, José María, 75, 76, 92–3, 110

Easton, David, 5
Ecclesia 15, 23, 28, 29, 46
Echarren, Ramón, 74, 80, 130
Eisenhower, Dwight 7
El Ciervo, 8, 36
El Cruzado Español, 26
El País, 93, 94, 95, 108, 131
Enrique y Tarancón, Vicente, 3, 9, 21, 25, 35–6, 40, 42–3, 44, 47, 48, 51, 52, 53, 62, 63, 64, 66, 67, 68, 69, 70, 72, 73, 74, 75, 76, 82, 83, 85–6,

Enrique y Tarancón, Vicente (*cont.*) 88, 90, 91, 92, 94, 95, 96, 99, 100, 101, 103, 104, 107, 108, 114, 125, 126, 133, 136; becomes Primate of Spain (Toledo), 25, Cardinal Archbishop of Madrid, 43, CEE President, 51; retirement and death of, 43; and the 'Añoveros affair', 67; and democracy, 42, 82; key role of in the transition, 42–4; at the 'extreme centre' of Church politics, 3, 43, 73, 120; and the Garrigues–Casaroli Concordat draft, 35–6; and homily at King Juan Carlos' enthronement, 85–6, 94, 99; 'Paul VI's man', 43; and the 'Popular Church' Assembly, 64; presides over 1971 Joint Assembly, 44; and reconciliation, 42–3, 64, 68–9; and regional autonomy, 103; and relations with Carrero Blanco, 53; and the 'Roman document', 51; and socialism, 43, 114; and the Vallecas Christian Assembly, 70
Erquicia, Anastasio, 69
Escrivá de Balaguer, José María, 10, 105
Estatuto de Centro Docentes, 105, 106
Estepa, José Manuel, 62, 64
Estrada, Juan 110
ETA, 26, 27, 28, 31, 64, 69, 70, 108, 109, 123, 133
Europa-Press, 51, 62
European Community (EC, later European Union – EU), 122, 130
European Economic Community (EEC), 70
Euskadiko Ezkerra, 109

Falange, 6, 10, 25, 30–1, 48
'Fr Paco' *see* García Salve, Francisco
FERE, 124
Fernández Miranda, Torcuato, 89
Fernández Ordóñez, Francisco, 106, 107
Financial Times, 48
FLP ('*Felipe*'), 8
FOESSA report 24, 30, 40
Forcano, Benjamín, 128

Fraga Iribarne, Manuel, 80, 89–90, 93, 123
Franco Bahamonde, Francisco, 6, 7, 14, 15, 17, 18, 19, 21, 22, 23, 26, 29, 30, 31, 32, 33, 34, 35, 42, 43, 45, 46–7, 48, 50–1, 52, 53–4, 60, 61, 62, 64, 68, 71, 74, 75, 132; designates Juan Carlos as successor, 30; death of, 71; and the *Caputxinada*, 18; and Catholic Action, 14, 19; and the *derecho de presentación*, 7, 22, 23, 35, 52–3, 55, 67; and the Joint Assembly, 46–7, 50–1; and relations with Paul VI, 17, 22, 23, 29, 30, 62, 70; socio-political regime of, 1, 2, 3, 5, 6, 7, 9, 11, 14, 15, 17, 18, 19, 20, 21, 28, 31, 33, 34, 36, 37–8, 40, 42, 43–4, 49, 50, 51, 52, 55, 56, 57, 61, 62, 67, 70, 72, 79, 81, 82, 83, 89, 94, 114, 131; and Vatican II, 14, 15
Frente Revolucionario Anti-Fascista Patriótico (FRAP), 48, 70
Friedrich Ebert Foundation, 117
Fuerza Nueva: as political party, 97; as publication, 26

García Huelga, Carlos, 29
García Salve, Francisco ('Fr Paco'), 47, 63, 80
Gea, José, 135, 136
González Márquez, Felipe, 92, 102, 113, 123, 133, 135
González Martín, Marcelo, 26, 32, 47, 52, 97, 106
González Moralejo, Rafael, 28, 32, 45, 49–50
González Ruiz, José María, 75
Guerra Campos, José, 20, 21, 34, 36, 43, 51, 52, 97, 123
Guerrilleros de Cristo Rey, 26, 48, 64
Guix, José María, 130

heresy, 1, 3, 5, 12, 41, 50, 119, 138, 139
Hernández, Carmen, 76
Hermandad Sacerdotal, 26, 31, 44, 46, 62, 70, 83, 97–8; and the Joint Assembly, 46

Index

Herri Gaztedi, 8
HOAC (Hermandad Obrera de Acción Católica), 7, 8, 9, 10, 11, 20, 21, 22, 25, 44, 70, 73, 78, 80, 90, 93, 112, 114, 115, 131

Iglesia-Mundo, 26, 32, 46
Iglesia Popular, 63, 87
Iglesia Viva, 17, 46, 87
Incunable, 8
Infantes Florido, José Antonio, 28
Informations Catholiques Internationales, 50
Iniesta, Alberto, 62, 70, 71, 74, 80, 93
Innocenti, Antonio, 104, 106, 109, 113
'International Catholic Conversations', 9
Iribarren, Jesús, 96
Izquierda Unida (IU), 126, 128, 136, 137

JOC (Juventud Obrera Católica), 7, 8, 9, 10, 20, 21, 22, 25, 48, 73, 90, 131
John XXIII, Pope, 2, 3, 12, 13, 17, 19, 84, 119; summons Vatican II, 2; *Mater et Magistra* (1962), 12, 14; *Pacem in Terris* (1963), 12, 17
John XXIII Theological Association (*Asociación Juan XXIII*), 114, 132
John Paul II, Pope, 3, 4, 59, 76, 84, 98, 100, 101, 104, 105, 106, 110, 111, 112, 114, 116, 117, 119, 120, 125, 126, 127, 139; succeeds Paul VI, 84; anti-communism of, 84, 100, 110, 119; conservative appointments of, 125; evangelisation strategy of, 84, 100, 119, 120, 127, 139; first visit to Spain by, 116–17; and 'neopaganism' of Spanish society, 76, 127; *Laborem Exercens* (1981), 3, 110, 111, 113, 114; *Centesimus Annus* (1991), 127; *Veritatis Splendor* (1993), 136; *Evangelium Vitae* (1995), 136
Joint Assembly (1971), 44–7, 50, 51, 54, 63, 70

Juan de Borbón, 30
Juan Carlos I, 30, 48, 62, 79, 85, 89, 99, 107
Jubany, Narcís, 47, 48, 75, 103, 124; and Catalan regional autonomy, 103
Justice and Peace Commission, 32–3, 49–50, 70, 73–4, 80, 87–8, 93, 112

Kada, Lajos, 132, 133
Kennedy, John Fitzgerald, 12
Khrushchev, Nikita, 13
Knoll, August, 5
Küng, Hans, 59

Laín Entralgo, Pedro, 9–10
Lamet, Pedro Miguel, 128
Larrauri, José María, 108
Larrea, Luis María, 108
Las Palmas Assembly, 70
La Vanguardia, 131
Leo XIII, Pope, 12; *Rerum Novarum* (1891), 12
liberalism, 10, 58, 123, 131
liberation theology, 25, 37, 44, 74, 114, 121, 125
LOAPA, 109
LODE, 124
LOGSE, 126
López Hernández Herrera, Francisco, 78
López Martínez, Alfredo, 32
López Rodó, Laureano, 30, 38, 62, 63
Llanos, José María, 64, 75, 92

Maisterra, Bernardo, 69
Marías, Julián, 26
Martín Descalzo, José Luis, 92
Martín Patino, José María, 100
Martín Velasco, Juan de Dios, 128
Martínez Loza, Fernando, 105
Martínez Somalo, Eduardo, 105
marxism, 3, 12, 21, 33, 41, 50, 56, 57, 58, 61, 72, 74, 75, 78, 83, 85, 86–7, 90, 93, 94, 100, 102, 110, 112
Matesa scandal, 31
Medellín, 25
media, 38, 55, 77, 94, 101, 107, 111, 121–2, 131, 133, 134, 135

Index

Miret Magdalena, Enrique, 117
Misión Abierta, 128
Misión del Sur, 111–12
modernity, 2, 3, 4, 5, 7, 12, 39, 100, 119, 128, 138, 140; *see also* postmodernity
Mondragón, 21
Montero, Antonio, 45, 108, 113
Montini, Giovanni Battista *see* Paul VI
Morcillo, Casimiro, 20, 21, 25, 29, 32, 35, 43, 45
Movimiento Católico de Empleados, 8
Mussolini, Benito, 68

National Catholicism, 8, 11, 14, 16, 19, 26, 30, 31, 46, 65, 75, 83, 121
National Movement, 26, 29, 30, 32, 62, 69
NATO, 110
Neocatechumen Communities, 76

Oliver, Victorio, 48, 62, 80
Opus Dei 1, 2, 10, 17, 30–1, 38, 44, 46, 48, 51, 62, 70, 89, 104–5, 107, 116, 117, 125, 137, 138; economic policy of, 10, 38, 44; holding key political positions, 10, 31, 38; and the Joint Assembly, 46; *prelatura nullius* of, 104–5; as pressure group, 10; and the 'Roman document', 51; as religious organisation, 10
Oriol y Urquijo, Antonio, 14, 35
Osés, Javier, 5, 40, 74, 112
Ostpolitik, 25, 84

Palenzuela, Antonio, 74
Parliament *see* Cortes
Partial Agreements (1979), 100–1, 106, 109, 113, 126, 134
Partido Comunista Español (PCE), 9, 21, 90–1, 92, 93, 94, 96, 97, 101, 102, 106, 117; attitude to the Church of, 90–1, 97, 101
Partido Nacionalista Vasco (PNV), 109, 133

Partido Socialista Obrera Español (PSOE), 90, 92, 93, 94, 97, 98, 101, 102, 105, 106, 113, 114, 115, 116, 117, 119, 120, 121, 122, 123, 125, 126, 127–8, 129, 131, 132, 134, 135, 136, 137; abandons marxism, 90, 102; attitude to the Church of, 90, 97, 106, 121, 127–8, 133, 135; secular view of society of, 90, 120, 121
Partido Popular (PP), 123, 127, 132, 135, 136, 137, 138; *see also* Alianza Popular
Pastoral Misionera, 17, 46
Paul VI, Pope (Giovanni Battista Montini), 4, 17, 22–3, 25, 29, 30, 31, 32, 35, 36, 39, 40, 43, 44, 51, 52, 53, 56, 57, 58, 59, 61, 62, 67, 70, 74, 83–4, 119; succeeds John XXIII, 17; death of, 84; on doctrinal relativism, 39; favours Tarancón, 43; Ostpolitik, 25, 84; and relations with Franco, 17, 22–3, 29, 30, 62; on 'right teaching', 59; and the 'Roman document', 51; and self-doubt, 58; strategy of in appointing bishops, 23, 32; *Humanae Vitae* (1968), 39, 84; *Octogesima Adveniens* (1971), 56, 58
Peces-Barba, Gregorio, 101
Pentecostalism, 76
people of God (community of believers), 1, 88, 125, 126, 129, 140
Piñar López, Blas, 26, 50, 97
Pius XII, Pope, 7
Pla y Deniel, Enrique, 9, 20
Political Reform Law, 81
Popular Alliance *see* Alianza Popular
Popular Christian Communities *see* Comunidades Cristianas Populares
Popular Church *see* Iglesia Popular
Popular Liberation Front *see* FLP
Popular Party *see* Partido Popular
Posible, 87
postmodernity, 4–5, 138–9
Press and Publications Law, 20
Priestly Brotherhood *see* Hermandad Sacerdotal

Index

Primo de Rivera, Miguel, 132
proceso 1001, 63, 64
Public Order Tribunal, 80
Puebla, 110

¿Qué Pasa?, 26

Rahner, Karl, 20
Reagan, Ronald, 84
reconciliation, 6, 17, 33, 37, 42–3, 45, 64, 68–9, 79, 80, 85, 133
regime: system, distinction between, 5, 79
religious freedom, 2, 12, 14, 15, 16, 17, 55, 90, 101, 105, 106, 113
Riberi, Antonio, 22
right of patronage *see* derecho de presentación
Romero, Carmen, 136
Ruiz Giménez, Joaquín, 17, 89
Ruiz Rico, Juan José, 5
Rural Youth *see* Herri Gaztedi

Sábado Gráfico, 66
San Antonio María Claret, 98
Sánchez, José, 134
Sánchez-Covisa, Mariano, 48
Sebastián, Fernando, 121, 134
Second Republic (1931–6), 6, 7, 11, 22, 43, 45, 53, 86, 95
Second Vatican Council (Vatican II), 1, 2, 3, 4, 5, 6–7, 9, 12, 13, 14, 15, 17, 18, 19, 20, 22, 25, 28, 31, 33, 39, 40, 42, 46, 55, 57, 59, 78, 81, 82, 83–4, 85, 100, 119, 125, 128, 129, 137, 138, 140; and attempt to dialogue with modernity, 2, 3, 4, 12, 39, 78, 84, 100, 119, 140; and freedom of conscience, 5, 40, 128, 138; and human and civil rights, 2, 12, 14; *Gaudium et Spes*, 2, 23, 85, 140; *Lumen Gentium* 129, 140
secularisation, 1, 2, 3, 4, 5, 12, 18, 24, 40, 41, 60, 77, 78, 98, 99, 117, 118, 119, 139; definition of, 1; as Church's intangible enemy, 5, 78
Setién, José María, 81, 108, 133
Silva Muñoz, Federico, 65

socialism, 12, 13, 42, 43, 45, 58, 71, 73, 74, 75, 86, 87, 90, 93, 110, 112, 114, 116, 119, 122, 127
Social Workers' Vanguard *see* VOS
Solé Tura, Jordi, 101, 106
Soviet bloc, 7, 58
Soviet Union, 12, 110
Spanish Bishops' Conference *see* Conferencia Episcopal Española
Spanish Church: attitude of to socioeconomic justice, 8, 13, 14, 16, 19, 23, 27, 28, 36–7, 42, 44, 57–8, 72, 74–5, 111, 129–30, 131–2, 134; Catholic Action *see* separate entry; as community of believers (people of God), 1, 88, 125, 126, 129, 140; clergy *see* separate entry; and the confessionality of the State, 2, 7, 15, 16, 43, 55, 91, 98; conflict within, 1, 2, 3, 8, 18, 19, 39, 44, 71, 119; financing of and dependence on the State, 16, 23, 34, 43, 53, 54, 56, 57, 60, 66, 71, 74, 93, 96, 97, 100, 134; and human and civil rights, 14, 18–19, 27, 28–9, 31, 32–3, 37, 48, 51, 63, 64–5, 68, 70–1, 72, 81–2, 85, 99, 112, *see also* HOAC, JOC, Justice and Peace Commission
as institution (hierarchy), 1, 74–5, 83, 139, 140; alliance with Francoism, 2, 3, 4, 5, 6–7, 8, 11, 18, 19, 20, 21, 22, 23–4, 52, 57, 60, 68, 74; and the Burgos trial, 31; and the Concordat (1953), 7, 28, 35–6, 85; as instrument of social control, 2, 7, 11, 32, 61; as legitimiser of the regime, 2, 6, 7, 19, 20, 30, 61; and religious freedom, 14, 15, 17, 55; and the Spanish Civil War, 6, 22, 42–3, 45, 47, 69; and the 1968 state of emergency, 27; *changing sociopolitical direction*, 2–3, 7, 31, 32, 33, 40–1, 42, 43, 55, 61; as rallying-point of opposition, 61; and the '*Catholic identity*' *of Spain*, 15–16, 18, 21, 34, 41, 56, 76–7, 82, 86, 95,

Spanish Church: (*cont.*)
116–17, 120, 121; *changing selfperception* of, 137; *defence of priests* by, 27, 28–9, 47; *divisions within*, 22, 27, 31–2, 34, 42, 44, 45, 54, 73, 74, 93, 97, 106, 124, 129; *'extreme centre' strategy* of, 3, 43, 57, 73, 75, 89, 94, 104, 120; as *guardian* of Church's unity and purity of the faith, 14, 17–18, 39, 59; *influence* of, 3, 34, 57, 76–7, 84, 85, 96–7; desire to maintain, 34, 82, 83, 84–5, 95, 96, 99, 119, 120, 121; loss of, 23–4, 39, 40, 59, 77, 98, 117–18, 139; traditional spheres of, 7, 33–4, 84–5, 102 (anti-abortion, 39, 85, 94, 97, 101, 102, 116, 123–4, 127, 129, 133, 135, 136, 138; anti-contraception 39, 40, 85, 122; divorce, 39, 85, 91, 97, 100, 101, 102, 104, 105, 106–7, 116; education, 3, 7, 11, 33–4, 44, 54, 55–6, 85, 91–2, 94, 95, 97, 100, 101, 104, 105, 124, 126, 127, 133, 134, 138; marriage, 3, 18, 33, 39, 40, 85, 91, 94, 97, 100, 106, 127); *lack of consultation* by, 36, 135; and the *media*, 55, 94, 101, 107, 111, 121–2, 131, 133, 134, 135; and *post-Enlightenment thought*: capitalism, 1, 2, 3, 8, 16, 23, 36, 37, 39, 42, 57, 60, 71, 72, 75–6, 85, 86, 87, 88, 112, 129, 130; communism, 2, 5, 14, 16, 19, 127; marxism, 3, 21, 33, 41, 56, 61, 72, 74, 75, 78, 85, 86–7, 93, 94, 110; modernity, 3, 5, 7, 84, 128, 138; socialism, 42, 43, 58, 71, 75, 86, 87, 114, 119; *post-Franco sociopolitical position of*, 84–5; attempts to recover public role, 119, 120; and 'camouflaged confessionality', 95; cold-shoulders left-wing Christian Democracy, 88, 93; on the 1978 Constitution, 95–8; on democracy, 3, 43, 61, 82, 84–5, 99, 114, 119; on elections, 91, 92, 93, 94, 98, 101–2, 113–14, 135–6; on the Partial Agreements (1979), 100–1, 113, 126, 134; and preferred political option, 74, 92, 105, 120; favours UCD, 88–9, 92, 93, 94, 101–2, 105; and professed political independence, 84–5, 88, 92, 94, 113, 135, 136; and reactions to the *Tejerazo*, 107–8; and regional autonomy, 103, 109–10; and relations with the PSOE government, 119, 120–2, 123–5, 126–8, 130, 131, 133–4, 135, 136–7; *reactions to Vatican II*, 2, 13–18, 22, 81–2; *teaching authority*, 39–40, 59, 77–8, 83, 84, 128; reins in theologians, 39–40, 110, 128–9; Joint Assembly *see* separate entry; Justice and Peace Commission *see* separate entry; levels of religious observance and disaffection, 3, 11–12, 23–4, 40, 59–60, 76, 77, 117–18, 138; Opus Dei *see* separate entry; pluralism of, 3, 17, 39, 44, 76, 120, 128–9, 138; as sanctuary, 47, 80, 82; universities of, 105; 'We are Church', 129

Spanish Civil War (1936–9), 2, 6, 11, 14, 22, 25, 33, 43, 45, 46–7, 69; Church and, 6, 22, 45, 46–7; as 'Crusade', 6, 22, 46–7, 49; Joint Assembly resolution on, 45

Spanish Communist Party *see* Partido Comunista Español

Spanish Socialist Party *see* Partido Socialista Obrero Español

Suárez, Adolfo, 81, 89, 93, 98, 102, 105, 106, 107

Suquía, Angel, 125, 126, 127, 133, 134, 135; becomes CEE President, 125; succeeds Tarancón as Archbishop of Madrid, 125

Tabera, Arturo, 27
The Tablet, 46
Tácitos, 89
Tagliaferri, Mario, 125, 132
Tarancón *see* Enrique y Tarancón, Vicente
Tejerazo, 107–8
Tejero, Antonio, 107, 108
Thomas Aquinas, St, 78

Index 183

trade unions: banned under Franco, 6, 19, 37; in democracy, 83, 122, 123, 130, 131; *see also* Confederación Nacional de Trabajo; Unión General de Trabajadores; Comisiones Obreras

Ubieta López, José Angel, 28, 66
Unión de Centro Democrático (UCD), 81, 88, 89, 90, 92, 93, 94, 96–7, 98, 101, 102, 105, 107, 109, 112, 113, 116, 121, 122, 126; favoured by the Church hierarchy, 88, 89, 92, 93, 94, 101, 102, 105
Unión General de Trabajadores (UGT), 8
United States of America, 4, 7, 12, 15, 25, 58, 84, 110
Uriarte, Juan María, 108
Urrutia, Víctor, 135
Utopia, 140

Vallecas Christian Assembly, 69–70
Valorek, Mariano, 104
Vanguardias Obreras, 8, 21
Vatican I, 12, 14

Vatican II *see* Second Vatican Council
Vatican III, 140
Vida Nueva, 9, 29, 76, 77, 104, 128, 129
Vidal i Barraquer, Francesc, 11
Villot, Jean, 35, 36, 51
VOJ (Vanguardia Obrera Juvenil), 8, 73
VOS (Vanguardia Obrera Social), 8, 73

Warriors of Christ the King *see* Guerrilleros de Cristo Rey
Workers' Commissions *see* Comisiones Obreras
Workers' Vanguards *see* Vanguardias Obreras

Xirinachs, Lluis, 69

Yanes, Elías, 45, 91, 96, 124, 129, 134, 135, 136; becomes CEE President, 134
Young Workers' Vanguard *see* VOJ

Zamora prison, 28, 53, 62, 63
Zubiri, Javier, 9